Contents Table

~ Welcome & What You'll Learn

Section A: Getting Started with JIRA and Confluence

1. Introduction to JIRA and Confluence
2. Setting Up Your JIRA Account and Project
3. Navigating the JIRA Interface
4. Getting Started with Confluence

Section B: Working with JIRA Software

5. Creating and Managing Issues
6. Using Agile Boards: Scrum and Kanban
7. Advanced Issue Search and Filters
8. Configuring Workflows

Section C: JIRA for Agile Project Management

9. Planning and Running Sprints
10. Backlog Management and Grooming
11. Reporting and Dashboards
12. Time Tracking and Estimation

Section D: JIRA Administration

13. User and Group Management
14. Project Roles and Permissions
15. Customizing Fields and Screens
16. Automation Rules and Triggers

Section E: Advanced JIRA Topics

17. Integrating JIRA with Other Tools
18. Using JIRA Query Language (JQL)
19. Best Practices for JIRA Administration
20. Migrating and Upgrading JIRA Instances

Section F: Confluence for Documentation and Collaboration

21. Creating and Managing Spaces
22. Building and Organizing Pages
23. Using Templates and Blueprints
24. Collaborating with Team Members

Section G: Confluence Administration and Advanced Features

25. User and Permissions Management in Confluence

26. Integrating Confluence with JIRA
27. Advanced Formatting and Macros
28. Best Practices for Confluence Administration

Section H: Real-World Examples and Case Studies

29. Setting Up a Project from Scratch
30. Real-World Use Cases for JIRA
31. Real-World Use Cases for Confluence
32. Lessons Learned and Tips for Success

Appendices

- Appendix A: JIRA Cheat Sheet
- Appendix B: Confluence Cheat Sheet
- Appendix C: Additional Resources for Further Learning

~ Conclusion

Welcome & What You'll Learn

Welcome to "Mastering JIRA for Agile Projects: A Practical Guide with Real-World Examples (Confluence Included)!" This book is designed to be your comprehensive guide to leveraging the power of JIRA and Confluence for seamless collaboration and efficient project management. Whether you're new to these tools or an experienced user looking to expand your knowledge, this book will equip you with the practical skills and real-world insights needed to streamline your workflows, enhance team productivity, and successfully deliver projects on time and within budget.

What You'll Learn

Throughout this book, you will gain a deep understanding of JIRA and Confluence, both individually and as a powerful integrated solution. Here's a glimpse of the key topics we'll cover:

Section A: Getting Started with JIRA and Confluence

- A solid foundation in the core concepts of JIRA and Confluence
- Step-by-step guidance on setting up your JIRA account and project
- Practical tips for navigating the JIRA interface effectively
- An introduction to the world of Confluence and its collaborative capabilities

Section B: Working with JIRA Software

- Creating, managing, and tracking issues like a pro
- Harnessing the power of Agile boards (Scrum and Kanban) to visualize and manage your work
- Advanced search techniques to find the information you need quickly
- Configuring workflows to automate and streamline your processes

Section C: JIRA for Agile Project Management

- Planning and executing sprints with precision
- Effective backlog management and grooming
- Generating insightful reports and dashboards
- Time tracking and estimation techniques for accurate project planning

Section D: JIRA Administration

- User and group management to ensure the right people have the right access
- Defining project roles and permissions for optimal security
- Customizing fields and screens to tailor JIRA to your specific needs
- Harnessing automation rules and triggers to eliminate manual tasks

Section E: Advanced JIRA Topics

- Integrating JIRA with other tools to create a seamless ecosystem
- Leveraging JIRA Query Language (JQL) for complex queries and reports
- Best practices for JIRA administration to ensure optimal performance
- Guidance on migrating and upgrading JIRA instances

Section F: Confluence for Documentation and Collaboration

- Creating and managing spaces to organize your team's knowledge
- Building and structuring pages for clear and concise documentation
- Utilizing templates and blueprints for standardized content creation
- Fostering collaboration and communication within your team

Section G: Confluence Administration and Advanced Features

- User and permissions management to control access to your Confluence spaces
- Integrating Confluence with JIRA for seamless traceability and knowledge sharing
- Mastering advanced formatting and macros for visually appealing content
- Best practices for Confluence administration to ensure smooth operation

Section H: Real-World Examples and Case Studies

- Practical examples of setting up JIRA and Confluence projects from scratch
- Real-world use cases showcasing how JIRA and Confluence are used in various industries
- Lessons learned and valuable tips for achieving success

Appendices

- Handy cheat sheets for JIRA and Confluence commands
- Additional resources to further your learning journey

By the time you complete this book, you'll be well-equipped to harness the full potential of JIRA and Confluence to drive collaboration, streamline workflows, and deliver successful projects. Let's get started on this exciting journey!

Section A:
Getting Started with JIRA and Confluence

Introduction to JIRA and Confluence

Outline

- What is JIRA?
- JIRA features
- What is Confluence?
- Confluence Features
- Chapter Summary

What is JIRA?

JIRA, developed by Atlassian, is a robust and multifaceted software development tool that serves as the central nervous system for teams involved in planning, tracking, and releasing software. It primarily functions as a comprehensive issue tracker, allowing teams to efficiently manage tasks, bugs, and other work items throughout their entire lifecycle. However, JIRA's capabilities extend far beyond simple issue tracking. It empowers teams with a wide range of features, including project management tools for planning, scheduling, and resource allocation. Additionally, JIRA's Agile boards enable teams to embrace Agile methodologies such as Scrum and Kanban, fostering iterative development and continuous improvement.

One of JIRA's key strengths is its high degree of customizability. It can be tailored to fit the specific needs and workflows of different teams and projects. Users can create custom workflows to define the steps an issue progresses through, from creation to resolution. This flexibility allows teams to adapt JIRA to their unique processes, ensuring seamless integration into their existing systems and methodologies.

JIRA's reporting and dashboard features provide teams with valuable insights into project progress, enabling them to identify bottlenecks, measure performance, and make data-driven decisions. By providing real-time visibility into project status, JIRA empowers teams to proactively address challenges and ensure project success.

Overall, JIRA's comprehensive feature set, combined with its adaptability and customization options, makes it an indispensable tool for teams across various industries and project types. Whether you're developing software, managing marketing campaigns, or coordinating complex projects, JIRA can streamline your workflows, enhance collaboration, and drive successful outcomes.

JIRA Features

JIRA offers a comprehensive suite of features designed to streamline project management and enhance team collaboration:

- **Issue Tracking:** At its core, JIRA excels at issue tracking, allowing teams to create, assign, and monitor the progress of various work items throughout their lifecycle. These issues can represent tasks, bugs, user stories, or any other relevant unit of work. JIRA provides a structured framework

for capturing issue details, assigning ownership, setting priorities, and tracking progress through customizable statuses.
- **Project Management:** JIRA goes beyond issue tracking by incorporating robust project management capabilities. Teams can utilize JIRA to plan projects, define timelines, allocate resources, and monitor overall progress. The platform supports the creation of project roadmaps, Gantt charts, and other visual representations of project plans, facilitating efficient coordination and execution.
- **Agile Boards:** JIRA is particularly well-suited for Agile development methodologies. It offers native support for Scrum and Kanban boards, providing teams with visual representations of their work in progress. These boards allow teams to easily track sprints, manage backlogs, and visualize the flow of work, fostering transparency and adaptability.
- **Workflows:** JIRA enables the creation of custom workflows that mirror the unique processes of different teams or projects. These workflows define the steps an issue transitions through, from creation to resolution. By automating routine tasks and enforcing standardized procedures, workflows streamline operations and ensure consistent outcomes.
- **Reporting and Dashboards:** JIRA's reporting capabilities empower teams with valuable insights into their project's health and performance. Teams can generate a variety of reports and create customizable dashboards to visualize key metrics, such as progress against goals, burndown charts, and team velocity. These data-driven insights facilitate informed decision-making and proactive course correction.

What is Confluence?

Confluence, another powerful tool developed by Atlassian, serves as a collaborative workspace where teams can converge to create, organize, and share knowledge, documentation, and other essential information. Think of it as a central repository, a digital library where all the collective wisdom and insights of your team reside. It's a place where ideas are born, projects are documented, and decisions are made.

But Confluence is more than just a static storage space. It's a dynamic platform that actively fosters collaboration. By providing a user-friendly interface and intuitive tools, Confluence empowers team members to contribute their knowledge and expertise effortlessly. Whether it's creating detailed project plans, documenting meeting minutes, or sharing best practices, Confluence makes it easy for everyone to add their voice to the conversation.

One of the key strengths of Confluence is its ability to organize information in a way that makes sense. With features like spaces, pages, and hierarchies, teams can structure their knowledge base in a logical and intuitive manner. This makes it easy for team members to find the information they need, when they need it.

Confluence also promotes collaboration through features like comments, mentions, and collaborative editing. Team members can provide feedback, ask questions, and work together in real time to refine documents and ideas. This not only improves the quality of the content but also fosters a sense of shared ownership and teamwork.

Confluence Features

Confluence boasts a wide array of features that empower teams to collaborate effectively and create a comprehensive knowledge base:

- **Page Creation and Organization:** Confluence provides a rich text editor that allows users to craft visually appealing and informative pages. With a variety of formatting options, including headers, tables, images, and multimedia embeds, users can create engaging content that is easy to consume. Additionally, Confluence's organization features, such as spaces and hierarchies, enable

teams to structure their content in a way that is logical and intuitive, making it easy to find the information they need.
- **Templates and Blueprints:** Confluence streamlines the content creation process through templates and blueprints. Templates provide pre-formatted structures for common types of documents, such as meeting notes, project plans, and product requirements. Blueprints take this a step further by offering step-by-step guides for creating complex documentation, ensuring consistency and reducing the learning curve for new users.
- **Collaboration Tools:** Confluence fosters collaboration through a range of tools that facilitate communication and feedback. Users can comment on pages, mention colleagues to draw their attention to specific points, and even collaborate in real-time on the same document. This creates a dynamic environment where ideas can be exchanged freely, and knowledge can be shared seamlessly.
- **Integration with JIRA:** Confluence seamlessly integrates with JIRA, creating a powerful synergy between project management and knowledge sharing. Teams can link Confluence pages to JIRA issues, providing context and documentation for project tasks. This integration streamlines workflows, improves traceability, and ensures that everyone has access to the information they need to make informed decisions.
- **Search and Discovery:** Confluence's powerful search engine enables users to quickly locate the information they need. Whether you're searching for a specific page, a keyword within a document, or an attachment, Confluence's search functionality can help you find it in seconds. This eliminates the frustration of searching through endless folders and files, saving time and boosting productivity.

Chapter Summary

In this introductory chapter, we delved into the fundamental concepts of JIRA and Confluence, two powerful tools developed by Atlassian that play a pivotal role in modern project management and collaboration. We explored JIRA's versatile capabilities as an issue tracker, project management platform, and Agile development tool, highlighting its customizable workflows, reporting features, and adaptability to diverse methodologies. Additionally, we introduced Confluence as a collaborative workspace that facilitates knowledge sharing, documentation, and communication within teams. We touched upon Confluence's rich text editor, organization features, templates, collaborative tools, integration with JIRA, and powerful search functionality. Understanding these core concepts will lay the groundwork for mastering JIRA and Confluence in the subsequent chapters. As we progress through this book, we will delve deeper into the intricacies of these tools, providing practical examples and real-world use cases to help you harness their full potential and streamline your workflows.

Setting Up Your JIRA Account and Project

Outline

- JIRA Deployment Options
- Creating Your JIRA Cloud Account
- Creating Your First JIRA Project
- Essential JIRA Project Configurations
- Chapter Summary

JIRA Deployment Options

Before diving into the nitty-gritty of setting up your JIRA account and project, it's crucial to understand the different deployment options available to you. Atlassian offers two primary ways to deploy JIRA:

1. **JIRA Cloud:** This is a cloud-based solution hosted by Atlassian on their servers. It's the simplest way to get started with JIRA as it requires minimal setup and maintenance. Atlassian takes care of all the technical aspects, including infrastructure, security, and updates.
2. **JIRA Server/Data Center:** These are self-hosted options where you install and manage JIRA on your own servers or data center. This gives you more control and customization flexibility but also requires more technical expertise and resources for maintenance.

Pros and Cons of JIRA Cloud

Pros:

- **Ease of setup and maintenance:** Atlassian handles everything, so you can focus on using JIRA.
- **Automatic updates:** You always have the latest features and security patches.
- **Scalability:** Easily scale your JIRA instance as your team or organization grows.
- **Lower upfront costs:** No need to invest in server hardware or infrastructure.

Cons:

- **Limited customization:** You cannot modify the underlying code or install custom plugins.
- **Less control over data:** Your data is stored on Atlassian's servers.
- **Potential for downtime:** Although rare, cloud services can experience occasional outages.

Pros and Cons of JIRA Server/Data Center

Pros:

- **Greater customization:** You have full control over the JIRA environment and can tailor it to your specific needs.
- **More control over data:** Your data resides on your own servers.
- **Increased security:** You can implement your own security measures to protect your data.

Cons:

- **Higher upfront costs:** You need to invest in server hardware, software licenses, and IT resources.
- **More maintenance required:** You are responsible for updates, backups, and troubleshooting.
- **Scalability challenges:** Scaling up a self-hosted JIRA instance can be more complex.

Choosing the Right Deployment Option

The best deployment option for you depends on your specific requirements and priorities. Consider the following factors when making your decision:

- **Budget:** JIRA Cloud is generally more affordable for smaller teams, while larger organizations might find JIRA Server/Data Center more cost-effective in the long run.
- **Technical expertise:** JIRA Cloud requires minimal technical knowledge, while JIRA Server/Data Center demands more IT expertise.
- **Customization needs:** If you need extensive customization, JIRA Server/Data Center is the better choice.
- **Data control and security:** If data control and security are top priorities, self-hosting with JIRA Server/Data Center is the preferred option.

For most users, especially those new to JIRA, the simplicity and convenience of JIRA Cloud make it an excellent starting point. However, if you have specific customization needs or stringent security requirements, JIRA Server/Data Center might be a more suitable choice.

In this book, we will primarily focus on JIRA Cloud as it is the most accessible and widely used deployment option. However, the core concepts and principles we cover are applicable to all JIRA deployment options.

Creating Your JIRA Cloud Account

Setting up your JIRA Cloud account is a straightforward process. Here's a step-by-step guide to get you started:

1. **Navigating to the JIRA website:** Open your web browser and go to the Atlassian website (https://www.atlassian.com/). Locate the JIRA Cloud product page. You can usually find it in the navigation menu or through a search on the site.
2. **Starting the free trial:** Once you're on the JIRA Cloud product page, look for the option to start a free trial. This trial typically lasts for a limited period (e.g., 7 days) and allows you to explore JIRA's features and functionalities before deciding on a paid plan. Click the button or link to begin the trial.
3. **Providing account information:** You'll be prompted to provide some basic information to create your account. This includes your email address, which will be used as your JIRA username, and a secure password. You might also be asked to provide your name and company name (optional). Fill in the required details accurately.
4. **Selecting a site name:** The site name is a unique identifier for your JIRA Cloud instance. It will be part of the URL you use to access JIRA. Choose a name that is relevant to your organization or project. For example, if your company is called "Acme Corporation," you could use "acme" as your site name. The URL for your JIRA instance would then be something like "acme.atlassian.net."
5. **Verifying the email address:** After completing the sign-up process, check your email inbox for a verification message from Atlassian. Click the verification link in the email to confirm your account and activate your JIRA Cloud trial.

Congratulations! You've successfully created your JIRA Cloud account. You can now log in and start exploring the platform. Remember that during the free trial period, you can experiment with different features, create projects, and invite team members to collaborate. Once the trial ends, you'll have the option to choose a suitable paid plan based on your needs and usage.

Creating Your First JIRA Project

Now that you have your JIRA Cloud account up and running, it's time to create your first project. This is where you'll start organizing your work, tracking tasks, and collaborating with your team.

1. **Accessing the project creation page:** After logging into your JIRA Cloud instance, look for the "Create project" button or link. It's usually prominently displayed on the dashboard or in the navigation menu. Click it to access the project creation page.
2. **Choosing a project template:** JIRA offers a variety of project templates designed for different methodologies and use cases. Some of the most common templates include:
    - **Scrum:** Ideal for Agile software development teams that work in sprints.
    - **Kanban:** Suitable for teams that prefer a continuous flow of work and visualize their workflow on a Kanban board.
    - **Bug tracking:** Designed for tracking and resolving software bugs.
    - **Content management:** Geared towards managing content creation and publishing processes.
    - **Task management:** A simple template for general task tracking and management.
3. Choose the template that best aligns with your project's goals and workflow. You can always customize it later.
4. **Naming the project:** Give your project a clear and descriptive name that reflects its purpose. This will make it easy for you and your team members to identify the project within JIRA. Avoid using generic names like "Project 1" or "New Project."
5. **Defining project key:** The project key is a short code that uniquely identifies your project in JIRA. It's typically a combination of letters and numbers (e.g., MKT-123 for a marketing project). Choose a project key that is meaningful and easy to remember.
6. **Customizing project settings:** After creating the project, you can customize its settings to match your specific requirements. This includes:
    - Defining the types of issues (tasks, bugs, stories) that can be created in the project.
    - Configuring workflows to define the steps an issue goes through.
    - Customizing screens to control the information displayed when creating or editing issues.
7. For now, you can leave these settings at their defaults and revisit them later as you become more familiar with JIRA.

By following these steps, you'll have your first JIRA project ready to go. In the next chapter, we'll dive deeper into the JIRA interface and explore how to navigate and use its various features effectively.

Essential JIRA Project Configurations

Creating a JIRA project is just the first step. To truly harness its power, you'll need to configure it to align with your team's specific workflows and requirements. Here are the essential configurations you should focus on:

- **Issue Types:** Issue types are labels that categorize different kinds of work items in your project. Common issue types include "Task" (for general tasks), "Bug" (for defects or errors), "Story" (for user requirements in Agile projects), and "Epic" (for large bodies of work). You can also create custom issue types to match your specific needs. To create or modify issue types, go to your project settings and look for the "Issue types" section.
- **Workflows:** Workflows define the lifecycle of an issue, outlining the different statuses it can transition through (e.g., "To Do," "In Progress," "Done") and the transitions between them. Each issue type can have its own workflow. You can customize workflows by adding or removing statuses, defining transitions, and setting conditions for when transitions can occur. JIRA's workflow editor makes this process intuitive.
- **Screens:** Screens control the information displayed when creating or editing an issue. JIRA comes with default screens, but you can customize them by adding, removing, or rearranging fields. For instance, you might want to add a "Priority" field to all issue types or a "Due Date" field to tasks. Navigate to the "Screens" section in your project settings to make these adjustments.
- **Fields:** Fields are the individual data points you capture within an issue. JIRA offers a wide range of field types, including text fields, number fields, date fields, user picker fields, and more. You can

add custom fields to your project to capture specific information relevant to your work. This can be done in the "Fields" section of your project settings.
- **User Management:** Effective collaboration in JIRA relies on proper user management. You need to add your team members to the project and assign them appropriate roles and permissions. Roles determine what actions a user can perform (e.g., create issues, edit workflows), while permissions control access to specific projects or issues. You can manage users and roles in the "Project settings" area.

These essential configurations lay the foundation for a well-organized and efficient JIRA project. By tailoring issue types, workflows, screens, fields, and user management to your specific needs, you can create a JIRA environment that seamlessly supports your team's unique processes and goals. As you become more familiar with JIRA, you can explore additional configurations and customizations to further enhance your project management experience.

Chapter Summary

In this chapter, we explored the essential steps involved in setting up your JIRA Cloud account and creating your first project. We discussed the different deployment options available for JIRA, highlighting the pros and cons of JIRA Cloud and JIRA Server/Data Center. We then walked you through the process of creating your JIRA Cloud account, from navigating to the website to verifying your email address. Next, we guided you through the steps of creating your first JIRA project, emphasizing the importance of choosing the right template and configuring essential project settings such as issue types, workflows, screens, fields, and user management. By completing these initial steps, you've laid the groundwork for effectively utilizing JIRA to manage your projects and collaborate with your team. In the upcoming chapters, we will delve deeper into the JIRA interface, exploring its various features and functionalities in more detail.

Navigating the JIRA Interface

Outline

- The JIRA Dashboard
- The Top Navigation Bar
- The Sidebar
- The Issue View
- Additional Tips for Navigation
- Chapter Summary

The JIRA Dashboard

Upon logging into JIRA, the first screen you encounter is the dashboard. This serves as your personalized command center, providing a comprehensive overview of your work and projects. Think of it as a control panel where you can monitor progress, access essential information, and quickly navigate to different areas of JIRA.

Key Functions of the Dashboard

The JIRA dashboard is designed to streamline your workflow and keep you informed about the most relevant aspects of your work. Here are some of its key functions:

- **Project Overview:** The dashboard typically displays a list of your active projects, allowing you to easily jump to the project you want to work on.
- **Recent Activity:** It provides a snapshot of recent activity across your projects, such as newly created issues, updated issues, and upcoming deadlines.
- **Assigned Issues:** You can see a list of issues that are currently assigned to you, helping you prioritize your tasks.
- **Filters and Gadgets:** JIRA dashboards are highly customizable. You can add various filters and gadgets to display specific information, such as charts showing project progress, calendars with upcoming deadlines, or activity streams for specific projects or teams.

Customization

One of the most powerful aspects of the JIRA dashboard is its flexibility. You can personalize your dashboard to display the information that is most relevant to you. This might include adding gadgets that show your team's progress on a specific project, filtering the activity stream to only show updates from certain projects, or rearranging the layout to suit your preferences. JIRA offers a wide range of built-in gadgets, and you can also install third-party gadgets to extend the dashboard's functionality further.

Why Customize Your Dashboard?

By customizing your JIRA dashboard, you can:

- **Focus on what matters:** Prioritize the information that is most important for your daily work.
- **Stay informed:** Get a quick overview of project progress and potential issues.
- **Increase productivity:** Access the tools and information you need more efficiently.

In the next sections, we will explore the other elements of the JIRA interface, such as the top navigation bar and sidebar, which will further enhance your ability to navigate and utilize JIRA effectively.

The Top Navigation Bar

The top navigation bar is a consistent element that you'll find at the top of every page within the JIRA interface. It serves as a central hub for accessing key functionalities and navigating through the platform. Let's delve into the primary functions of this navigation bar:

- **Search:** The search bar is your gateway to quickly finding anything within JIRA. Simply type in a keyword, issue key, project name, or any other relevant term, and JIRA will display a list of matching results. This is a powerful tool for locating specific issues, projects, or even users. You can use advanced search operators to refine your queries further.
- **Create:** The Create button is your starting point for creating new JIRA entities. Clicking on this button opens a dropdown menu that allows you to create various items, including:
    - **Issue:** Create a new task, bug, story, or other type of issue.
    - **Project:** Initiate a new project from scratch or using a template.
    - **Filter:** Create a custom filter to view specific sets of issues.
    - **Dashboard:** Design a personalized dashboard to display relevant information.
- **Profile and Settings:** On the right side of the navigation bar, you'll find your profile icon or avatar. Clicking on it reveals a dropdown menu with several options:
    - **Profile:** View and edit your personal profile information.
    - **Settings:** Manage your JIRA settings, such as notifications, keyboard shortcuts, and language preferences.
    - **Account:** Access your Atlassian account settings, where you can manage your subscription, billing information, and connected apps.
    - **Log out:** Safely exit your JIRA session.

The top navigation bar is designed to be intuitive and user-friendly, providing easy access to essential JIRA features regardless of where you are within the platform. By mastering the functions of this navigation bar, you'll be able to navigate JIRA efficiently and streamline your workflow.

The Sidebar

The sidebar in JIRA serves as your trusty navigator, providing quick and easy access to various sections and features within the platform. It typically resides on the left side of the screen and remains consistent across different pages, ensuring you can always find your way around. Let's break down the key sections of the sidebar:

- **Projects:** This section is your gateway to all the projects you're involved in. It usually displays a list of your recent projects for easy access. You can also use the search bar within this section to find specific projects or browse through all projects available to you. Clicking on a project name takes you directly to its dashboard.
- **Boards:** Agile teams will find this section particularly useful. It provides direct links to the Agile boards associated with your projects. Whether you're using Scrum or Kanban, you can quickly jump to the board to visualize your workflow, manage sprints (in Scrum), and track the progress of your issues.
- **Issues:** This section is your hub for managing individual issues. It offers various views and filters to help you find the issues you need. You can access lists of your assigned issues, recently viewed issues, or issues that match specific criteria. You can also create and manage filters to narrow down the issue list and focus on specific tasks.
- **Dashboards:** Your personalized dashboards are housed in this section. You can create multiple dashboards to visualize different aspects of your work, such as project progress, team performance, or upcoming deadlines. Clicking on a dashboard will open it in the main content area of JIRA.
- **Apps:** JIRA's extensive marketplace offers a wide array of apps and add-ons that can enhance its functionality. These apps can integrate JIRA with other tools, automate tasks, provide additional

reporting capabilities, and much more. The Apps section in the sidebar allows you to access and manage the apps installed in your JIRA instance.

By utilizing the sidebar effectively, you can effortlessly navigate between projects, boards, issues, and dashboards, making your JIRA experience more efficient and productive. Additionally, the sidebar gives you quick access to the powerful apps that can further customize and optimize your JIRA workflow.

The Issue View

The issue view in JIRA is where the magic happens. It's the heart of your interaction with individual work items. When you click on an issue from a list or board, you're taken to its dedicated issue view, a comprehensive page that provides all the details and context you need to understand and address the task at hand.

Key Elements of the Issue View

The issue view is packed with information and interactive elements. Here's a breakdown of the key components you'll encounter:

- **Summary:** This is the title or a brief description of the issue. It gives you a quick overview of what the issue is about. Think of it as the headline of a news article – it should be concise yet informative.
- **Description:** Below the summary, you'll find the description field, where the issue's details are elaborated. This is where you'll typically find a more comprehensive explanation of the task, bug, or requirement. The description can include steps to reproduce a problem, acceptance criteria, relevant attachments, and other pertinent information.
- **Comments:** The comments section is a collaborative space where team members can discuss the issue, share updates, ask questions, and provide feedback. It's like a threaded conversation that allows everyone involved to stay informed and contribute their insights.
- **Activity:** The activity stream is a chronological log of all the actions taken on the issue. It records changes to the issue's status, assignee, priority, comments, and other updates. This historical record provides valuable context and helps you track the issue's progress over time.
- **People:** This section shows you who is currently assigned to the issue and who is watching it. The assignee is the person responsible for completing the task or resolving the problem. Watchers are individuals who have expressed interest in the issue and want to stay informed about its progress.

Additional Elements

In addition to these core elements, the issue view often includes other sections, depending on your JIRA configuration and the specific issue type. These may include:

- **Details:** This section may display additional metadata about the issue, such as its type, priority, due date, and related issues.
- **Subtasks:** If the issue has been broken down into smaller subtasks, they will be listed in this section.
- **Time Tracking:** If your team uses JIRA for time tracking, you might see fields here to log the time spent on the issue.
- **Links:** This section shows any links to external resources or other JIRA issues that are related to the current issue.
- **Attachments:** You can attach files, images, or other documents to the issue for reference.

The issue view is a dynamic and interactive workspace. You can edit most of the fields, add comments, transition the issue through its workflow, and perform other actions depending on your permissions. By mastering the issue view, you gain the ability to effectively manage individual tasks within JIRA, ensuring smooth progress and collaboration with your team.

Additional Tips for Navigation

As you become more familiar with JIRA, here are some additional tips and tricks to enhance your navigation experience and boost your productivity:

- **Keyboard Shortcuts:** JIRA offers a plethora of keyboard shortcuts that can significantly speed up your workflow. For instance, you can press "c" to create a new issue, "e" to edit an issue, or "/" to initiate a search. Take some time to learn these shortcuts, and you'll find yourself zipping through tasks in no time. You can access a complete list of shortcuts by pressing "?" within JIRA.
- **Saved Filters:** If you frequently find yourself searching for specific sets of issues, saved filters are your best friend. You can create custom filters based on various criteria, such as project, issue type, status, assignee, or any other relevant field. Once you've created a filter, you can save it for easy access later. This saves you the hassle of re-entering the same search criteria repeatedly.
- **Project Shortcuts:** If you work on multiple projects simultaneously, project shortcuts can be a lifesaver. These shortcuts allow you to quickly jump to a specific project's dashboard or board without navigating through the project list. You can create project shortcuts by right-clicking on a project in the sidebar and selecting "Add project shortcut."
- **Customizing the Interface:** JIRA offers various options for personalizing the interface to your liking. You can adjust the theme, change the color scheme, rearrange the sidebar, and even customize the columns displayed on your boards. Explore the JIRA settings to discover the available customization options and tailor the interface to your preferences.

By incorporating these tips into your daily JIRA usage, you can streamline your workflow, save time, and become a true JIRA navigation ninja. Remember, practice makes perfect, so don't hesitate to experiment and find the navigation techniques that work best for you.

Chapter Summary

In this chapter, we've embarked on a guided tour of the JIRA interface, equipping you with the essential knowledge to navigate the platform effectively. We began by exploring the JIRA dashboard, your personalized command center for monitoring projects and staying informed about recent activity. Next, we delved into the top navigation bar, highlighting its powerful search functionality, the ability to create new JIRA entities, and the options available under your profile for settings and account management. We then explored the sidebar, your navigational compass for accessing projects, boards, issues, dashboards, and apps. We also ventured into the issue view, where you can interact with individual work items, view details, add comments, and track progress. Finally, we shared additional navigation tips, including keyboard shortcuts, saved filters, project shortcuts, and interface customization options, to empower you to become a JIRA navigation pro. With this solid foundation in navigating the JIRA interface, you're well-prepared to dive deeper into the world of JIRA and harness its full potential for project management and collaboration.

Getting Started with Confluence

Outline

- What is Confluence?
- Confluence Deployment Options
- Creating a Confluence Cloud Account
- Creating Your First Confluence Space
- Chapter Summary

What is Confluence?

Confluence, developed by Atlassian, is a dynamic and versatile collaborative workspace and knowledge base platform. It serves as a centralized hub where teams can seamlessly create, organize, and share information, fostering a culture of collaboration and knowledge exchange.

At its core, Confluence empowers teams to work together more effectively. It provides a shared space where team members can contribute their knowledge, ideas, and insights, regardless of their physical location. This collaborative environment breaks down silos and promotes open communication, enabling teams to harness their collective intelligence and achieve better outcomes.

Beyond collaboration, Confluence excels at knowledge management. It acts as a repository for valuable information, ensuring that it is easily accessible to everyone who needs it. With Confluence, teams can create and maintain documentation, wikis, how-to guides, meeting notes, project plans, and other essential resources. This not only saves time by preventing the need to recreate information but also ensures that knowledge is preserved and shared across the organization.

Furthermore, Confluence streamlines documentation processes. Its rich text editor and powerful formatting options make it easy to create professional-looking documents. Templates and blueprints help standardize documentation formats, ensuring consistency and reducing the effort required to create new documents. With version history and commenting features, teams can track changes, provide feedback, and collaborate on improving documentation over time.

Confluence Deployment Options

Similar to JIRA, Confluence also offers two main deployment options:

1. **Confluence Cloud:** This cloud-based option is hosted on Atlassian's servers, offering a hassle-free setup and maintenance experience. Atlassian manages the infrastructure, security, and updates, allowing you to focus solely on utilizing Confluence for collaboration and knowledge sharing.
2. **Confluence Server/Data Center:** These self-hosted options involve installing and managing Confluence on your own servers or data center. While this provides greater control and customization capabilities, it also necessitates technical expertise and resources for upkeep.

Pros and Cons of Confluence Cloud

Pros:

- **Easy setup and maintenance:** Atlassian handles all technical aspects, eliminating the need for server setup or ongoing maintenance.
- **Automatic updates:** You always have access to the latest features, improvements, and security patches without manual intervention.

- **Scalability:** Confluence Cloud effortlessly scales with your team or organization's growth, ensuring smooth performance even with increased usage.
- **Lower upfront costs:** There's no need to invest in server hardware or infrastructure, making it a cost-effective option, especially for smaller teams.

Cons:

- **Limited customization:** You have less control over the underlying infrastructure and cannot modify the source code or install certain custom apps.
- **Data residency:** Your data is stored on Atlassian's servers, which might be a concern for organizations with strict data residency requirements.

Pros and Cons of Confluence Server/Data Center

Pros:

- **Greater customization:** You have full control over the Confluence environment, enabling you to tailor it precisely to your organization's specific needs and processes.
- **Data control:** Your data resides on your own servers, giving you complete ownership and control over it.
- **Enhanced security:** You can implement your own security measures to protect your sensitive information.

Cons:

- **Higher upfront costs:** You need to invest in server hardware, software licenses, and IT resources to set up and maintain Confluence Server/Data Center.
- **More maintenance required:** You are responsible for managing updates, backups, and troubleshooting, demanding more technical expertise.

Choosing the Right Deployment Option

The optimal deployment option for you hinges on your unique circumstances and priorities. To make an informed decision, consider the following factors:

- **Budget:** Confluence Cloud is typically more budget-friendly for smaller teams, while larger organizations might find Confluence Server/Data Center more cost-effective in the long term.
- **Technical resources:** Confluence Cloud requires minimal technical know-how, whereas Confluence Server/Data Center necessitates dedicated IT personnel.
- **Customization needs:** If extensive customization is a priority, Confluence Server/Data Center offers greater flexibility.
- **Data control and security:** For organizations with strict data governance policies or sensitive information, Confluence Server/Data Center provides more control.

In this book, we will primarily focus on Confluence Cloud due to its user-friendliness and widespread adoption. However, the principles and concepts we cover are applicable to both deployment options, allowing you to adapt your knowledge to your specific Confluence environment.

Creating a Confluence Cloud Account

Setting up your Confluence Cloud account is a breeze. Follow these steps to get started:

1. **Visit the Confluence website:** Open your web browser and navigate to the Atlassian Confluence website. You can typically find it by searching for "Atlassian Confluence" or going directly to their website (https://www.atlassian.com/software/confluence).

2. **Start a free trial:** Look for the option to start a free trial on the Confluence Cloud product page. This trial allows you to explore the platform's features and functionalities before committing to a paid plan. Click the button or link to initiate the trial.
3. **Enter account details:** You'll be asked to provide some basic information to create your account. This includes:
    - **Email address:** This will serve as your Confluence username and be used for communication.
    - **Password:** Choose a strong password to secure your account.
    - **Name (optional):** Enter your name for personalization.
    - **Company name (optional):** If you're using Confluence for work, you can enter your company's name.
4. **Choose a site name:** The site name is a unique identifier for your Confluence Cloud instance. It will be part of the URL you use to access Confluence. Select a name that is meaningful and easy to remember for your team. For instance, if your company is named "ABC Enterprises," you might choose "abc-enterprises" as your site name.
5. **Verify the email address:** After submitting your information, check your email inbox for a verification message from Atlassian. Click the link in the email to confirm your account and activate your Confluence Cloud trial.

Congratulations! You've successfully created your Confluence Cloud account. You can now log in and start exploring the platform's features. During the free trial, you can experiment with creating spaces, pages, and collaborating with your team members. Once the trial period ends, you have the option to select a suitable paid plan based on your team's size and needs.

Creating Your First Confluence Space

After setting up your Confluence Cloud account, the next step is to create your first space. In Confluence, a **space** serves as a dedicated area for organizing and collaborating on a specific topic or project. It's like a virtual folder where you can store related pages, documents, and other content.

Types of Spaces

Confluence offers several types of spaces to cater to different needs:

- **Team Spaces:** These are designed for teams to collaborate on ongoing work. They typically contain meeting notes, project plans, team calendars, and other collaborative documents.
- **Project Spaces:** These spaces are focused on specific projects and contain all the relevant information, such as project goals, timelines, deliverables, and status updates.
- **Personal Spaces:** These are private spaces for individual users to organize their own notes, drafts, and personal projects.

Creating a Space

To create your first space, follow these simple steps:

1. **Access the space creation page:** After logging into Confluence, look for the "Create space" button or link. It's usually prominently displayed on the dashboard or in the navigation menu.
2. **Choose a space type:** Select the type of space that best suits your purpose. If you're unsure, start with a team space or a project space.
3. **Name your space:** Give your space a clear and descriptive name that reflects its purpose. For example, if you're creating a space for your marketing team, you could name it "Marketing Team Workspace."

4. **Customize your space:** Confluence offers various customization options to personalize your space. You can choose a space theme to give it a unique look and feel. You can also set permissions to control who can access and contribute to the space.

Customization Options

While you can always customize your space later, here are some options to consider:

- **Space themes:** Confluence provides a variety of themes to change the appearance of your space. Choose a theme that aligns with your team's preferences or your organization's branding.
- **Permissions:** By default, all members of your Confluence site can access and contribute to team spaces. However, you can restrict access to specific users or groups if needed. Project spaces and personal spaces offer more granular permission controls.

By following these steps, you'll have your first Confluence space ready to use.

Chapter Summary

In this chapter, we introduced Confluence as a powerful collaborative workspace and knowledge base platform designed to enhance team communication, knowledge management, and documentation. We explored the two main deployment options, Confluence Cloud and Confluence Server/Data Center, discussing their respective advantages and disadvantages in terms of cost, setup, maintenance, customization, and control. We then provided a step-by-step guide on how to create a Confluence Cloud account, from visiting the website to verifying your email address. Finally, we delved into the process of creating your first Confluence space, explaining the different types of spaces, their purposes, and the customization options available. With this foundational knowledge, you are now equipped to start exploring the full potential of Confluence for fostering collaboration and building a comprehensive knowledge base for your team or organization.

Section B:
Working with JIRA Software

Creating and Managing Issues

Outline

- Understanding JIRA Issues
- Creating Issues
- Essential Issue Fields
- Managing Issues
- Advanced Issue Management
- Chapter Summary

Understanding JIRA Issues

In the world of JIRA, issues are the fundamental building blocks of your project. They represent individual pieces of work that need to be tracked and completed. Whether it's a task to be done, a bug to be fixed, a user story to be implemented, or any other item that requires attention, it can be represented as an issue within JIRA.

The Lifecycle of a JIRA Issue

Every JIRA issue goes through a lifecycle, which typically consists of the following stages:

1. **Creation:** The issue is created, either manually by a user or automatically through a trigger.
2. **Triage:** The issue is reviewed and assigned to the appropriate team or individual.
3. **Prioritization:** The issue is given a priority level based on its importance and urgency.
4. **Work in Progress:** The assigned team member starts working on the issue.
5. **Review:** The completed work is reviewed by a designated reviewer.
6. **Testing:** The issue undergoes testing to ensure it meets the specified requirements.
7. **Resolution:** The issue is marked as resolved, indicating that the work has been completed.
8. **Closure:** The issue is closed after a final review and verification.

This lifecycle can be customized to fit your specific workflow and project requirements.

Assigning, Prioritizing, and Moving Issues

JIRA provides a flexible framework for managing issues throughout their lifecycle. Here's how you can interact with issues:

- **Assigning Issues:** You can assign issues to specific team members or groups, making it clear who is responsible for working on them.
- **Prioritizing Issues:** JIRA allows you to set priority levels for issues, such as "Highest," "High," "Medium," or "Low," to indicate their relative importance.
- **Moving Issues Through a Workflow:** By transitioning issues through their workflow stages, you can track their progress and ensure they are completed according to your defined process. You can

typically move issues by dragging and dropping them on an Agile board or by using the transition buttons in the issue view.

By understanding the concept of JIRA issues and how to manage them effectively, you'll be well on your way to mastering JIRA and utilizing it to streamline your project management and collaboration efforts.

Creating Issues

Creating a new issue in JIRA is a simple process that involves a few straightforward steps:

1. **Click the "Create" button:** Locate and click the "Create" button, usually prominently displayed in the JIRA interface. This button is typically located at the top-right corner of the screen or in the project sidebar.
2. **Select the appropriate project and issue type:** After clicking "Create," you'll be presented with a dialog or a new page where you need to select the project the issue belongs to. Choose the correct project from the available list. Next, select the issue type that best represents the nature of your work. Common issue types include "Task," "Bug," "Story," and "Epic." If you have custom issue types defined for your project, you'll see those as well.
3. **Fill out the required fields:** The next step is to provide the necessary details for the issue. The required fields may vary depending on your JIRA configuration and the chosen issue type. However, the most common required fields include:
   - **Summary:** A concise and descriptive title for the issue (e.g., "Implement user login feature").
   - **Description:** A more detailed explanation of the issue, outlining its purpose, requirements, and any relevant context.
   - **Assignee:** If you know who will be working on the issue, you can assign it to them at this stage.
   - **Priority:** Indicate the relative importance of the issue (e.g., "Highest," "High," "Medium," or "Low").
4. **Assign the issue to a team member (optional):** As mentioned above, you can assign the issue to a specific team member during the creation process. If you're not sure who will be working on it yet, you can leave this field blank and assign it later.
5. **Set the issue's priority (optional):** If you haven't already set the issue's priority, you can do so now. Choose a priority level that reflects the issue's urgency and importance in relation to other tasks in your project.
6. **Click "Create" to save the issue:** After filling in all the necessary information, click the "Create" button to save the issue. JIRA will generate a unique issue key (e.g., PROJ-123) and add the issue to your project's issue tracker.

Congratulations! You've successfully created your first JIRA issue. Now you can start tracking its progress, collaborating with your team, and moving it through your workflow until it's resolved.

Essential Issue Fields

When you create an issue in JIRA, you'll encounter several fields that are essential for capturing and organizing information about the work item. These fields provide crucial context and help team members understand the nature, scope, and progress of the issue. Here's a breakdown of the essential issue fields you'll typically find in JIRA:

- **Summary:** This is the title or headline of your issue. It should be a brief, yet descriptive, summary of what the issue is about. The summary should be clear enough to give anyone a quick understanding of the task or problem at hand. For example, a good summary might be "Implement new user registration form" or "Fix bug causing crashes on iOS devices."
- **Description:** The description field provides space for a more detailed explanation of the issue. Here, you can provide all the necessary context, including:

- **Steps to Reproduce (for bugs):** If the issue is a bug, outline the exact steps someone would take to encounter the problem.
- **Acceptance Criteria (for stories):** If the issue is a user story, describe the conditions that must be met for the story to be considered complete.
- **Relevant Information:** Include any other details that would be helpful for someone working on the issue, such as error messages, screenshots, or links to related resources.
- **Issue Type:** This field categorizes the issue based on its nature. Common issue types include:
  - **Task:** A general task or piece of work that needs to be done.
  - **Bug:** A defect or error in the software.
  - **Story:** A user requirement or feature request in Agile projects.
  - **Epic:** A large body of work that can be broken down into smaller stories or tasks.
- **Priority:** The priority field indicates the relative importance of the issue compared to other tasks in the project. You can typically choose from a range of options, such as "Highest," "High," "Medium," or "Low." Setting priorities helps teams focus their efforts on the most critical issues.
- **Assignee:** This is the person who is responsible for working on the issue. Assigning an issue to a team member makes it clear who is accountable for its completion.
- **Reporter:** This field records the name of the person who initially created the issue. It can be useful for providing context or asking follow-up questions if needed.

These essential fields provide a solid foundation for tracking and managing issues in JIRA. By carefully filling out these fields, you ensure that your team has all the necessary information to understand and address each issue effectively.

Managing Issues

Once you have created issues in JIRA, it's essential to actively manage them throughout their lifecycle. This involves viewing, editing, transitioning, commenting, and watching issues to ensure smooth progress and effective collaboration.

- **Viewing and Editing Issues:** To view the details of an issue, simply click on its summary or key in any issue list or board. This will open the issue view, where you can see all the relevant information, including the description, comments, activity history, and people involved. To edit an issue, click the "Edit" button in the issue view and make the necessary changes to the fields.
- **Transitioning Issues:** Issues in JIRA follow a workflow, which defines the stages an issue progresses through, from creation to resolution. You can transition an issue to a different status by clicking the available buttons in the issue view or dragging and dropping it on an Agile board. For instance, when you start working on an issue, you would transition it from "To Do" to "In Progress." When you complete the work, you would transition it to "Done."
- **Commenting on Issues:** Comments are a crucial aspect of collaboration in JIRA. You can add comments to an issue to provide updates, ask questions, share ideas, or collaborate with team members. To add a comment, scroll to the comments section in the issue view and type your message in the comment box. You can also mention other users using the "@" symbol to notify them directly.
- **Watching Issues:** If you want to stay updated on an issue's progress, you can "watch" it. This means you'll receive notifications whenever changes are made to the issue, such as new comments or status updates. To watch an issue, click the "Watch" button in the issue view. You can also unwatch an issue if you no longer need to receive notifications.

By actively managing issues in JIRA, you can ensure that work progresses smoothly, keep your team informed, and collaborate effectively to achieve your project goals.

Advanced Issue Management

As you become more proficient in using JIRA, you can leverage advanced issue management techniques to further streamline your workflow and enhance collaboration:

Linking Issues

JIRA allows you to establish relationships between issues by linking them together. This is particularly useful for representing dependencies, hierarchies, or related work items. Some common types of issue linking include:

- **Blocks/Blocked By:** This link indicates that one issue cannot be completed until another issue is resolved. For example, a development task might be blocked by a design issue.
- **Relates To:** This link signifies a general relationship between two issues that are not necessarily dependent on each other.
- **Clones/Cloned By:** This link indicates that an issue is a duplicate of another issue.
- **Parent/Sub-task:** This link establishes a hierarchical relationship where one issue is the parent and the other is a sub-task.

To link issues, open the issue view and navigate to the "Link" section. You can then select the link type and choose the issue you want to link to.

Cloning Issues

Cloning an issue creates an exact copy of it, including its summary, description, and other fields. This can be useful if you need to create a similar issue or want to use an existing issue as a template. To clone an issue, open the issue view and click the "More" button, then select "Clone."

Converting Issue Types

Sometimes, you might need to change the type of an issue. For example, you might realize that what you initially thought was a bug is actually a task. JIRA allows you to convert issue types as long as it's allowed by your project's workflow. To convert an issue type, open the issue view and click the "More" button, then select "Convert to."

Deleting Issues

In some cases, you might need to delete an issue. This should be done with caution, as deleted issues cannot be recovered. To delete an issue, open the issue view and click the "More" button, then select "Delete."

Bulk Editing

If you need to make the same change to multiple issues, you can use JIRA's bulk edit feature. This allows you to select multiple issues and modify them simultaneously. To bulk edit issues, select the issues you want to modify in the issue list or board, then click the "More" button and select "Bulk Change."

By mastering these advanced issue management techniques, you can unlock the full potential of JIRA and streamline your workflow for even greater efficiency and productivity.

Chapter Summary

In this chapter, we delved into the intricacies of creating and managing issues in JIRA, a fundamental aspect of utilizing this powerful project management tool. We began by understanding the core concept of JIRA issues, their lifecycle, and how they can be assigned, prioritized, and moved through workflows. Next, we provided a step-by-step guide on how to create new issues, emphasizing the importance of filling out essential fields such as summary, description, issue type, priority, assignee, and reporter. We then explored the various ways to manage issues in JIRA, including viewing, editing, transitioning, commenting, and watching. Finally, we introduced you to advanced issue management techniques, such as linking issues, cloning issues, converting issue types, deleting issues, and bulk editing, to further enhance your proficiency in using JIRA. By mastering these concepts and techniques, you're now equipped to effectively create, track, and manage issues in JIRA, paving the way for successful project management and collaboration within your team.

Using Agile Boards: Scrum and Kanban

Outline

- Introduction to Agile Boards
- Scrum Boards
- Kanban Boards
- Choosing the Right Agile Board for Your Project
- Chapter Summary

Introduction to Agile Boards

In the realm of agile project management, visibility and collaboration are paramount. Agile boards provide a dynamic and intuitive way to visualize and manage work items throughout a project's lifecycle. Imagine them as digital whiteboards where tasks, bugs, and user stories are represented as cards or sticky notes. These cards move across columns that represent different stages of the workflow, offering a real-time snapshot of your project's progress.

Agile boards serve as a central hub for teams, allowing them to track progress, visualize workflow, and identify bottlenecks. By seeing the status of each work item at a glance, team members can easily understand what's been done, what's in progress, and what's next. This transparency fosters a sense of shared responsibility and accountability, driving collaboration and ensuring everyone is on the same page.

Facilitating Project Management

Agile boards simplify project management by providing a clear visual representation of the work to be done. Teams can easily prioritize tasks, assign resources, and identify dependencies, leading to more efficient planning and execution. The ability to visualize the workflow helps teams identify bottlenecks or areas where work is getting stuck, enabling them to address these issues proactively.

Benefits of Agile Boards

The use of agile boards in JIRA offers numerous benefits, including:

- **Improved Transparency:** Everyone on the team can see the status of each work item, fostering open communication and reducing the need for status update meetings.
- **Enhanced Collaboration:** Team members can easily collaborate on tasks, share updates, and discuss challenges directly on the board.
- **Increased Productivity:** By visualizing the workflow and identifying bottlenecks, teams can optimize their processes and focus their efforts on the most critical tasks.
- **Better Decision-Making:** Agile boards provide real-time data on project progress, enabling teams to make informed decisions and adapt to changing circumstances.

JIRA supports two primary types of agile boards: Scrum boards and Kanban boards. In the following sections, we'll dive deeper into each of these board types, exploring their unique features and how they can be used to effectively manage your agile projects.

Scrum Boards

Scrum boards are a visual representation of the workflow in a Scrum project. They help teams manage and track their work throughout a sprint, fostering transparency and collaboration.

Structure of a Scrum Board

A typical Scrum board is divided into vertical columns, each representing a different stage in the workflow. The most common columns are:

- **To Do:** This column contains tasks that are yet to be started. These tasks are typically drawn from the product backlog, which is a prioritized list of user stories or features to be implemented.
- **In Progress:** Tasks that are currently being worked on are moved to this column. This helps the team see who is working on what and what the current focus of the sprint is.
- **Done:** When a task is completed, it is moved to this column, indicating that it has been reviewed and meets the acceptance criteria.

Some teams may also use additional columns, such as "In Review" or "Blocked," to further refine their workflow.

Swimlanes

In addition to columns, Scrum boards can also be divided into horizontal swimlanes. Swimlanes are used to group tasks based on different criteria, such as:

- **User Stories:** Each swimlane represents a different user story, and tasks related to that story are placed within the corresponding swimlane.
- **Epics:** Epics are larger bodies of work that can be broken down into multiple user stories. Swimlanes can be used to group user stories under their respective epics.
- **Team Members:** If your team has distinct roles (e.g., frontend developers, backend developers, testers), you can create swimlanes for each role to see who is responsible for which tasks.
- **Priorities:** You can also create swimlanes for different priority levels (e.g., High, Medium, Low) to ensure that the most critical tasks are addressed first.

Using swimlanes helps to organize the board and make it easier to see how the work is progressing. The choice of swimlanes depends on the specific needs of your team and project.

Key Components of a Scrum Board

A Scrum board is a dynamic tool with several key components that work together to provide a comprehensive view of your project's progress:

- **Issues:** In JIRA, each task, bug, or user story is represented as an issue. On a Scrum board, these issues appear as cards. Each card contains essential information about the issue, such as its summary, assignee, priority, and status. You can click on a card to open the issue view and access more details.
- **Columns:** The columns on a Scrum board represent the different stages of your workflow, typically "To Do," "In Progress," and "Done." As work progresses on an issue, you move the corresponding card from one column to the next. This gives you a visual representation of where each issue is in the development process.
- **Swimlanes:** Swimlanes are horizontal rows that divide the board into sections. They are used to group issues based on different criteria, such as user stories, epics, team members, or priorities. Swimlanes help you organize your board and make it easier to see how the work is distributed and progressing across different categories.
- **Quick Filters:** Quick filters allow you to quickly filter the issues displayed on the board based on specific criteria. For example, you can filter by assignee, priority, issue type, or any other field. This is useful when you want to focus on a specific set of issues, such as all high-priority tasks or all bugs assigned to a particular team member.
- **Estimation Points:** Estimation points, often referred to as story points, are a relative measure of the effort required to complete a task. They are typically assigned to user stories during sprint planning and help the team estimate how much work they can realistically commit to in a sprint.

Estimation points are usually displayed on the issue card and can be used to track the team's progress over time.

By understanding these key components and how they interact, you can effectively utilize a Scrum board to plan, track, and manage your work in JIRA. This visual representation of your project's progress enhances transparency, facilitates collaboration, and enables you to identify and address any potential bottlenecks in your workflow.

Using a Scrum Board

A Scrum board is a dynamic tool that evolves throughout a sprint. Here's a step-by-step guide on how to use it effectively:

1. **Create and Prioritize the Backlog:** The product backlog is a living document that contains a prioritized list of all the features, enhancements, and bug fixes that need to be addressed in the product. This is where you'll define the user stories, which are short descriptions of desired functionality from the end user's perspective. Prioritize these stories based on their business value and dependencies.
2. **Plan Sprints:** A sprint is a time-boxed period, typically 1-4 weeks, during which the team commits to delivering a set of user stories. During sprint planning, the team selects user stories from the top of the prioritized backlog that they believe they can complete within the sprint timeframe. These stories are then added to the sprint backlog, which is a subset of the product backlog.
3. **Track Progress:** As work progresses during the sprint, team members move the corresponding issue cards across the columns of the Scrum board. For example, when a developer starts working on a task, they would move the card from the "To Do" column to the "In Progress" column. When the task is completed and reviewed, it would be moved to the "Done" column. This allows the team to visualize their progress and identify any potential blockers or issues that need to be addressed.
4. **Review and Retrospective:** At the end of each sprint, the team conducts a sprint review to demonstrate the completed work to stakeholders and gather feedback. This is followed by a sprint retrospective, where the team reflects on the sprint, identifies what went well and what could be improved, and creates action items for the next sprint. These meetings help the team continuously learn and adapt their processes to improve their performance.

By following these steps and regularly updating the Scrum board, your team can maintain visibility into the sprint's progress, collaborate effectively, and deliver high-quality results. The Scrum board serves as a powerful tool for managing work, tracking progress, and ensuring that everyone is aligned towards the common goal of delivering value to the customer.

Kanban Boards

Kanban boards provide a visual representation of workflow in a Kanban project, emphasizing continuous flow and limiting work in progress. They are ideal for teams seeking flexibility and adaptability in their processes.

Structure of a Kanban Board

A Kanban board is divided into vertical columns, each representing a different stage in the workflow. However, unlike Scrum boards, Kanban boards don't have fixed time-boxed iterations (sprints). Instead, work items flow through the board as they are completed, promoting a continuous delivery model.

The columns on a Kanban board typically include:

- **To Do:** This is where new tasks or ideas are initially placed before work begins.
- **In Progress:** Tasks actively being worked on are moved to this column.
- **In Review/Testing:** (Optional) For tasks that require additional review or testing before completion.

- **Done:** Completed tasks are moved to this column, indicating they are ready for delivery.

Work-in-Progress (WIP) Limits

A crucial aspect of Kanban boards is the implementation of WIP limits. Each column has a maximum number of work items that can be in progress simultaneously. This limit helps prevent bottlenecks and encourages the team to focus on completing tasks before starting new ones. The WIP limit is typically displayed at the top of each column.

Swimlanes

Similar to Scrum boards, Kanban boards can also utilize swimlanes to categorize and organize work items. Swimlanes can be used to group issues based on various criteria, such as:

- **Classes of Service:** Prioritize work items based on urgency or importance (e.g., Expedite, Fixed Delivery Date, Standard).
- **Team Members:** Assign swimlanes to individual team members to visualize their workload and ensure balanced distribution.
- **Types of Work:** Categorize work items by type (e.g., features, bugs, maintenance) for better prioritization and resource allocation.

By combining columns, WIP limits, and swimlanes, Kanban boards provide a powerful visual tool for managing work, optimizing workflow, and promoting continuous improvement. They enable teams to focus on delivering value to customers consistently and efficiently.

Key Components of a Kanban Board

A Kanban board is a dynamic tool with several essential components that collaborate to provide a comprehensive view of your project's workflow:

- **Issues:** Similar to Scrum boards, each task or work item in JIRA is represented as an issue on the Kanban board. These issues appear as cards that can be easily moved across the board as their status changes. Each card typically displays a summary of the issue, its assignee, and any relevant labels or priority indicators. Clicking on the card opens the issue view for more details.
- **Columns:** The columns on a Kanban board represent the different stages of your workflow, from the initial "To Do" stage to the final "Done" stage. As work progresses on an issue, the corresponding card is moved from one column to the next, visually representing its current status in the process. The number of columns and their names can be customized to match your specific workflow.
- **Swimlanes:** Swimlanes are horizontal rows that divide the Kanban board into sections. They can be used to categorize issues based on various criteria, such as classes of service, team members, or types of work. Swimlanes help you organize the board and make it easier to see how work is distributed across different categories.
- **Work-in-Progress (WIP) Limits:** WIP limits are a key feature of Kanban boards. They restrict the number of issues that can be in progress in each column at any given time. This helps prevent bottlenecks and encourages the team to focus on completing tasks before starting new ones. WIP limits are typically displayed at the top of each column.
- **Quick Filters:** Quick filters allow you to filter the issues displayed on the board based on specific criteria. This is helpful when you want to focus on particular types of work or issues assigned to specific team members. You can create custom quick filters based on any field or attribute of the issues on your board.

By understanding these key components and how they function together, you can effectively utilize a Kanban board to manage your work, visualize your workflow, and continuously improve your processes. The Kanban board provides a real-time snapshot of your project's status, enabling you to identify bottlenecks, prioritize tasks, and deliver value to your customers more efficiently.

Using a Kanban Board

A Kanban board is a living representation of your work, designed to evolve and adapt as your project progresses. Here's a step-by-step guide on how to use it effectively:

1. **Visualize the Workflow:** Start by creating columns on your board to represent the different stages of your workflow. These could be simple stages like "To Do," "In Progress," and "Done," or more detailed steps like "Backlog," "Analysis," "Development," "Testing," and "Deployment." Each column should reflect a distinct phase of your work process.
2. **Set WIP Limits:** For each column, establish a work-in-progress (WIP) limit. This is the maximum number of issues that can be in that column at any given time. The WIP limit helps prevent bottlenecks by ensuring that work items don't pile up in any particular stage. The ideal WIP limit depends on your team's capacity and the nature of the work.
3. **Add Issues:** Now, populate your board with issues. These could be tasks, bugs, user stories, or any other work items relevant to your project. You can create issues directly on the board or import them from a backlog. Prioritize the issues based on their urgency and importance, placing the most critical ones at the top of the "To Do" column.
4. **Manage the Flow:** As work progresses, move issues across the columns. When someone starts working on an issue, they move it to the "In Progress" column. When it's completed, they move it to the "Done" column. Ensure that you don't exceed the WIP limits for each column. If a column is full, focus on completing the tasks in that column before pulling in new ones.
5. **Continuous Improvement:** Regularly review your Kanban board to identify bottlenecks and areas where work is getting stuck. Analyze the cycle time (the time it takes for an issue to move from "To Do" to "Done") and lead time (the time it takes from the initial request to completion). Use this data to identify inefficiencies and make adjustments to your workflow, WIP limits, or team capacity to optimize your process.

By consistently using and refining your Kanban board, you can improve your team's efficiency, reduce waste, and deliver value to your customers more effectively. The Kanban board serves as a visual management tool that empowers your team to take ownership of their work, collaborate effectively, and continuously strive for improvement.

Choosing the Right Agile Board for Your Project

The choice between Scrum and Kanban boards in JIRA depends on several factors, including your project type, team structure, and desired level of flexibility versus predictability. Let's explore these factors to help you make an informed decision:

Project Type and Goals

- **Scrum:** If your project has well-defined deliverables, clear milestones, and a fixed timeline, Scrum might be the better choice. The structured sprints in Scrum provide a rhythm for regular deliveries and help you measure progress against a set schedule. Scrum is well-suited for projects where predictability and planning are paramount.
- **Kanban:** If your project is ongoing, with evolving requirements and priorities that change frequently, Kanban might be a more suitable option. Kanban's emphasis on continuous flow and limiting work in progress allows you to adapt quickly to changing circumstances. It's ideal for projects where flexibility and responsiveness are key.

Team Structure and Preferences

- **Team Size:** Smaller, co-located teams often find Scrum's close collaboration and regular meetings beneficial. Larger or distributed teams might prefer Kanban's focus on individual work and asynchronous communication.

- **Team Experience:** Teams with experience in Agile methodologies might be comfortable with the structured sprints and ceremonies of Scrum. Teams new to Agile might find Kanban's simplicity and visual workflow easier to adopt.
- **Communication Style:** Teams that thrive on frequent interaction and collaboration might prefer Scrum's daily stand-ups and sprint reviews. Teams that prefer more autonomy and less formal communication might find Kanban's emphasis on visual management and self-organization more appealing.

Flexibility vs. Predictability

- **Scrum:** Emphasizes predictability through time-boxed sprints and well-defined roles and responsibilities. This can be beneficial for projects with strict deadlines and clear expectations.
- **Kanban:** Prioritizes flexibility and responsiveness to change. It allows you to adapt your workflow and priorities as needed, which can be advantageous in dynamic environments.

Making the Decision

Ultimately, the choice between Scrum and Kanban boards comes down to what works best for your specific project and team. There's no one-size-fits-all answer, and you might even find that a hybrid approach, combining elements of both Scrum and Kanban, is the most effective solution.

Consider the factors discussed above, experiment with both board types, and gather feedback from your team to determine which approach best aligns with your goals and working style.

Chapter Summary

In this chapter, we explored the powerful world of Agile boards in JIRA, highlighting their role in facilitating project management, enhancing collaboration, and boosting productivity. We delved into the specific structures and key components of both Scrum and Kanban boards, elucidating how they visually represent work items and enable teams to track progress effectively.

For Scrum boards, we discussed their columnar structure representing workflow stages, the use of swimlanes for categorization, and elements like issues, quick filters, and estimation points. We also outlined the steps involved in using a Scrum board, from creating and prioritizing the backlog to planning sprints, tracking progress, and conducting reviews and retrospectives.

With Kanban boards, we emphasized the continuous flow of work, the significance of WIP limits for each column, and the similar use of swimlanes for organization. We outlined the key components, including issues, columns, and quick filters. Additionally, we provided a guide on using Kanban boards, covering workflow visualization, setting WIP limits, managing the flow of work, and leveraging the board for continuous improvement.

Finally, we discussed the critical factors to consider when choosing between Scrum and Kanban boards, such as project type and goals, team structure and preferences, and the desired balance between flexibility and predictability. Armed with this knowledge, you can confidently select the Agile board that best suits your project's unique needs and your team's working style.

Advanced Issue Search and Filters

Outline

- Basic Issue Search
- JIRA Query Language (JQL)
- Advanced Search Operators
- Saved Filters
- Sharing Filters
- Dashboards and Gadgets
- Chapter Summary

Basic Issue Search

JIRA offers a powerful search functionality that lets you quickly locate specific issues within your projects. Even with the basic search, you can efficiently find the information you need without delving into the complexities of JIRA Query Language (JQL).

The Search Bar

The search bar is prominently located at the top of the JIRA interface, usually in the center of the navigation bar. It's your primary tool for initiating a search.

How to Search

1. **Access the search bar:** Click on the search bar to activate it.
2. **Enter your search query:** Type in a keyword, issue key, project name, or any combination of these terms.
   - **Keywords:** If you're looking for issues related to a specific topic or feature, simply type in relevant keywords that you think might appear in the issue's summary or description.
   - **Issue keys:** If you know the unique identifier of an issue (e.g., PROJ-123), you can enter it directly into the search bar to find that specific issue.
   - **Project names:** To narrow down your search to a particular project, include the project name or key in your search query.
3. **View the results:** JIRA will display a list of issues that match your search criteria. You can click on an issue to open its detailed view.

Refining Your Search

JIRA's basic search provides some additional options to refine your results:

- **Recent Issues:** By default, JIRA shows you recent issues that match your search query. You can click on the "All" tab to see all matching issues.
- **Project Filter:** If you want to search within a specific project, you can select it from the project dropdown menu in the search bar.
- **Assignee Filter:** You can also filter the results by the assignee of the issue. This is useful if you want to see all the issues assigned to a particular team member.

Additional Tips

- **Use quotation marks:** Enclose multiple words in quotation marks to search for an exact phrase (e.g., "new feature request").

- **Use wildcards:** Use an asterisk (*) as a wildcard to match any number of characters (e.g., "implement*" to find issues related to implementing something).

While the basic search in JIRA is a powerful tool on its own, it has limitations for complex queries. In the next section, we'll introduce you to JIRA Query Language (JQL), which allows you to create more sophisticated and precise searches.

JIRA Query Language (JQL)

JIRA Query Language (JQL) is a flexible and powerful tool that allows you to construct complex search queries in JIRA. While the basic search is sufficient for simple queries, JQL gives you the ability to create highly specific filters and find exactly the information you need.

The Power of JQL

JQL extends the capabilities of basic search by providing a structured syntax for expressing search criteria. It allows you to combine multiple fields, operators, and values to create complex queries that go beyond simple keyword matching. With JQL, you can:

- Search across multiple projects.
- Filter issues based on specific fields, such as assignee, priority, status, or custom fields.
- Combine multiple search criteria using logical operators (AND, OR, NOT).
- Use functions to perform calculations or comparisons on field values.

Basic JQL Syntax

A basic JQL query consists of the following elements:

- **Field:** The field you want to search in (e.g., `project`, `assignee`, `status`, `summary`).
- **Operator:** The operator that defines the relationship between the field and the value (e.g., =, !=, >, <, >=, <=, ~, !~).
- **Value:** The value you want to search for (e.g., "PROJ-123", "John Doe", "Open").

Here's a simple example of a JQL query:

```
project = "MyProject" AND assignee = currentUser()
```

This query will return all issues in the project "MyProject" that are currently assigned to the user running the query.

Additional Notes

- JQL is case-insensitive, except for text searches that use the ~ or !~ operators.
- You can use parentheses to group clauses and control the order of evaluation.
- JQL provides a wide range of functions that you can use to perform calculations, comparisons, or transformations on field values.

In the following sections, we'll explore advanced search operators and functions in more detail, allowing you to unlock the full potential of JQL and create highly customized searches in JIRA.

Advanced Search Operators

While the basic syntax of JQL covers simple queries, advanced search operators significantly expand its capabilities, allowing you to craft highly precise and targeted searches within JIRA. Let's explore these operators and their applications:

Comparison Operators

Comparison operators are used to compare field values in JQL queries. Here are the common ones:

- **= (equals):** Finds issues where the field value exactly matches the specified value. For example, `status = "Done"` finds all issues with the status "Done."
- **!= (not equals):** Finds issues where the field value does not match the specified value. For example, `assignee != "John Doe"` finds all issues not assigned to John Doe.
- **> (greater than), < (less than), >= (greater than or equals), <= (less than or equals):** These operators are used for numerical and date comparisons. For example, `created >= "2023-01-01"` finds all issues created on or after January 1, 2023.

Logical Operators

Logical operators combine multiple clauses in a JQL query.

- **AND:** Returns issues that match all the specified conditions. For example, `project = "MyProject" AND status = "In Progress"` finds all issues in the project "MyProject" that are currently in progress.
- **OR:** Returns issues that match at least one of the specified conditions. For example, `assignee = "John Doe" OR assignee = "Jane Smith"` finds all issues assigned to either John Doe or Jane Smith.
- **NOT:** Excludes issues that match the specified condition. For example, `project != "MyProject"` finds all issues that are not in the project "MyProject."

Functions

JQL functions provide additional flexibility by allowing you to perform calculations, comparisons, or transformations on field values. Here are some common functions:

- `currentUser()`: Returns the current user's username.
- `membersOf("group name")`: Returns a list of users belonging to the specified group.
- `startOfDay()`, `endOfDay()`: Returns the start or end of the current day.
- `updatedDate > startOfMonth()`: Returns issues updated since the start of the current month

Text Search

Text search operators are used to find issues that contain or do not contain specific text.

- **~ (contains):** Finds issues where the field value contains the specified text. For example, `summary ~ "bug"` finds all issues with the word "bug" in their summary.
- **!~ (does not contain):** Finds issues where the field value does not contain the specified text.

Date/Time Functions

JIRA offers powerful date and time functions to filter issues based on specific dates or date ranges.

- **AFTER, BEFORE:** Filter issues with dates after or before a specified date.
- **DURING:** Filter issues within a specified date range.
- **BY, ON:** Filter issues due or completed by a specific date.

By understanding and utilizing these advanced search operators and functions, you can create highly targeted JQL queries to efficiently retrieve the information you need from JIRA.

Saved Filters

In the fast-paced world of project management, efficiency is key. JIRA's saved filters feature is designed to streamline your workflow by allowing you to save frequently used JQL queries for quick and easy access. Imagine having a library of pre-made searches that you can instantly apply to your project's data – that's precisely what saved filters offer.

Why Use Saved Filters?

Saved filters bring several benefits to your JIRA experience:

- **Time-Saving:** Instead of manually entering complex JQL queries each time you need to find specific issues, you can simply select a saved filter and get the results instantly. This saves you valuable time and effort, especially for recurring searches.
- **Consistency:** Saved filters ensure that you apply the same search criteria consistently across different searches. This helps maintain accuracy and avoid inconsistencies in your results.
- **Collaboration:** You can share your saved filters with other team members, allowing everyone to access the same filtered views and work from a common understanding of the project's data.

Creating and Managing Saved Filters

Creating a saved filter is a straightforward process:

1. **Construct your JQL query:** Start by building your JQL query using the search bar or the advanced JQL search interface. Make sure the query accurately captures the specific issues you want to find.
2. **Save the filter:** Once you're satisfied with your query, click the "Save as" button next to the search bar. Give your filter a descriptive name that clearly indicates its purpose. You can also add a description to provide additional context.
3. **Organize filters (optional):** If you have multiple saved filters, you can organize them into folders for easier management. This is especially useful when you have a large number of filters.

Sharing Saved Filters

To share a saved filter with others:

1. **Access the filter configuration:** Navigate to the saved filter's configuration page. You can usually find this by clicking on the filter name in the saved filters list or dropdown menu.
2. **Set sharing options:** Look for the sharing settings on the filter configuration page. Here, you can choose to share the filter with specific users, groups, or make it available to everyone on your JIRA site.

By creating and sharing saved filters, you empower your team with quick and easy access to the information they need, fostering collaboration and driving efficiency in your JIRA projects.

Sharing Filters

JIRA's ability to share saved filters is a game-changer for team collaboration. It allows everyone to access the same filtered views, ensuring everyone is on the same page and can easily access the information they need.

Why Share Filters?

Sharing filters is a simple yet powerful way to enhance collaboration in JIRA. Here's why it's beneficial:

- **Transparency and Visibility:** When filters are shared, everyone on the team can see the same set of issues, promoting transparency and reducing the need for redundant communication.
- **Standardized Views:** Shared filters provide a standardized way of looking at project data, ensuring everyone is using the same criteria to evaluate progress and identify issues.
- **Reduced Effort:** Team members don't have to recreate filters individually, saving time and effort.
- **Improved Decision-Making:** By sharing filters that highlight critical issues or bottlenecks, teams can make faster and more informed decisions.

How to Share Filters

Sharing a saved filter in JIRA is a simple process:

1. **Access the filter configuration:** Navigate to the saved filter you want to share. You can find it in the "Saved filters" section of the sidebar or by searching for it in the search bar. Click on the filter name to open its configuration page.
2. **Choose who to share with:** In the filter configuration page, you'll see a section for sharing. Click on the "Edit Permissions" button or a similar option.
3. **Add users or groups:** You can share the filter with specific users by entering their names or email addresses. You can also share it with entire groups by selecting them from a list. If you want the filter to be accessible to everyone on your JIRA site, choose the "Anyone" option.
4. **Set permissions:** You can control whether the recipients can only view the filter results or if they can also edit the filter itself.
5. **Save changes:** After selecting the recipients and setting permissions, save your changes.

Example

Let's say you've created a filter that shows all high-priority bugs in a specific project. You can share this filter with your development team, allowing them to quickly access and address these critical issues. This eliminates the need for them to manually search for high-priority bugs, saving time and ensuring everyone is working on the most important tasks.

Additional Notes

- **Filter subscriptions:** You can also set up filter subscriptions to automatically receive email notifications whenever new issues match a saved filter. This helps you stay on top of critical issues without having to constantly check JIRA.
- **Managing shared filters:** As a filter owner, you can modify the sharing settings at any time. You can also delete the filter if it's no longer needed.

By leveraging the filter sharing feature, you can significantly enhance collaboration and communication within your JIRA projects. It's a simple step that can have a big impact on your team's efficiency and effectiveness.

Dashboards and Gadgets

In JIRA, dashboards act as control centers that provide you with an overview of your projects at a glance. They offer a visual representation of your project data, making it easier to track progress, monitor key metrics, and identify potential issues. A crucial element in creating these informative dashboards is the use of gadgets, and JQL filters play a pivotal role in customizing these gadgets to display precisely the information you need.

Gadgets: The Building Blocks of Dashboards

Think of gadgets as the building blocks of your JIRA dashboard. They are mini-applications that display specific information in a visual format. JIRA comes with a variety of built-in gadgets, such as:

- **Pie Chart:** Displays the distribution of issues across different categories.
- **Created vs. Resolved Chart:** Shows the trend of created versus resolved issues over time.
- **Two-Dimensional Filter Statistics:** Provides a breakdown of issue counts based on two selected fields.
- **Activity Stream:** Displays a list of recent activity within the project.

You can also install additional gadgets from the Atlassian Marketplace to extend the capabilities of your dashboards.

JQL Filters: The Power Behind Gadgets

Most JIRA gadgets rely on JQL filters to determine the data they display. By creating a JQL filter, you can precisely define the criteria for the issues you want to include in a gadget. For example, you can create a filter to show only high-priority bugs, or only issues that are due in the next week.

Once you have created a filter, you can add it to a gadget to display the filtered data. For instance, you could add a pie chart gadget that shows the distribution of high-priority bugs by assignee, or a two-dimensional filter statistics gadget that shows the number of issues in each status for the next week.

Benefits of Dashboards and Gadgets

Dashboards and gadgets offer several benefits for JIRA users:

- **Visual Clarity:** They present complex project data in a visually appealing and easy-to-understand format.
- **Real-Time Insights:** They provide up-to-date information on project progress and health.
- **Customizable:** You can tailor dashboards and gadgets to your specific needs and preferences.
- **Collaboration:** You can share dashboards with your team members to foster transparency and collaboration.

Creating and Customizing Dashboards

To create a new dashboard, click on the "Dashboards" link in the JIRA sidebar and select "Create dashboard." You can then give your dashboard a name and description. Once you have created a dashboard, you can add gadgets to it by clicking the "Add gadget" button. You can then configure each gadget by selecting the appropriate JQL filter and customizing other settings.

By mastering the use of JQL filters and gadgets, you can create powerful dashboards that provide valuable insights into your project's performance and help you stay on top of your work.

Chapter Summary

In this chapter, we delved into the advanced search and filtering capabilities of JIRA, empowering you to efficiently find and analyze information within your projects. We began by introducing the basic search functionality and how it can be used to locate issues using keywords, issue keys, or project names. However, we quickly realized that the true power of JIRA search lies in its query language, JQL.

We explored the basic syntax of JQL, including fields, operators, and values, and how they can be combined to create complex queries. We then dove into advanced search operators, such as comparison operators, logical operators, functions, text search, and date/time functions, showcasing how they can be leveraged to construct highly specific searches.

To further streamline your workflow, we introduced the concept of saved filters, which allow you to store and reuse frequently used JQL queries. We also discussed how to share these filters with your team members, fostering collaboration and ensuring everyone has access to the same relevant information.

Finally, we explored the role of JQL filters in creating custom dashboards and gadgets. We highlighted how dashboards provide visual representations of project data, allowing teams to easily track progress and identify potential issues. By mastering JQL filters and gadgets, you can create tailored dashboards that offer valuable insights into your projects, promoting data-driven decision-making and effective project management. With these advanced search and filtering techniques at your disposal, you are now equipped to navigate the vast landscape of JIRA data with precision and efficiency.

Configuring Workflows

Outline

- Understanding Workflows
- Elements of a Workflow
- Creating and Customizing Workflows
- Workflow Best Practices
- Chapter Summary

Understanding Workflows

In JIRA, a workflow acts as a roadmap that guides an issue through its lifecycle, from its initial creation to its ultimate resolution. It's a series of steps, represented by statuses, that an issue transitions through as work progresses. Each step signifies a specific stage in the issue's journey, such as "To Do," "In Progress," "In Review," and "Done."

Think of a workflow as a conveyor belt in a factory. Raw materials enter the conveyor belt (issue creation), and they undergo various processes (statuses) before emerging as finished products (issue resolution). Similarly, in JIRA, issues enter the workflow and move through different stages until they are completed.

Workflows play a crucial role in promoting consistency and standardization within teams. By defining a clear path for issues to follow, workflows ensure that everyone adheres to the same process. This reduces confusion, minimizes errors, and streamlines collaboration. For instance, if everyone knows that an issue must be reviewed before it can be marked as done, it eliminates the possibility of work being prematurely considered complete.

Moreover, workflows can be designed to automate routine tasks. For example, you can set up a workflow to automatically assign an issue to a specific team member when it reaches a particular status. You can also configure workflows to send notifications to relevant stakeholders when an issue transitions between statuses. This automation saves time, reduces manual effort, and ensures that everyone stays informed about the progress of work items.

Benefits of Using Workflows

The use of workflows in JIRA offers numerous advantages:

- **Improved Visibility:** Workflows provide a clear visual representation of the progress of each issue. This transparency allows team members to easily track the status of work items and identify any bottlenecks or delays.
- **Enhanced Collaboration:** Workflows facilitate collaboration by providing a structured framework for team members to work together. Everyone understands the process and knows what is expected of them at each stage.
- **Increased Efficiency:** By automating routine tasks and enforcing standardized procedures, workflows streamline processes and eliminate unnecessary steps. This frees up time for team members to focus on more valuable activities.
- **Enforced Consistency:** Workflows ensure that everyone follows the same process, reducing errors and ensuring that work is completed to a high standard.
- **Adaptability:** Workflows can be customized to match your team's unique needs and processes. You can add or remove statuses, define transitions, and configure conditions and validators to tailor the workflow to your specific requirements.

Elements of a Workflow

To fully harness the power of JIRA workflows, it's essential to understand the building blocks that make them up. Let's break down the key elements that constitute a JIRA workflow:

- **Statuses:** Statuses are the fundamental building blocks of a workflow. They represent the various stages that an issue progresses through during its lifecycle. Think of them as checkpoints along a journey. Common statuses include "To Do" (indicating the issue is pending), "In Progress" (signifying active work), "In Review" (denoting that the issue is being evaluated), and "Done" (marking the issue as complete). You can customize the names and number of statuses to match your team's specific process.
- **Transitions:** Transitions are the links that connect statuses, enabling issues to move from one stage to the next. They define the valid paths an issue can take within the workflow. For instance, a transition might be "Start Progress" (moving an issue from "To Do" to "In Progress") or "Resolve Issue" (moving an issue from "In Review" to "Done"). You have control over which transitions are allowed between statuses, providing flexibility in designing your workflow.
- **Conditions and Validators:** Conditions and validators act as gatekeepers for transitions. They impose rules and constraints that must be met before an issue can move to the next status. For example, you could set a condition that requires a code review to be completed before an issue can transition from "In Progress" to "In Review." Validators ensure that certain fields are filled out or that specific criteria are met before a transition is allowed.
- **Post Functions:** Post functions are automated actions that trigger after a successful transition. They are used to streamline processes and eliminate manual intervention. Common post functions include:
    - **Assigning the issue:** Automatically assigning the issue to the next responsible person.
    - **Sending notifications:** Notifying relevant stakeholders about the issue's progress.
    - **Updating fields:** Automatically updating specific fields based on the transition (e.g., setting the resolution date when an issue is resolved).
    - **Triggering webhooks:** Integrating with external systems to perform actions outside of JIRA.

By strategically combining statuses, transitions, conditions, validators, and post functions, you can create comprehensive workflows that precisely reflect your team's processes, enhance efficiency, and ensure quality control throughout the lifecycle of every JIRA issue.

Creating and Customizing Workflows

To create and customize workflows in JIRA, follow these steps:

1. **Access the workflow editor:** Start by navigating to your JIRA project. Click on the **Project settings** gear icon (usually located in the sidebar or project menu). In the settings menu, find and click on **Issues**, then select **Workflows**. This will open the workflow editor, where you can view and modify existing workflows or create new ones.
2. **Add and configure statuses:**
    - To add a new status, click the **Add status** button and provide a name and description for the status. You can also choose a status category (e.g., "To Do," "In Progress," or "Done") and an icon to represent the status visually.
    - To edit an existing status, click the pencil icon next to it. You can modify its name, description, category, or icon.
    - You can also reorder statuses by dragging and dropping them within the workflow diagram.
3. **Define transitions:**
    - Transitions are represented as arrows between statuses. To create a transition, click on the **Add transition** button that appears when you hover over a status. Select the destination status and provide a name for the transition.

- Click on the transition to open its properties. Here, you can add conditions (rules that determine whether the transition is available) and validators (rules that validate the input before the transition is executed).
- You can also specify who can perform the transition by setting permissions.

4. **Set up post functions:**
   - Post functions are automated actions that trigger after a transition. To add a post function, click the **Post functions** tab in the transition properties.
   - JIRA provides various built-in post functions, such as assigning the issue, adding a comment, or updating fields. You can also install additional post functions from the Atlassian Marketplace.
   - Configure each post function according to your needs. For example, if you want to assign the issue to a specific user after a transition, you can use the "Assign to" post function and select the user.

5. **Associate workflow with issue types:**
   - Once you have customized your workflow, you need to associate it with specific issue types within your project.
   - Go to the **Workflow schemes** section in the project settings. Click on the **Edit** button next to the workflow scheme you want to modify.
   - Select the issue types you want to associate with your customized workflow and choose the workflow from the dropdown menu.

By following these steps, you can create tailored workflows that streamline your team's processes and ensure consistent issue management in JIRA. Remember, workflows are flexible and can be modified as your project needs evolve. Regular review and refinement of your workflows will help you maintain optimal efficiency and productivity.

Workflow Best Practices

Designing and managing effective workflows in JIRA is crucial for maximizing the platform's benefits and ensuring smooth project execution. Here are some best practices to follow:

- **Keep it Simple:** Avoid overcomplicating your workflows initially. Start with a basic structure and gradually add complexity as needed. A simple workflow is easier to understand, maintain, and adapt to changing project requirements.
- **Involve Stakeholders:** Collaborate with your team members and other stakeholders to gather input on the workflow design. Ensure that it accurately reflects their actual processes and addresses their needs. This collaborative approach fosters buy-in and ensures that the workflow is practical and effective.
- **Document the Workflow:** Create clear and concise documentation that outlines the workflow steps, statuses, transitions, and any associated conditions or validators. This documentation serves as a reference for team members and helps new members quickly understand the process.
- **Use Conditions and Validators Wisely:** Conditions and validators add control and enforce business rules within your workflow. Use them judiciously to prevent invalid transitions and ensure that issues follow the correct path. However, avoid excessive or overly complex conditions that might hinder flexibility.
- **Leverage Post Functions for Automation:** JIRA's post functions allow you to automate various actions, such as assigning issues, updating fields, or sending notifications. Utilize these features to eliminate manual tasks, reduce errors, and save time. This automation can significantly streamline your workflow and boost productivity.
- **Regularly Review and Refine:** Workflows are not static; they should evolve as your team's processes and project requirements change. Regularly review your workflows to identify bottlenecks, inefficiencies, or areas where the process can be improved. Gather feedback from team members and make necessary adjustments to optimize the workflow.

By adhering to these best practices, you can design and manage JIRA workflows that are both effective and adaptable. Well-designed workflows enhance collaboration, improve visibility into project progress, and ultimately contribute to the successful completion of your projects.

Chapter Summary

In this chapter, we delved into the intricacies of configuring workflows in JIRA, a pivotal aspect of maximizing the platform's effectiveness in project management. We began by defining workflows as a series of steps that guide an issue through its lifecycle, emphasizing their role in standardizing processes, enforcing consistency, and automating tasks. We then broke down the essential elements of a workflow, including statuses, transitions, conditions, validators, and post functions, explaining their individual roles and how they interact to create a streamlined process.

Furthermore, we provided a step-by-step guide on how to create and customize workflows in JIRA, from accessing the workflow editor to associating the customized workflow with specific issue types. We also shared valuable best practices for designing and managing workflows, such as keeping them simple, involving stakeholders, documenting the process, using conditions and validators judiciously, leveraging post functions for automation, and regularly reviewing and refining the workflow to ensure optimal efficiency. By mastering these concepts and techniques, you are now equipped to tailor JIRA workflows to your specific project needs, fostering collaboration, improving visibility, and ultimately driving project success.

Section C:
JIRA for Agile Project Management

Planning and Running Sprints

Outline

- What is a Sprint?
- Sprint Planning
- Sprint Backlog
- Running the Sprint
- Sprint Review
- Sprint Retrospective
- Chapter Summary

What is a Sprint?

In the world of Agile project management, a sprint is a time-boxed iteration, a short, focused period during which a development team works collaboratively to complete a set amount of work. This work is typically defined as a collection of tasks or user stories that have been prioritized and selected from the project's backlog.

The duration of a sprint can vary, but it typically ranges from one to four weeks. This time-boxed nature ensures that the team remains focused on delivering a specific set of deliverables within a defined timeframe. The goal of each sprint is to produce a potentially shippable product increment, meaning that the completed work is of high enough quality that it could be released to users if desired.

The Benefits of Sprints

Sprints offer several key benefits in the Agile development process:

- **Focus:** By breaking down work into smaller, manageable chunks, sprints help teams maintain focus and avoid getting overwhelmed by the larger project scope.
- **Collaboration:** Sprints encourage collaboration and communication among team members. The daily stand-up meetings foster a sense of shared responsibility and accountability, ensuring everyone is aligned on goals and progress.
- **Regular Delivery of Value:** The completion of each sprint results in a tangible product increment, providing regular feedback and opportunities for course correction. This iterative approach allows for early detection of issues and reduces the risk of project failure.
- **Adaptability:** Sprints provide a framework for adapting to change. As new information or requirements emerge, the team can adjust their priorities and plans for upcoming sprints.
- **Transparency:** The use of visual tools like JIRA's Agile boards makes it easy to track progress and visualize the workflow, increasing transparency and ensuring everyone is aware of the project's status.

By incorporating sprints into your project management approach, you can promote a more agile, responsive, and efficient way of working. JIRA's robust features for sprint planning, tracking, and review make it an ideal tool for implementing and managing sprints within your Agile projects.

Sprint Planning

Sprint planning is a crucial ceremony in the Scrum framework, and JIRA provides robust tools to facilitate this collaborative process. It's a dedicated time for the entire team to come together, align their efforts, and set a clear direction for the upcoming sprint. The goal of sprint planning is to ensure that everyone understands the sprint goals, the work involved, and their individual responsibilities.

The Importance of Sprint Planning

Sprint planning is not just a formality; it's a strategic activity that significantly impacts the success of a sprint. By investing time in thorough planning, teams can:

- **Set realistic goals:** By assessing their capacity and the complexity of the user stories, teams can set achievable goals for the sprint, avoiding overcommitment.
- **Identify potential roadblocks:** Early identification of potential challenges or dependencies allows for proactive planning and mitigation strategies.
- **Enhance collaboration:** Sprint planning fosters a collaborative environment where everyone's input is valued, leading to better decision-making and a stronger sense of ownership.
- **Increase transparency:** By clearly defining the sprint goals and tasks, everyone on the team understands what needs to be done and can track progress effectively.

Collaborative Activities in Sprint Planning

During sprint planning, the team engages in several collaborative activities:

- **Select user stories:** The product owner presents the prioritized product backlog, and the team selects the user stories they believe they can realistically complete within the sprint. This selection is based on the user stories' priority, complexity, and the team's estimated capacity.
- **Define sprint goals:** The team collaboratively defines the sprint goals, which are overarching objectives that guide the work during the sprint. These goals should be specific, measurable, achievable, relevant, and time-bound (SMART).
- **Create tasks:** Once the user stories are selected, the team breaks them down into smaller, more manageable tasks. This process helps clarify the work involved and allows for better task assignment and tracking.
- **Estimate effort:** The team estimates the effort required for each task, typically using story points. Story points are a relative measure of complexity rather than absolute time units, allowing for more accurate estimation.

JIRA's Role in Sprint Planning

JIRA provides several features that support and streamline the sprint planning process:

- **Backlog management:** JIRA's backlog management features allow you to easily prioritize user stories and visualize their relationships.
- **Sprint creation and management:** You can create sprints in JIRA, define their start and end dates, and add selected user stories to the sprint backlog.
- **Task creation and assignment:** JIRA facilitates the creation of tasks from user stories and their assignment to team members.
- **Estimation tools:** JIRA supports various estimation techniques, including story points, allowing teams to estimate the effort required for each task.

By utilizing JIRA's features for sprint planning, teams can collaborate effectively, set clear goals, and create a solid plan for the upcoming sprint.

Sprint Backlog

Once the sprint planning phase is complete, the team's commitments are captured in the sprint backlog. This is a dynamic and ever-evolving list that details all the tasks the team has pledged to accomplish during the sprint. Think of it as the team's to-do list for the next one to four weeks, outlining the specific steps needed to achieve the sprint goal.

A Living Artifact

The sprint backlog is not a static document; it's a living artifact that adapts and changes as the sprint progresses. As team members work on tasks, they update their progress in JIRA, reflecting the current state of the sprint. New tasks might be added if unforeseen requirements arise, or existing tasks might be removed if they become irrelevant. This flexibility allows the team to respond to changes and ensure that the sprint backlog accurately reflects the work that needs to be done.

Viewing and Managing the Sprint Backlog in JIRA

JIRA provides a user-friendly interface for viewing and managing the sprint backlog. It typically appears as a column on your Scrum board, labeled "Sprint Backlog" or similar. Here, you can see all the tasks for the current sprint, along with their details, such as assignee, priority, and status.

You can interact with the sprint backlog in several ways:

- **Update task progress:** Team members can update the status of their tasks (e.g., "In Progress," "Done") as they work on them. This provides real-time visibility into the sprint's progress for the entire team.
- **Identify blockers:** If a task is blocked or facing challenges, team members can flag it as such in JIRA. This allows the Scrum Master or other team members to step in and help resolve the issue.
- **Reorder tasks:** You can drag and drop tasks within the sprint backlog to re-prioritize them as needed.
- **Add or remove tasks:** If new tasks arise during the sprint, or if certain tasks become unnecessary, you can add or remove them from the sprint backlog.
- **Track sprint status:** JIRA provides various reports and charts that visualize the sprint's progress, such as burndown charts and velocity charts. These reports help you track the team's performance and identify any trends or issues that need attention.

By actively managing the sprint backlog in JIRA, you can ensure that your team stays on track, addresses any challenges promptly, and delivers the sprint goal successfully.

Running the Sprint

Once your sprint is underway, the focus shifts to the daily execution and management of the work. JIRA plays a vital role in facilitating this process, providing tools to keep the team aligned, track progress, and address any obstacles that may arise.

Daily Scrum (Daily Stand-up)

A cornerstone of the Scrum methodology, the daily scrum is a brief, time-boxed meeting where the team synchronizes their efforts. Typically held at the same time and place each day, the daily scrum serves three primary purposes:

1. **Progress Update:** Each team member briefly shares what they accomplished since the last meeting, what they plan to work on today, and any obstacles they are facing.
2. **Collaboration:** The daily scrum fosters collaboration and communication by providing a platform for team members to discuss challenges, offer help, and coordinate their work.
3. **Planning:** The team can adjust their plans for the day based on the updates and discussions during the scrum, ensuring they stay on track towards the sprint goal.

While JIRA doesn't directly facilitate the daily scrum meeting itself, it provides the context for these discussions. Team members can refer to the sprint backlog in JIRA to discuss their tasks and progress.

Updating Tasks

In JIRA, team members update the status of their tasks as they work on them. This is typically done by moving the task card across the columns of the Scrum board. For example, when a task is started, it would be moved from the "To Do" column to the "In Progress" column. When it's completed, it would be moved to the "Done" column. This provides real-time visibility into the status of each task, allowing everyone on the team to see the overall progress of the sprint.

Monitoring Progress

JIRA offers various tools for monitoring the sprint's progress:

- **Agile Boards:** The Scrum board provides a visual overview of the sprint's status. You can see which tasks are in progress, which are completed, and which are still to be started. This helps you identify any bottlenecks or areas where work is getting stuck.
- **Reports:** JIRA offers a range of reports, such as burndown charts and sprint reports, that provide detailed insights into the sprint's progress. These reports can help you track the team's velocity, identify trends, and make data-driven decisions to optimize your workflow.
- **Dashboards:** You can create custom dashboards in JIRA to display specific metrics and charts related to your sprint. This allows you to tailor your view of the data to your specific needs and preferences.

By utilizing these tools, you can stay on top of your sprint's progress, identify any potential issues early on, and take corrective action as needed. This proactive approach ensures that your sprint stays on track and delivers the expected results.

Sprint Review

As a sprint nears its conclusion, the sprint review takes center stage. It's a collaborative meeting where the development team showcases the work completed during the sprint to key stakeholders, such as product owners, clients, or other interested parties. The primary goals of the sprint review are to:

1. **Demonstrate Progress:** The team presents a working demonstration of the completed user stories or features, highlighting the functionality and value delivered during the sprint.
2. **Gather Feedback:** Stakeholders provide feedback on the completed work, offering insights, suggestions, and potential changes that can be incorporated into future sprints.
3. **Adjust the Product Backlog:** Based on the feedback received, the product owner may adjust the product backlog, re-prioritizing items or adding new ones.
4. **Celebrate Success:** The sprint review is also an opportunity to celebrate the team's accomplishments and recognize their hard work.

JIRA's Role in Sprint Review

JIRA plays a pivotal role in facilitating and enhancing the sprint review process:

- **Showcasing Completed Tasks:** The Scrum board in JIRA provides a visual representation of the completed tasks. The team can easily filter the board to show only the issues that have been moved to the "Done" column, providing a clear overview of the sprint's deliverables.
- **Generating Reports:** JIRA offers various reports that can be used to highlight the sprint's achievements. For example, the sprint report provides a summary of the sprint's progress, including the number of completed issues, the remaining work, and the team's velocity. Other reports, such as the burndown chart, can be used to visualize the team's progress over time.
- **Facilitating Discussion:** JIRA's issue view allows stakeholders to easily access the details of each completed task, including its description, acceptance criteria, and any associated discussions or attachments. This facilitates a more informed and productive discussion during the sprint review.

By leveraging JIRA's capabilities, teams can conduct more effective sprint reviews, ensuring that stakeholders are well-informed about the progress of the project, providing valuable feedback, and contributing to the ongoing success of the product.

Sprint Retrospective

The sprint retrospective is the final ceremony of the Scrum sprint cycle, serving as a crucial opportunity for the team to reflect, learn, and grow. It's a dedicated time for team members to inspect their processes, identify what went well and what didn't, and develop actionable plans for improvement in future sprints. This continuous improvement mindset is at the heart of Agile methodologies and is essential for fostering a high-performing team.

Key Goals of the Sprint Retrospective

- **Inspect and Adapt:** The team examines their processes, tools, communication, and collaboration during the previous sprint. They identify strengths to build upon and weaknesses to address.
- **Identify Improvement Opportunities:** The team pinpoints specific areas where they can improve their performance, efficiency, or collaboration. These could be related to technical practices, communication, or even team dynamics.
- **Create Action Items:** Based on their insights, the team formulates concrete action items or experiments to try out in the next sprint. These actions should be aimed at addressing the identified weaknesses and improving the overall process.
- **Foster a Culture of Continuous Improvement:** The retrospective encourages a culture of open communication, learning, and continuous improvement within the team. It provides a safe space for team members to share feedback, raise concerns, and suggest ideas for making the process better.

JIRA's Role in Sprint Retrospectives

JIRA can be a valuable tool in supporting sprint retrospectives:

- **Documenting Findings:** You can create a dedicated issue in JIRA to capture the key findings, insights, and action items from the retrospective. This creates a record of the discussions and decisions made, which can be referenced later.
- **Tracking Improvement Actions:** The action items identified during the retrospective can be turned into tasks or sub-tasks in JIRA. This allows you to track their progress, assign them to team members, and ensure they are completed in subsequent sprints.
- **Analyzing Trends:** By reviewing past retrospective issues, you can identify recurring patterns or trends in your team's challenges and successes. This data can help you make more informed decisions about process improvements.
- **Integrating with Confluence:** You can link the retrospective issue in JIRA to a Confluence page where you can elaborate on the discussion, provide more context, and document the team's action plan in detail.

Conclusion

The sprint retrospective is a powerful tool for fostering continuous improvement in Agile teams. By utilizing JIRA to document and track retrospective findings and action items, you can ensure that the valuable insights gained during these meetings are not lost and are effectively implemented to enhance your team's performance and collaboration in future sprints.

Chapter Summary

In this chapter, we explored the key phases of planning and running sprints within the Agile project management framework, focusing on the role JIRA plays in streamlining these processes. We began by defining what a sprint is, highlighting its time-boxed nature and the importance of delivering incremental value. Next, we delved into the collaborative process of sprint planning, discussing how teams select user stories, define sprint goals, create tasks, and estimate effort. We also explored how JIRA facilitates this process with features like backlog management, sprint creation, task assignment, and estimation tools.

We then moved on to the sprint backlog, describing it as a living document that lists the tasks the team commits to completing during the sprint. We explained how JIRA enables teams to view and manage the backlog, update task progress, identify blockers, and track the overall sprint status. Furthermore, we discussed the daily activities involved in running a sprint, including daily scrums, task updates, and monitoring progress using JIRA's Agile boards and reports.

Finally, we explored the sprint review and sprint retrospective, highlighting their significance in showcasing the completed work to stakeholders, gathering feedback, reflecting on the process, and identifying areas for improvement. We illustrated how JIRA can be used to document retrospective findings and track the implementation of improvement actions, ensuring that the lessons learned are applied to future sprints. By understanding and effectively implementing these sprint processes within JIRA, your team can foster a culture of continuous improvement and deliver high-quality results in a timely and efficient manner.

Backlog Management and Grooming

Outline

- What is a Backlog?
- The Importance of Backlog Management
- Backlog Grooming Techniques
- Managing the Backlog in JIRA
- Chapter Summary

What is a Backlog?

In Agile project management, the product backlog serves as the central repository of all the work that needs to be done to complete a project. It's a comprehensive and ever-evolving list that encompasses everything from new features and enhancements to bug fixes and technical debt. The product backlog is not merely a static list; it's a dynamic artifact that constantly adapts to the project's changing landscape.

Think of the backlog as a wish list for your product. It captures all the ideas, requests, and requirements from stakeholders, customers, and the development team itself. Each item in the backlog, whether it's a user story, a technical task, or a bug report, represents a piece of work that needs to be addressed.

The product backlog is more than just a collection of items; it's a prioritized list. The items at the top of the backlog are considered the most important and valuable, while those at the bottom are less urgent or lower in priority. This prioritization ensures that the team focuses its efforts on the work that will deliver the most value to the customer or stakeholder.

The backlog is not set in stone. It evolves throughout the project's lifecycle as new information emerges, priorities shift, and requirements change. New items may be added to the backlog, existing items may be modified or removed, and priorities may be adjusted. This dynamic nature allows the team to respond to feedback, adapt to changing circumstances, and ensure that the product backlog remains a relevant and accurate reflection of the work that needs to be done.

The Importance of Backlog Management

In Agile methodologies, the product backlog acts as the project's compass, guiding the team towards successful completion. Effective backlog management is the key to ensuring that the compass points in the right direction, leading to a product that truly meets the needs of its users.

Benefits of a Well-Managed Backlog

A well-managed backlog offers a myriad of benefits that contribute to the overall success of Agile projects:

- **Prioritization of Work:** A well-organized backlog ensures that the most important and valuable items rise to the top, while less urgent or lower-priority items are addressed later. This helps the team focus on delivering maximum value to the customer or stakeholder with each sprint.
- **Maintaining Focus:** By having a clear and prioritized backlog, the team knows exactly what needs to be done next. This prevents distractions, reduces confusion, and keeps everyone focused on the most critical tasks. It also helps avoid scope creep, where the project's scope expands uncontrollably, leading to delays and cost overruns.
- **Adaptability to Change:** In the fast-paced world of Agile development, change is inevitable. A well-maintained backlog allows the team to easily adapt to new information, evolving requirements,

or shifting priorities. By regularly reviewing and updating the backlog, the team can ensure that it remains aligned with the project's goals and the needs of the customer.
- **Accurate Effort Estimation:** A well-groomed backlog, with clear and detailed user stories, enables the team to estimate the effort required for each item more accurately. This, in turn, facilitates better sprint planning and resource allocation. The team can confidently commit to delivering a certain amount of work within a sprint, knowing they have a realistic understanding of the effort involved.

Poor Backlog Management Consequences

On the other hand, neglecting backlog management can lead to several issues that can derail a project:

- **Misaligned Priorities:** If the backlog is not properly prioritized, the team might end up working on less important or less valuable tasks first, delaying the delivery of critical features.
- **Scope Creep:** An unmanaged backlog can easily become bloated with new requests and ideas, leading to scope creep and making it difficult to deliver the project on time and within budget.
- **Wasted Effort:** Working on irrelevant or outdated backlog items results in wasted effort and resources.
- **Unrealistic Expectations:** Inaccurate effort estimations, resulting from a poorly groomed backlog, can lead to unrealistic expectations and missed deadlines.

By understanding the importance of backlog management and investing time and effort in maintaining a well-groomed backlog, teams can set themselves up for success in their Agile projects. In the following sections, we will explore techniques for effective backlog grooming and how JIRA can be leveraged to streamline this process.

Backlog Grooming Techniques

Backlog grooming, also known as backlog refinement, is the ongoing process of maintaining and refining the product backlog. It's a collaborative effort involving the product owner, the development team, and other stakeholders. The goal is to ensure that the backlog remains up-to-date, prioritized, and contains well-defined items that are ready to be worked on in upcoming sprints.

Key Techniques for Backlog Grooming

Several techniques can be employed to effectively groom the backlog:

1. **Review and Update Items:** Regularly review each item in the backlog to ensure it's still relevant and accurate. As the project progresses, requirements may change, new information may emerge, or priorities may shift. Updating backlog items ensures that the backlog reflects the current understanding of the project's needs.
2. **Add Details and Clarify Requirements:** User stories in the backlog should be clear, concise, and actionable. If a user story lacks sufficient details, work with the stakeholders to refine it. Add acceptance criteria, define the desired outcome, and clarify any ambiguities. This will help the development team understand the requirements thoroughly and avoid misunderstandings later in the development process.
3. **Estimate Effort:** Accurately estimating the effort required for each backlog item is crucial for sprint planning and resource allocation. Involve the development team in the estimation process, as they have the technical expertise to assess the complexity of the work involved. Use techniques like story points or planning poker to arrive at a consensus on effort estimates.
4. **Prioritize Items:** Prioritization is an ongoing activity in backlog grooming. As the project progresses, new information and feedback may necessitate adjustments to the backlog's priority order. Use techniques like the MoSCoW method (Must have, Should have, Could have, Won't have) or value-based prioritization to rank items based on their value and importance to the stakeholders.

5. **Remove Irrelevant Items:** As the project evolves, some backlog items might become obsolete or irrelevant. It's essential to regularly review the backlog and remove any items that no longer align with the project's goals or priorities. This keeps the backlog lean and focused, ensuring that the team doesn't waste time on unnecessary work.

Backlog Grooming Frequency

The frequency of backlog grooming sessions depends on the project's complexity and pace of change. Some teams might find it beneficial to have short grooming sessions weekly, while others might prefer longer, less frequent sessions. The key is to find a cadence that works for your team and ensures that the backlog is always in a healthy state.

Managing the Backlog in JIRA

JIRA provides a comprehensive suite of tools and features that facilitate efficient backlog management, making it easier to prioritize, refine, and organize your project's work items.

Creating and Editing Backlog Items

In JIRA, backlog items are represented as issues. To create a new backlog item, simply click the "Create" button and select the appropriate project and issue type (e.g., Story, Task, Bug). Fill in the required fields, such as the summary and description, and add any relevant details or attachments. You can also assign the issue to a team member and set its priority.

To edit an existing backlog item, open the issue view and click the "Edit" button. You can then modify any of the fields, add comments, or change the issue's status.

Prioritizing and Ranking Items

JIRA offers several ways to prioritize and rank backlog items:

- **Drag-and-drop:** You can easily reorder backlog items by dragging and dropping them within the backlog view. This allows you to quickly adjust the priority order as needed.
- **Priority field:** Each issue has a priority field where you can select a predefined priority level (e.g., Highest, High, Medium, Low).
- **Rank field:** In some JIRA configurations, you may also have a Rank field that assigns a numerical value to each backlog item, indicating its relative priority.

Estimating Effort

Effort estimation is a crucial aspect of backlog management. JIRA supports various estimation techniques, including story points, which are a relative measure of the effort required to complete a task. You can add story point estimates to your backlog items during backlog grooming or sprint planning sessions.

Linking Issues

JIRA allows you to link issues together to create relationships between them. This is particularly useful for representing dependencies, hierarchies, or related work items. For example, you can link a user story to the tasks required to implement it, or you can link multiple user stories together to create an epic. Linking issues provides better visibility into the project's structure and helps you track dependencies between work items.

Filtering and Searching

JIRA's powerful search functionality allows you to quickly find specific backlog items. You can use the basic search bar to search for keywords, issue keys, or project names. For more advanced searches, you can use JIRA Query Language (JQL) to create complex queries that filter issues based on specific criteria, such as status, assignee, or due date.

By leveraging these backlog management features in JIRA, you can maintain a well-organized and prioritized backlog, ensuring that your team is always working on the most important and valuable tasks. This, in turn, contributes to the overall success of your Agile projects.

Chapter Summary

In this chapter, we delved into the intricacies of backlog management and grooming, a cornerstone of Agile project management. We defined the product backlog as a prioritized list of all the work required to complete a project, emphasizing its dynamic and evolving nature. We then discussed the crucial role of backlog management in prioritizing work, maintaining focus, adapting to change, and estimating effort accurately. Furthermore, we explored various techniques for backlog grooming, including reviewing and updating items, adding details, estimating effort, prioritizing items, and removing irrelevant ones.

We also highlighted JIRA's robust features for backlog management, such as creating and editing backlog items, prioritizing and ranking items, estimating effort, linking issues, and filtering and searching. By harnessing these features, teams can effectively manage their backlog, ensuring that it remains a valuable tool for guiding their Agile projects toward success. With a well-maintained backlog, teams can focus on delivering maximum value to their customers or stakeholders while adapting to the ever-changing demands of the project.

Reporting and Dashboards

Outline

- Introduction to JIRA Reporting
- Types of JIRA Reports
- Creating and Customizing Dashboards
- JIRA Reporting Best Practices
- Chapter Summary

Introduction to JIRA Reporting

In the realm of project management, data is king. The ability to collect, analyze, and interpret data is essential for understanding your project's progress, identifying areas for improvement, and ultimately, ensuring successful delivery. This is where JIRA's reporting capabilities come into play. JIRA offers a robust reporting framework that empowers teams to gain valuable insights into their work, making it an indispensable tool for data-driven decision-making.

The Importance of Reporting in Project Management

Reporting is not merely a formality; it's a strategic activity that provides a window into the heart of your project. It allows you to answer critical questions, such as:

- Are we on track to meet our deadlines?
- Which tasks are causing bottlenecks?
- How is our team performing?
- Are there any areas where we can improve?

By providing answers to these questions, reporting enables you to:

- **Track progress:** Monitor your project's advancement against planned timelines and goals.
- **Identify issues:** Spot potential problems early on before they escalate into major setbacks.
- **Measure performance:** Evaluate the effectiveness of your team and processes.
- **Make informed decisions:** Base your decisions on data rather than assumptions or gut feelings.

JIRA's Reporting Capabilities

JIRA's reporting features offer a comprehensive suite of tools to help you gather and analyze project data. You can generate various reports that provide insights into different aspects of your project, such as:

- **Sprint progress:** Track how your team is progressing through the current sprint, identifying completed tasks and remaining work.
- **Team velocity:** Measure the amount of work your team typically completes in a sprint, helping you forecast future performance.
- **Burndown charts:** Visualize the remaining work in a sprint, showing how quickly the team is burning through the backlog.
- **Cumulative flow diagrams:** Analyze the flow of work through your workflow, identifying bottlenecks and areas for improvement.
- **Issue analysis reports:** Understand the distribution and trends of issues based on various parameters like issue type, priority, status, and assignee.
- **Time tracking reports:** Track the time spent on tasks, allowing you to analyze your team's time utilization and identify areas where you can improve efficiency.

- **User workload report:** Visualize how work is distributed among your team members, ensuring that no one is overloaded or underutilized.

JIRA also allows you to create custom reports and dashboards, tailoring the information you see to your specific needs. This flexibility makes JIRA a powerful tool for tracking project health, team performance, and individual contributions, ultimately empowering you to make data-driven decisions that lead to project success.

Types of JIRA Reports

JIRA offers a diverse range of reports to cater to different aspects of project management and analysis. These reports provide valuable insights into various dimensions of your project, empowering you to make informed decisions and take corrective actions when necessary. Let's delve into the different types of reports available in JIRA:

- **Agile Reports:** These reports are specifically designed for Agile projects and provide key metrics to track the progress and performance of your sprints. Some of the essential Agile reports include:
    - **Sprint Report:** This report summarizes the overall progress of a sprint, showing the completed work, remaining work, and any scope changes.
    - **Velocity Chart:** It tracks the team's velocity over time, helping you estimate how much work the team can realistically complete in future sprints.
    - **Burndown Chart:** This chart visualizes the remaining work in a sprint, indicating whether the team is on track to complete all the planned work by the end of the sprint.
    - **Cumulative Flow Diagram:** This diagram illustrates the flow of work through your workflow, highlighting bottlenecks and areas where work is getting stuck.
- **Issue Analysis Reports:** These reports delve into the details of individual issues and provide insights into their distribution and trends. Some useful issue analysis reports include:
    - **Created vs. Resolved Issues Report:** This report compares the number of issues created versus resolved over time, revealing patterns in workload and throughput.
    - **Pie Chart Report:** This report displays the distribution of issues across different categories, such as issue type, priority, or status.
    - **Average Age Report:** This report shows the average age of unresolved issues, helping you identify issues that are taking longer to resolve than expected.
    - **Time to Resolution Report:** This report tracks how long it takes to resolve issues, providing insights into your team's efficiency and responsiveness.
- **Time Tracking Reports:** If your team tracks time spent on JIRA issues, you can utilize time tracking reports to analyze how time is being allocated. These reports can help you identify areas where you might be spending too much or too little time, allowing you to optimize your resource utilization.
- **User Workload Report:** This report provides a visual representation of the workload distribution among your team members. It shows you who is assigned to which issues and how many issues each person is currently working on. This can help you ensure that the workload is balanced across the team and that no one is overloaded.

By leveraging the diverse range of reports available in JIRA, you can gain a comprehensive understanding of your project's performance. These reports empower you to track progress, identify bottlenecks, measure team efficiency, and make data-driven decisions to improve your project's overall success.

Creating and Customizing Dashboards

JIRA dashboards are your personalized windows into the world of your project data. They offer a versatile canvas where you can arrange and customize various gadgets to visualize and monitor key metrics, trends, and progress in real time.

What are Gadgets?

Gadgets are the visual building blocks of your JIRA dashboard. They are interactive components that display specific data views, such as:

- **Charts and Graphs:** These can visualize trends over time, comparisons between different data sets, and distributions of data points. Examples include pie charts, bar graphs, line graphs, and scatter plots.
- **Tables and Lists:** These provide structured views of data, often with filtering and sorting capabilities.
- **Other Visualizations:** JIRA offers various other gadgets, such as calendars, activity streams, and progress bars, to display project data in different formats.

Each gadget is designed to present a specific piece of information or insight, allowing you to tailor your dashboard to focus on the most critical aspects of your project.

Creating a New Dashboard

To create a new dashboard in JIRA:

1. **Navigate to Dashboards:** Click on the "Dashboards" link in the JIRA sidebar or main navigation menu.
2. **Click "Create dashboard":** This button is usually located at the top right of the Dashboards page.
3. **Name and describe your dashboard:** Give your dashboard a meaningful name that reflects its purpose. You can also add a description to provide more context.
4. **Select the dashboard type:** Choose between a system dashboard (shared with everyone) or a private dashboard (visible only to you).
5. **Click "Create":** Your new dashboard will be created, and you can start adding gadgets to it.

Adding Gadgets

To add a gadget to your dashboard:

1. **Click "Add gadget":** This button is usually located at the top right of the dashboard.
2. **Browse the gadget directory:** JIRA offers a wide range of built-in gadgets. You can also search for and install additional gadgets from the Atlassian Marketplace.
3. **Select a gadget:** Choose the gadget that best suits your needs.
4. **Configure the gadget:** Most gadgets require some configuration, such as selecting the project, filter, or data fields to display. You can also customize the appearance of the gadget, such as its colors, labels, and chart type.
5. **Save the gadget:** Once you have configured the gadget, click "Save" to add it to your dashboard.

Customizing Dashboards

You can customize your dashboard in several ways:

- **Drag and drop gadgets:** Rearrange the gadgets on your dashboard by dragging and dropping them.
- **Resize gadgets:** Click and drag the edges of a gadget to resize it.
- **Edit gadget settings:** Click the pencil icon on a gadget to edit its configuration.
- **Delete gadgets:** Click the trash can icon on a gadget to remove it from the dashboard.

By creating and customizing dashboards, you can transform raw JIRA data into actionable insights, making it easier to track progress, identify issues, and make informed decisions.

JIRA Reporting Best Practices

To truly harness the power of JIRA reporting and dashboards, consider incorporating these best practices into your project management workflow:

- **Identify Key Metrics:** Not all data is created equal. Start by identifying the key metrics that align with your project goals and objectives. These metrics could be related to sprint progress (e.g., velocity, burndown), issue resolution (e.g., time to resolution, average age of unresolved issues), or team performance (e.g., user workload distribution). Focus on the metrics that provide actionable insights and drive decision-making.
- **Regularly Review Reports:** Don't just create reports and forget about them. Make it a habit to review them regularly, ideally on a weekly or bi-weekly basis. This allows you to track progress, identify trends, and detect potential issues early on. By staying on top of your data, you can proactively address any problems that arise and keep your project on track.
- **Use Filters:** JIRA's filtering capabilities are essential for extracting meaningful insights from your data. Use filters to narrow down the data displayed in reports and dashboards, focusing on specific aspects of your project. For example, you can filter by project, issue type, assignee, or any other relevant field. This allows you to drill down into the details and uncover hidden patterns or trends.
- **Customize Dashboards:** Your JIRA dashboard should be your personalized command center. Customize it to display the most relevant gadgets and metrics for your role and responsibilities. Experiment with different layouts, colors, and gadgets to create a dashboard that is both visually appealing and informative. Don't be afraid to try new things and tailor the dashboard to your specific needs.
- **Share Dashboards:** Transparency is key to effective collaboration. Share your dashboards with team members and stakeholders to keep everyone informed about the project's progress. This promotes open communication, builds trust, and encourages collective ownership of the project's success. You can also use dashboards to facilitate discussions during sprint reviews and retrospectives.

By following these best practices, you can maximize the value of JIRA's reporting and dashboard features. Treat your data as a valuable asset, and use it to drive informed decision-making, improve team performance, and ultimately deliver successful projects.

Chapter Summary

In this chapter, we delved into the reporting and dashboard capabilities of JIRA, a powerful tool that enables teams to gain valuable insights into their project's progress and performance. We began by emphasizing the importance of reporting in project management and how JIRA's reporting features can aid in tracking project health, team performance, and individual contributions. We then explored the different types of reports available in JIRA, including Agile reports, issue analysis reports, time tracking reports, and user workload reports, highlighting how each type provides unique insights into various aspects of a project.

Furthermore, we explained how JIRA dashboards can be customized to create a personalized view of project data using interactive gadgets like charts, graphs, tables, and lists. We provided a step-by-step guide on creating and customizing dashboards, emphasizing their flexibility in adapting to individual and team preferences. Finally, we offered best practices for maximizing the effectiveness of JIRA's reporting and dashboard features. This includes identifying key metrics, regularly reviewing reports, utilizing filters, customizing dashboards, and sharing them with stakeholders to foster transparency and communication. By adhering to these best practices, you can leverage JIRA's reporting capabilities to make data-driven decisions, improve project performance, and ultimately achieve successful outcomes.

Time Tracking and Estimation

Outline

- The Importance of Time Tracking and Estimation in Agile
- Time Tracking in JIRA
- Estimation Techniques in JIRA
- Best Practices for Time Tracking and Estimation
- Chapter Summary

The Importance of Time Tracking and Estimation in Agile

In Agile project management, time tracking and estimation are essential practices that contribute significantly to the success and predictability of projects. They provide a framework for understanding the effort required to complete tasks, enabling teams to make informed decisions about planning, resource allocation, and budgeting.

Accurate Estimation: The Foundation of Agile Planning

Accurate estimation is the bedrock of Agile planning. It involves determining the relative size or complexity of work items, often expressed in story points or other relative units. By estimating the effort required for each task, teams can:

- **Plan Sprints Effectively:** Determine how much work can be realistically committed to in a sprint, ensuring that the team doesn't overcommit or underdeliver.
- **Forecast Project Timelines:** By aggregating the estimated effort for all backlog items, project managers can create a rough timeline for the entire project.
- **Allocate Resources:** Estimate the resources (people, time, budget) needed to complete the project, ensuring that you have the right people in the right roles at the right time.
- **Set Realistic Budgets:** Based on the estimated effort and resource requirements, project managers can create more accurate budgets, reducing the risk of cost overruns.

Time Tracking: Unveiling Insights and Improving Performance

Time tracking, on the other hand, focuses on recording the actual time spent on each task. This data provides valuable insights into:

- **Team Velocity:** By analyzing the time spent on completed tasks, you can calculate the team's velocity, which is the average amount of work the team completes in a sprint. This metric helps you forecast future sprint deliverables and adjust your plans accordingly.
- **Individual Performance:** Time tracking data reveals how much time each team member spends on different tasks, enabling you to identify high performers, address potential bottlenecks, and optimize resource allocation.
- **Task Complexity:** Comparing estimated time with actual time spent can help you refine your estimation process and improve its accuracy over time.
- **Project Progress:** Time tracking data can be used to generate reports that track the project's overall progress, allowing you to identify any deviations from the plan and take corrective action.

Combined Power

The combination of accurate estimation and detailed time tracking creates a powerful feedback loop. Estimations help you plan your work, while time tracking data allows you to evaluate the accuracy of those estimations and refine them for future sprints. This iterative process of planning, tracking, and adjusting ensures that your Agile projects stay on track and deliver maximum value to your customers.

In the next sections, we will explore how JIRA facilitates time tracking and estimation, providing you with the tools and techniques to harness their full potential for your Agile projects.

Time Tracking in JIRA

Built-in Time Tracking

JIRA offers a built-in time tracking feature that allows team members to log the time they spend working on issues directly within the platform. This feature is valuable for several reasons:

- **Monitoring Progress:** By tracking time spent on tasks, you can gain a clear understanding of how work is progressing and whether the team is on schedule.
- **Identifying Bottlenecks:** Time tracking data can help you pinpoint areas where work is getting stuck or taking longer than expected, allowing you to address these bottlenecks and improve efficiency.
- **Resource Allocation:** By analyzing how much time is spent on different types of tasks, you can make better decisions about resource allocation and ensure that your team members are working on the most impactful activities.
- **Billing and Reporting:** Time tracking data can be used for billing clients or for generating reports to track project costs and profitability.

Enabling and Configuring Time Tracking

Time tracking is typically enabled by default in JIRA Cloud, but you might need to configure certain settings to tailor it to your project's specific requirements. Here's how you can do it:

1. **Project Settings:** Navigate to your project settings and look for the "Time Tracking" section.
2. **Enable Time Tracking:** If it's not already enabled, click the toggle to activate time tracking for your project.
3. **Choose Estimation Statistic:** Decide whether you want to track time based on the "Original Estimate" (the initial estimate for the task) or the "Remaining Estimate" (the estimated time remaining to complete the task).
4. **Configure Time Format:** Choose how you want to display time values (e.g., hours, days, weeks).
5. **Set Up Worklog Attributes:** Define the attributes that you want to capture in worklogs. These typically include:
    - **Time Spent:** The actual time spent working on the issue.
    - **Remaining Estimate:** The estimated time remaining to complete the issue.
    - **Start Date:** The date when work on the issue started.
    - **Worklog Comments:** A space for adding comments or notes about the work performed.
6. **Add the Time Tracking Field to Screens:** Ensure that the "Time Tracking" field is added to the relevant issue screens (Create Issue, View Issue, Edit Issue) so that team members can log their work.

Once time tracking is enabled and configured, team members can log their work on issues directly from the issue view. They can enter the time spent, update the remaining estimate, and add any relevant comments. This data is then used to generate various time tracking reports, which we'll explore in more detail later in this chapter.

Worklog Attributes

When you or your team members log work on a JIRA issue, you create a worklog. Each worklog captures essential details about the work performed, providing a historical record of time spent and progress made. Let's delve into the key attributes of worklogs in JIRA:

- **Time Spent:** This is the core attribute of a worklog. It records the actual time spent working on the issue, typically in hours or minutes. It's crucial to log this accurately to get a realistic picture of the effort involved in completing tasks.
- **Remaining Estimate:** This attribute reflects the estimated time remaining to complete the issue after the worklog has been logged. It's helpful for adjusting project timelines and resource allocation based on the actual progress made.
- **Start Date:** This attribute indicates the date and time when the work on the issue started. It helps track the history of worklogs and understand when specific tasks were initiated.
- **Worklog Comments:** This field allows you to add additional notes or details about the work performed. You can describe the specific activities you worked on, mention any challenges you encountered, or provide any other relevant information that might be helpful for future reference or collaboration.

Example

Let's say you're a developer working on a JIRA issue titled "Implement user authentication feature." You spent 4 hours on Monday implementing the login functionality and another 2 hours on Tuesday integrating it with the backend. You would create two separate worklogs in JIRA:

- **Worklog 1:**
    - Time Spent: 4 hours
    - Remaining Estimate: 6 hours (assuming the original estimate was 10 hours)
    - Start Date: Monday, June 10, 2024
    - Worklog Comments: "Implemented the login form and basic authentication logic."
- **Worklog 2:**
    - Time Spent: 2 hours
    - Remaining Estimate: 4 hours
    - Start Date: Tuesday, June 11, 2024
    - Worklog Comments: "Integrated login functionality with the backend API."

These worklogs provide a detailed record of your progress on the issue, allowing you and your team to track the time spent and adjust estimates as needed.

By understanding and utilizing worklog attributes effectively, you can gain valuable insights into your team's work patterns, identify areas for improvement, and make data-driven decisions to optimize your project's timeline and resource utilization.

Third-Party Time Tracking Apps

While JIRA's built-in time tracking is a valuable tool, some teams might require more advanced features or functionalities. Luckily, there are several popular third-party time tracking apps available on the Atlassian Marketplace that seamlessly integrate with JIRA. These apps offer a range of additional capabilities, including:

- **Advanced reporting:** Gain deeper insights into time tracking data with customizable reports, dashboards, and visualizations.
- **Resource planning:** Plan and allocate resources more effectively based on team capacity and availability.
- **Budgeting and forecasting:** Track project budgets and forecast future costs based on time tracking data.
- **Invoicing and client billing:** Streamline invoicing and billing processes by integrating time tracking data with your accounting software.

- **Automatic time tracking:** Automatically track time spent on tasks based on activity or calendar events.

Some of the most popular third-party time tracking apps for JIRA include:

- **Tempo Timesheets:** Offers comprehensive time tracking, resource management, and reporting features, including budgeting, forecasting, and project portfolio management.
- **Harvest Time Tracking:** Provides a simple and intuitive interface for time tracking, invoicing, and reporting. It also integrates with other popular tools like Slack and Asana.
- **Everhour Time Tracking:** Offers a flexible time tracking solution with features like budgeting, invoicing, and team scheduling. It also integrates with project management tools like Trello and Basecamp.
- **Time Doctor Time Tracking Software:** Includes advanced features like screenshots, website and app monitoring, and productivity reports.

By exploring the various third-party time tracking apps available, you can find the one that best suits your team's specific needs and enhances your JIRA experience.

Estimation Techniques in JIRA

Estimating the effort required to complete tasks is a critical aspect of project planning and scheduling. In Agile methodologies, especially Scrum, story points are a widely used technique for estimation.

Story Points

Story points are a unitless measure of the relative effort required to complete a task or user story. Unlike absolute time estimates (e.g., hours or days), story points focus on the size or complexity of the work rather than the actual time it will take.

The team collaboratively assigns story points to each task or user story based on their understanding of its complexity, risk, and uncertainty. The values of story points are typically chosen from a Fibonacci sequence (1, 2, 3, 5, 8, 13, etc.), as it reflects the increasing uncertainty associated with larger tasks.

Benefits of Using Story Points

Using story points offers several advantages over traditional time-based estimates:

- **Improved Accuracy:** Story points encourage teams to focus on the relative effort required for different tasks, rather than getting bogged down in precise time estimations. This leads to more accurate estimations over time as the team gains experience and learns to compare the complexity of various tasks.
- **Flexibility:** Story points provide flexibility in planning and scheduling. Since they are not tied to specific time units, they can be adapted to different team velocities and project timelines.
- **Collaboration:** Story point estimation is a collaborative process that involves the entire team. This fosters a shared understanding of the work involved and promotes a sense of ownership among team members.
- **Reduced Pressure:** By focusing on relative effort rather than absolute time, story points reduce the pressure on team members to provide overly precise estimates, which can be challenging and stressful.

Example

Let's say your team is estimating the effort required for two user stories:

- **User Story A:** "As a user, I want to be able to log in to the application using my email address and password."

- **User Story B:** "As a user, I want to be able to reset my password if I forget it."

The team might agree that User Story A is relatively simple and assign it a story point value of 3. User Story B, on the other hand, might involve additional complexity, such as email verification and security considerations, and might be assigned a story point value of 5.

By using story points, the team can quickly assess that User Story B is likely to require more effort than User Story A, even without knowing the exact time it will take to complete each one. This information helps them prioritize their work and make informed decisions about sprint planning and resource allocation.

Planning Poker

Planning poker, also known as Scrum poker, is a gamified and collaborative technique used in Agile project management for estimating the effort required to complete tasks or user stories. It's a fun and engaging way to bring the team together to reach a consensus on story point estimations.

How Planning Poker Works

1. **Preparation:** The product owner or facilitator presents a user story or task to the team.
2. **Card Distribution:** Each team member receives a deck of cards with numbers representing different story point values (usually following the Fibonacci sequence: 0, 1, 2, 3, 5, 8, 13, 20, 40, 100).
3. **Estimation:** Team members privately select a card that represents their estimate of the effort required to complete the user story.
4. **Reveal:** Everyone simultaneously reveals their chosen card.
5. **Discussion:** If there's a wide range of estimates, the team discusses the reasons behind their choices. The team members with the highest and lowest estimates explain their reasoning.
6. **Re-Estimation:** The team members who provided outliers may choose to adjust their estimates based on the discussion.
7. **Repeat:** Steps 3-6 are repeated until the team reaches a consensus on the estimate.

Benefits of Planning Poker

- **Engaging and Collaborative:** Planning poker makes estimation more fun and interactive, encouraging active participation from all team members.
- **Shared Understanding:** The discussions during planning poker help team members better understand the requirements and complexities of the work, leading to more accurate estimations.
- **Reduced Bias:** The simultaneous reveal of cards prevents anchoring bias, where the first estimate influences subsequent estimates.
- **Consensus-Driven:** The goal is to reach a consensus, ensuring that the final estimate reflects the collective knowledge and experience of the team.

JIRA Support for Planning Poker

While JIRA doesn't have a built-in planning poker feature, there are numerous add-ons and plugins available on the Atlassian Marketplace that seamlessly integrate with JIRA. These add-ons provide a virtual planning poker environment where team members can participate in estimation sessions remotely or in person.

Some popular planning poker add-ons for JIRA include:

- **Planning Poker®:** This app offers a simple and intuitive interface for running planning poker sessions directly within JIRA. It allows for customizable card decks, voting options, and real-time results.

- **Agile Poker for Jira:** This add-on provides a comprehensive estimation toolkit with multiple estimation methods, including planning poker, affinity estimation, and t-shirt sizing. It also supports asynchronous estimation for distributed teams.
- **Scrumpy Planning Poker for Jira:** This app features a user-friendly interface, customizable card decks, real-time chat, and the ability to save estimates directly to JIRA issues.

By utilizing these add-ons, you can easily incorporate planning poker into your JIRA workflow, making estimation a more enjoyable and collaborative experience for your team.

Best Practices for Time Tracking and Estimation

To ensure accurate time tracking and estimation in JIRA, consider these practical tips and best practices:

- **Set Realistic Estimates:** Avoid the temptation to underestimate task complexity or overestimate your team's capacity. Base your estimations on historical data from similar projects or tasks, and consider factors like team experience, available resources, and potential risks. If you're new to a project, start with conservative estimates and adjust them as you gain more knowledge.
- **Track Time Consistently:** Encourage your team members to log their time regularly and accurately. This may involve setting aside time at the end of each day to update their worklogs or using a time tracking tool that automatically records their activity. Consistent time tracking ensures that you have reliable data to analyze and make informed decisions.
- **Review and Adjust Estimates:** Estimations are not set in stone. As work progresses, new information may arise, or unexpected challenges may occur. It's essential to regularly review your estimates and adjust them as needed to reflect the current reality of the project. This ensures that your timelines and resource allocation remain accurate.
- **Use Time Tracking Data to Improve Estimates:** Your time tracking data is a goldmine of information. Analyze it to identify patterns in how long certain types of tasks typically take. This information can be used to refine your estimation process and improve its accuracy over time. For example, if you notice that a particular type of task consistently takes longer than estimated, you can adjust your future estimates accordingly.
- **Integrate with Other Tools:** If your team uses other time tracking or project management tools, consider integrating them with JIRA. This can help you streamline your workflow and avoid duplicating data entry. Many integrations are available on the Atlassian Marketplace that can seamlessly connect JIRA with popular tools like Harvest, Tempo Timesheets, and Toggl.

By following these best practices, you can leverage the power of time tracking and estimation in JIRA to improve your project planning, resource allocation, and overall efficiency. Accurate time tracking and estimation are essential for delivering projects on time, within budget, and with high quality.

Chapter Summary

In this chapter, we explored the critical role of time tracking and estimation in Agile project management, highlighting their impact on planning, resource allocation, and overall project success. We discussed how accurate estimations help teams create realistic project timelines, allocate resources effectively, and set appropriate budgets. We also emphasized the importance of time tracking for gaining insights into team velocity, individual performance, task complexity, and project progress.

We then delved into JIRA's built-in time tracking capabilities, explaining how to enable and configure them for your projects. We also discussed the key attributes of worklogs, such as time spent, remaining estimate, start date, and comments, and how they contribute to a comprehensive understanding of work performed on issues. Additionally, we briefly mentioned the availability of third-party time tracking apps that integrate with JIRA, offering expanded features and functionalities for more robust time management.

Furthermore, we explored common estimation techniques in JIRA, with a focus on story points as a relative unit of measure for estimating effort. We discussed the benefits of story points over absolute time estimates and illustrated how planning poker can be used to collaboratively estimate story points in a fun and engaging way. We also highlighted JIRA's support for planning poker through add-ons and plugins.

Finally, we provided a set of best practices for time tracking and estimation in JIRA. These recommendations included setting realistic estimates, tracking time consistently, reviewing and adjusting estimates, using time tracking data to improve estimates, and considering integration with other tools. By following these best practices, you can leverage JIRA's time tracking and estimation features to optimize your project planning, enhance team productivity, and deliver projects on time and within budget.

Section D:
JIRA Administration

User and Group Management

Outline

- Introduction to User and Group Management
- Managing Users
- Managing Groups
- Project Roles and Permissions
- User Management Best Practices
- Chapter Summary

Introduction to User and Group Management

In the realm of JIRA administration, user and group management is a cornerstone. It's the process of creating and managing user accounts, organizing users into groups, and assigning roles and permissions to control access to different JIRA features and functionalities. Essentially, it's about deciding who can do what within your JIRA instance.

Imagine JIRA as a bustling city with various buildings representing projects and areas within those buildings representing specific tasks or issues. User and group management is like the city's security system, ensuring that only authorized personnel can enter certain buildings and access specific areas within them. Without proper security measures in place, chaos could ensue, and sensitive information could be compromised.

Similarly, in JIRA, effective user and group management is crucial for maintaining order, security, and efficiency. By defining clear roles and permissions, you ensure that only the right people have access to the right information and can perform the appropriate actions. This not only protects sensitive project data but also streamlines collaboration and prevents unauthorized changes or disruptions.

For instance, you might have a project manager who needs access to all aspects of a project, while a developer might only need access to specific issues related to their assigned tasks. By setting up appropriate roles and permissions, you can grant each user the necessary access without compromising security.

In this chapter, we'll delve into the intricacies of user and group management in JIRA. We'll explore how to create and manage user accounts, organize users into groups, assign project roles and permissions, and implement best practices to ensure the security and integrity of your JIRA instance. By the end of this chapter, you'll be equipped with the knowledge and skills to effectively manage users and groups in JIRA, creating a well-organized and secure environment for your team's collaboration.

Managing Users

Efficient user management is essential for maintaining a well-organized and secure JIRA environment. In this section, we'll cover the fundamental aspects of managing users within JIRA.

Creating User Accounts

JIRA offers two primary methods for creating user accounts:

1. **Manual Creation:**
    - Navigate to the User Management section within JIRA's administration settings.
    - Click on the "Create User" button.
    - Fill in the required details, such as the user's full name, email address (which will serve as their username), and a temporary password.
    - Optionally, you can add the user to relevant groups and assign them project roles at this stage.
    - Click "Create" to add the new user to JIRA.
2. **Bulk Import:**
    - If you have a large number of users to add, bulk import is a more efficient option.
    - Prepare a CSV file with the required user information (e.g., full name, email, groups).
    - In JIRA's User Management section, click on the "Bulk Create" button.
    - Upload your CSV file and follow the instructions to map the fields and create the user accounts.

Editing User Profiles

To modify a user's details or preferences:

1. Navigate to the User Management section.
2. Search for and select the user you want to edit.
3. Click on the "Edit" button next to the user's name.
4. Modify the desired fields, such as the user's name, email address, or notification preferences.
5. Click "Update" to save the changes.

Deactivating and Reactivating Users

If a user is no longer active or needs their access temporarily revoked, you can deactivate their account:

1. Go to the User Management section.
2. Locate the user and click the "Deactivate" button.
3. Confirm the deactivation. The user will no longer be able to log in.

To reactivate a deactivated user:

1. Navigate to the User Management section.
2. Select the "Deactivated Users" tab.
3. Find the user and click the "Reactivate" button.
4. Confirm the reactivation. The user will regain access to their account.

Deleting User Accounts

Deleting a user account should be done with caution, as it permanently removes the user's data and activity history from JIRA. Consider deactivating the account instead if there's a chance the user might return. If you need to delete an account:

1. Go to the User Management section.
2. Search for the user and click the "Delete" button.
3. Confirm the deletion. Note that this action cannot be undone.

By mastering these user management techniques, you'll be able to maintain a well-organized and secure JIRA environment, ensuring that the right users have the appropriate access to your projects and resources.

Managing Groups

In JIRA, groups are a powerful tool for streamlining user management and simplifying permission administration. By organizing users into groups, you can efficiently assign permissions and control access to various JIRA functionalities. Let's explore the benefits of using groups and how to manage them effectively.

Benefits of Using Groups

- **Simplified Permission Management:** Instead of assigning permissions to individual users, you can grant permissions to groups. This saves time and effort, especially when dealing with a large number of users.
- **Efficient Onboarding:** When new users join your organization, you can simply add them to the relevant groups, automatically granting them the necessary permissions.
- **Improved Security:** By controlling access through groups, you reduce the risk of unauthorized access to sensitive project data.
- **Enhanced Collaboration:** Groups can be used to foster collaboration by creating dedicated spaces for teams or departments to share information and work together.

Creating and Editing Groups

To create a new group in JIRA:

1. Navigate to the User Management section within JIRA's administration settings.
2. Click on the "Groups" tab.
3. Click the "Create group" button.
4. Enter a name for the group and an optional description.
5. Click "Create" to save the new group.

To add or remove users from an existing group:

1. Go to the "Groups" tab in the User Management section.
2. Search for and select the group you want to modify.
3. Click the "Add members" or "Remove members" button.
4. Select the users you want to add or remove from the group.
5. Click "Add" or "Remove" to update the group membership.

Group Types

JIRA offers several types of groups:

- **Project Roles:** These groups are automatically created for each project and represent different roles within the project (e.g., Administrators, Developers, Users).
- **Application Access Groups:** These groups control access to specific JIRA applications or features (e.g., JIRA Software, JIRA Service Management).
- **User-created Groups:** You can create custom groups to categorize users based on your organization's specific needs (e.g., Marketing Team, Engineering Team).

Nesting Groups

You can create nested groups to organize users hierarchically. For example, you might have a "Development Team" group that contains two subgroups: "Frontend Developers" and "Backend Developers." This allows you to assign permissions to the parent group, which will automatically apply to all its subgroups and members.

By understanding and utilizing groups effectively, you can streamline user management, simplify permission administration, and enhance collaboration within your JIRA instance.

Project Roles and Permissions

Project roles and permissions are fundamental to controlling who can do what within a JIRA project. They ensure that team members have the appropriate access to perform their tasks while safeguarding sensitive information and preventing unauthorized changes.

Project Roles

Project roles are predefined sets of permissions that define what actions a user can take within a project. JIRA comes with several default project roles, but you can also create custom roles to tailor permissions to your specific needs. Here are some common project roles and their typical permissions:

- **Administrator:** Has full control over the project, including managing users, configuring settings, and modifying workflows.
- **Project Lead/Manager:** Responsible for managing the project, including creating and assigning tasks, tracking progress, and generating reports.
- **Developer:** Works on developing and implementing features, typically with permissions to create and edit issues, transition issues through the workflow, and add comments.
- **Tester:** Tests the functionality of the software, typically with permissions to create and edit issues, transition issues through the workflow (e.g., marking issues as "Done"), and add comments.
- **User:** Has limited access to the project, typically with permissions to view issues, add comments, and create their own issues.

Permission Schemes

Permission schemes are collections of project roles and their associated permissions. Each project is associated with a permission scheme, which determines what actions users with different roles can perform within that project. JIRA provides default permission schemes, but you can customize them to align with your organization's specific requirements.

Assigning Project Roles

You can assign project roles to individual users or groups. This allows you to grant or restrict access to project features based on a user's role. To assign a project role:

1. **Go to Project Settings:** Navigate to your project's settings page.
2. **Select "People":** In the settings menu, click on the "People" tab.
3. **Add users or groups:** Search for the user or group you want to assign a role to and add them to the project.
4. **Assign roles:** Once the user or group is added, select the appropriate project role from the dropdown menu next to their name.

By carefully assigning project roles and managing your permission schemes, you can ensure that your JIRA projects are secure, organized, and efficient. Remember, it's crucial to follow the principle of least privilege, granting users only the minimum permissions necessary to perform their tasks. This helps to mitigate security risks and maintain the integrity of your project data.

User Management Best Practices

Efficient user and group management is not just about setting up accounts and permissions; it's an ongoing process that requires careful planning and continuous maintenance. Here are some best practices to help you optimize your JIRA user management:

1. **Plan Your User Structure:** Before creating user accounts or groups, take the time to plan your user structure. Consider your organization's hierarchy, team structures, and project roles. Decide how you want to group users (e.g., by department, project, or role) and what permissions each group should have. A well-thought-out user structure will make it easier to manage permissions and ensure that users have the appropriate access levels.
2. **Use Groups for Efficiency:** Leverage groups to simplify permission management. Instead of assigning permissions to individual users, grant permissions to groups and then add users to those groups. This saves time and effort, especially when you have a large number of users. If a user's role changes, you simply need to update their group membership, rather than modifying their individual permissions.
3. **Follow the Principle of Least Privilege:** This principle states that users should only be granted the minimum permissions necessary to perform their tasks. Avoid giving users excessive permissions, as this can increase the risk of accidental or intentional misuse of JIRA. Regularly review user permissions and revoke any unnecessary access.
4. **Regularly Review and Update Permissions:** User roles and responsibilities can change over time, so it's important to periodically review and update permissions. This ensures that users have the correct access levels and helps maintain the security of your JIRA instance. Conduct regular audits of user accounts and groups to identify any inactive or unauthorized users.
5. **Document Your User Management Processes:** Create clear and comprehensive documentation outlining your user management policies and procedures. This documentation should include information on how to create and manage user accounts, assign roles and permissions, handle deactivation and reactivation, and address any other relevant processes. This documentation will be invaluable for new administrators and will help maintain consistency in your user management practices.

By following these best practices, you can establish a robust and scalable user management system in JIRA. This will not only enhance the security and integrity of your JIRA instance but also improve collaboration and streamline your overall project management processes.

Chapter Summary

In this chapter, we delved into the intricacies of user and group management in JIRA, a critical aspect of ensuring the security, organization, and efficiency of your JIRA environment. We started by highlighting the importance of user and group management, explaining how it empowers administrators to control access to sensitive project data and functionalities.

We then provided a comprehensive guide on managing users, covering the creation of user accounts (manually or through bulk import), editing user profiles, deactivating and reactivating users, and deleting user accounts. We also discussed the benefits of using groups in JIRA, including simplified permission management, efficient onboarding, improved security, and enhanced collaboration. We explained how to create and edit groups, different types of groups, and the concept of nesting groups for hierarchical organization.

Additionally, we explored the relationship between project roles and permissions, describing common project roles and their associated permissions, as well as the concept of permission schemes. We outlined how to assign project roles to users or groups, allowing you to grant or restrict access based on their responsibilities.

Finally, we provided a set of best practices for JIRA user and group management. These recommendations included planning your user structure, leveraging groups for efficiency, following the principle of least privilege, regularly reviewing and updating permissions, and documenting your user management processes. By adhering to these best practices, you can establish a robust and scalable user management system that enhances collaboration, ensures security, and streamlines your project management workflow.

Project Roles and Permissions

Outline

- What are Project Roles?
- Default Project Roles in JIRA
- Customizing Project Roles
- Understanding Permissions
- Permission Schemes
- Assigning Project Roles
- Chapter Summary

What are Project Roles?

In the complex ecosystem of a JIRA project, **project roles** are the gatekeepers, determining who can access what and who can perform which actions. They are predefined sets of permissions that dictate the level of interaction a user can have within a specific project. Think of them as the different hats team members wear, each with its own set of responsibilities and corresponding access rights.

These roles are instrumental in maintaining project organization and security. By assigning appropriate roles to users, you ensure that only those who need access to specific information or functionalities have it. For example, a developer might need the ability to create and edit tasks, while a project manager might require broader permissions to oversee the entire project.

The concept of project roles is deeply rooted in the principle of least privilege, a security best practice that advocates for granting users only the minimum level of access necessary to perform their duties. This minimizes the risk of accidental or intentional misuse of JIRA, safeguarding sensitive data and ensuring the integrity of your projects.

Imagine a JIRA project as a construction site. Different workers have different roles and responsibilities. A construction worker needs access to tools and materials, but they don't need access to the project blueprints. The architect, on the other hand, needs access to the blueprints but doesn't need to operate heavy machinery. Similarly, in JIRA, project roles ensure that each user has the right tools and access levels for their specific role, promoting efficient collaboration and protecting sensitive information.

By carefully assigning and managing project roles, you create a structured and secure environment where everyone can contribute effectively without compromising the project's integrity. This not only streamlines your workflow but also fosters a sense of trust and accountability among team members.

Default Project Roles in JIRA

JIRA comes equipped with a set of default project roles, each designed to represent common responsibilities and tasks within a project. Understanding these roles and their associated permissions is crucial for effectively managing your team's access and collaboration within JIRA.

Administrator

The Administrator role is the most powerful role within a JIRA project. Users with this role have full control over the project and can perform any action, including:

- **Managing project settings:** Configuring workflows, issue types, screens, fields, and other project-level settings.

- **Managing users and permissions:** Adding and removing users, assigning project roles, and modifying permission schemes.
- **Creating and editing issues:** Creating, editing, assigning, and transitioning issues through the workflow.
- **Viewing and generating reports:** Accessing all project data and generating reports on project progress and performance.

Administrators are typically project managers, team leads, or system administrators responsible for the overall management and configuration of the project.

Project Lead/Manager

The Project Lead/Manager role is designed for individuals who are responsible for the day-to-day management of the project. They have a broad range of permissions, including:

- **Creating and assigning tasks:** Creating and assigning issues to team members, setting priorities, and managing the project backlog.
- **Tracking progress:** Monitoring the progress of the project through Agile boards, reports, and dashboards.
- **Communicating with stakeholders:** Providing updates to stakeholders and managing their expectations.
- **Resolving issues:** Addressing any issues or blockers that arise during the project.

Developer

The Developer role is intended for team members who are primarily responsible for developing and implementing features. Developers typically have the following permissions:

- **Creating and editing issues:** Creating and updating issues related to their assigned tasks, including bug reports, feature requests, and technical tasks.
- **Transitioning issues:** Moving issues through the workflow as they progress (e.g., from "In Progress" to "In Review" to "Done").
- **Adding comments:** Providing updates, asking questions, and collaborating with other team members through comments.
- **Viewing project information:** Accessing relevant project information, such as the project backlog, sprint boards, and reports.

Tester

The Tester role is designed for team members responsible for testing the functionality of the software. Testers typically have similar permissions to Developers, but they might also have additional permissions related to test case management and defect tracking.

User

The User role is the most basic role and is intended for individuals who need limited access to the project. Users typically have the following permissions:

- **Viewing issues:** Viewing the details of issues relevant to their work.
- **Adding comments:** Providing feedback or asking questions about issues.
- **Creating issues:** Reporting bugs or suggesting new features (if allowed by the project configuration).

By understanding the default project roles in JIRA and their associated permissions, you can effectively manage your team's access and ensure that everyone has the right level of authorization to contribute to the project while maintaining security and control.

Customizing Project Roles

While JIRA's default project roles cover many common scenarios, your team's specific needs might not always fit neatly into these predefined categories. That's where custom project roles come in. JIRA empowers administrators to create tailored roles that align precisely with your team's unique structure, responsibilities, and workflow.

Why Create Custom Project Roles?

Custom project roles offer several benefits:

- **Granular Control:** You can define specific permissions that go beyond the default roles, granting or restricting access to individual actions within JIRA.
- **Flexibility:** Custom roles allow you to adapt JIRA to your unique project requirements and organizational structure.
- **Enhanced Security:** By granting only the necessary permissions, you minimize the risk of unauthorized access or accidental changes.
- **Improved Collaboration:** Custom roles can clarify responsibilities and ensure that each team member has the right level of access to perform their tasks effectively.

Creating a Custom Project Role: Step-by-Step Guide

1. **Access Project Settings:** Navigate to your project's settings page.
2. **Select "Project Roles":** In the settings menu, click on the "Project Roles" tab.
3. **Click "Create Project Role":** You'll find this button on the Project Roles page.
4. **Name and Describe the Role:** Give your custom role a clear and descriptive name (e.g., "Marketing Specialist" or "UX Designer"). Add a brief description to explain the role's purpose and responsibilities.
5. **Assign Permissions:** This is the crucial step. Select the specific permissions you want to grant to this role. You can choose from a wide range of permissions, including creating and editing issues, transitioning issues through the workflow, viewing project reports, and managing project settings. Be sure to select only the permissions that are necessary for the role's responsibilities.
6. **Save the Role:** Once you've selected the permissions, click "Save" to create the custom role.

Example: Creating a "Marketing Specialist" Role

Let's say you want to create a custom role for marketing specialists who need access to JIRA but should not be able to modify project settings or workflows. You could create a "Marketing Specialist" role and assign the following permissions:

- Browse Projects
- Create Issues
- Edit Own Issues
- Transition Issues
- Add Comments

Assigning Custom Project Roles

Once you've created a custom role, you can assign it to users or groups just like you would with default roles. Go to the "People" tab in the project settings, add the user or group, and select the newly created custom role from the dropdown menu.

By leveraging custom project roles, you can tailor JIRA to your team's specific needs, ensuring everyone has the right level of access and responsibility to contribute effectively to the project.

Understanding Permissions

In JIRA, permissions are the fine-grained controls that govern what actions a user can and cannot perform within a project. They are the granular details that define a user's level of access, shaping their experience and interaction with the project's data and functionalities.

Permissions: The Building Blocks of Access Control

Think of permissions as a set of keys that unlock specific doors within your JIRA project. Each permission grants access to a particular action or piece of information. By combining different permissions, you create project roles, which are essentially bundles of keys that grant access to a defined set of actions and information.

Common JIRA Permissions and Their Implications

JIRA offers a wide range of permissions, covering various aspects of project management and collaboration. Here are some of the most common permissions and their implications:

- **Browse Projects:** This permission allows users to view the project and access its basic information, such as the project summary, description, and components.
- **Create Issues:** This permission allows users to create new issues within the project.
- **Edit Issues:** This permission grants users the ability to modify the details of existing issues, such as the summary, description, assignee, and priority.
- **Assign Issues:** This permission allows users to assign issues to themselves or other team members.
- **Transition Issues:** This permission allows users to move issues through the workflow by changing their status.
- **Add Comments:** This permission allows users to add comments to issues, facilitating communication and collaboration.
- **View Project Information:** This permission grants access to various project-related information, such as the project backlog, sprint boards, reports, and dashboards.
- **Manage Project Settings:** This permission is typically reserved for administrators and project leads. It allows users to modify project settings, such as workflows, issue types, screens, and fields.

Examples

Let's consider a few scenarios to illustrate how permissions work in practice:

- **Developer:** A developer might have the "Create Issues," "Edit Issues," "Transition Issues," and "Add Comments" permissions, allowing them to work on their assigned tasks but not modify project settings.
- **Tester:** A tester might have similar permissions to a developer, but they might also have the "Schedule Issues" permission, allowing them to schedule tests and track their results.
- **Project Manager:** A project manager might have broader permissions, including "Browse Projects," "Create Issues," "Edit Issues," "Assign Issues," "Transition Issues," "Add Comments," and "View Project Information," allowing them to oversee the entire project.
- **Stakeholder:** A stakeholder who only needs to view project progress might have the "Browse Projects" and "View Project Information" permissions, limiting their access to sensitive information.

By understanding the different permissions available in JIRA and their implications, you can effectively manage user access and ensure that each team member has the right level of authorization to contribute to the project while maintaining security and control.

Permission Schemes

In JIRA, a permission scheme is a structured framework that governs user access within a project. It's essentially a collection of project roles, each bundled with its corresponding set of permissions. This scheme acts as a rulebook, determining what actions users with different roles can perform within a specific project.

How Permission Schemes Work

Each project in JIRA is linked to a permission scheme. When you create a new project, JIRA automatically associates it with a default permission scheme, which includes the standard project roles (Administrator, Project Lead/Manager, Developer, Tester, User) and their typical permissions. However, you can modify this default scheme or create a custom scheme to tailor permissions precisely to your project's requirements.

The permission scheme acts as a filter, determining which actions are allowed or restricted for each user based on their assigned role. For example, if a user is assigned the "Developer" role and the permission scheme for the project allows developers to create and edit issues, then that user will be able to perform those actions. However, if the permission scheme does not grant developers the permission to delete issues, then they will not be able to do so.

Default vs. Custom Permission Schemes

JIRA's default permission schemes provide a good starting point for most projects. They cover common scenarios and ensure that essential permissions are granted to the appropriate roles. However, as your project evolves and your team's needs change, you might find that the default scheme doesn't fully meet your requirements.

In such cases, you can customize the default scheme or create a brand new custom scheme. This allows you to fine-tune the permissions granted to each role, adding or removing specific permissions as needed. For example, you might want to create a custom role for a "Marketing Manager" who needs to view project reports but doesn't need to edit issues.

Modifying and Customizing Permission Schemes

To modify or customize a permission scheme, navigate to your project's settings page and select the "Permissions" tab. Here, you can view the current permission scheme and make any necessary changes. You can add or remove project roles, modify the permissions associated with each role, or create a new scheme altogether.

By understanding and utilizing permission schemes effectively, you can ensure that your JIRA projects are secure, organized, and efficient. Each team member will have the appropriate level of access to perform their tasks, while sensitive information remains protected from unauthorized viewing or modification.

Assigning Project Roles

Assigning project roles is the final step in setting up your JIRA project's permissions structure. It's a crucial process that determines who can do what within the project, ensuring smooth collaboration and data security.

Importance of Assigning Appropriate Roles

Choosing the right project role for each user is essential for several reasons:

- **Efficiency:** Assigning the correct roles ensures that users have the necessary permissions to perform their tasks without being hindered by unnecessary restrictions.

- **Security:** It prevents unauthorized access to sensitive information and functionalities, protecting your project data.
- **Clarity:** Clearly defined roles help team members understand their responsibilities and expectations within the project.

How to Assign Project Roles

Here's a step-by-step guide on how to assign project roles to users or groups in JIRA:

1. **Navigate to Project Settings:** Go to your project's settings page.
2. **Select "People":** In the settings menu, click on the "People" tab. This will open a page where you can manage the users and groups associated with the project.
3. **Add Users or Groups:**
    - To add an individual user, click the "Add people" button and enter their name or email address.
    - To add a group, click the "Add groups" button and select the desired group from the list.
4. **Assign Roles:**
    - Once a user or group is added to the project, you'll see a dropdown menu next to their name. Select the appropriate project role from this menu. For example, you might assign the "Developer" role to a user who will be working on coding tasks or the "Project Lead" role to a user who will be overseeing the project's progress.

Managing Project Roles

Managing project roles is an ongoing process as your team's composition or project requirements may change over time. Here's how you can manage project roles:

- **Adding or Removing Users:** You can easily add or remove users from a project role by selecting the user or group on the "People" page and clicking the "Remove from project" or "Remove from role" button.
- **Modifying Permissions:** If you need to adjust the permissions associated with a project role, you can do so by editing the corresponding permission scheme. This allows you to fine-tune the access levels for each role without having to recreate the roles themselves.

By following these steps and adhering to best practices for assigning and managing project roles, you can ensure that your JIRA project is well-organized, secure, and conducive to effective collaboration.

Chapter Summary

In this chapter, we delved into the crucial topic of project roles and permissions within JIRA, a cornerstone of effective project management and collaboration. We defined project roles as sets of permissions that govern what actions users can perform within a project, highlighting their importance in maintaining project organization and security.

We explored the default project roles available in JIRA, including Administrator, Project Lead/Manager, Developer, Tester, and User, outlining their typical responsibilities and associated permissions. We then discussed how you can customize project roles to suit your unique needs, granting granular control and flexibility in defining access levels.

Further, we explained the concept of permissions in JIRA, detailing how they act as fine-grained controls over user actions within a project. We provided examples of common permissions and their implications within a project context. We also discussed permission schemes, which are collections of project roles and their associated permissions, and how they are linked to each project to determine user access.

Finally, we provided a detailed guide on how to assign project roles to users or groups, emphasizing the importance of selecting appropriate roles based on individual responsibilities. We also discussed how to manage project roles, including adding or removing users from roles and modifying permissions as needed. By understanding and implementing these concepts, you can create a well-structured and secure JIRA environment where everyone has the right level of access to contribute effectively to the project while safeguarding sensitive data.

Customizing Fields and Screens

Outline

- Introduction to Fields and Screens
- Managing Custom Fields
- Managing Screens and Screen Schemes
- Advanced Field and Screen Customization
- Chapter Summary

Introduction to Fields and Screens

In JIRA, fields are the fundamental building blocks for capturing information about issues. They act as containers for specific data points, such as the issue's summary, description, assignee, priority, due date, and many more. Fields are essential for organizing and tracking the details of your work items, making it easy to find, filter, and report on specific information.

JIRA provides two types of fields:

- **System Fields:** These are built-in fields that are included in JIRA by default. They capture essential information common to most projects, such as the issue type, summary, description, priority, and status. System fields are usually mandatory and cannot be deleted.
- **Custom Fields:** These are user-defined fields that you can create to capture additional information specific to your project or organization. For example, you might create a custom field to track the customer associated with an issue, the estimated effort in hours, or a specific project phase. Custom fields can be of various types, including text, number, date, user picker, and more.

Screens, on the other hand, are collections of fields that determine which fields are displayed and editable when creating or viewing an issue. JIRA comes with default screens for different issue operations (e.g., create, edit, view), but you can customize these screens to tailor the information displayed based on your project's specific needs.

Importance of Customizing Fields and Screens

Customizing fields and screens is crucial for aligning JIRA with your unique workflows and processes. By creating custom fields, you can capture the specific data points that are most relevant to your projects. For example, if you're working on a software development project, you might want to create custom fields for tracking the software version, the affected components, or the root cause of a bug.

Similarly, customizing screens allows you to streamline data entry and ensure that users only see the relevant fields for each issue operation. For instance, you might want to create a simplified screen for creating new issues and a more detailed screen for viewing or editing existing issues. This can significantly improve user experience and reduce the risk of errors during data entry.

By customizing fields and screens, you can:

- **Capture relevant data:** Ensure that you're collecting all the necessary information about your issues.
- **Improve visibility:** Make it easier for team members to find the information they need.
- **Streamline workflows:** Simplify data entry and reduce the risk of errors.
- **Enhance collaboration:** Create a shared understanding of the information that's important for your projects.

In the following sections, we'll delve deeper into the process of managing custom fields, creating and customizing screens, and exploring advanced customization techniques.

Managing Custom Fields

JIRA's built-in fields are designed to capture common information relevant to most projects. However, your projects might have unique requirements that necessitate the collection of additional data. This is where custom fields come into play. Custom fields allow you to tailor JIRA to your specific needs by adding fields that capture information not covered by the default options.

Creating a Custom Field

1. **Navigate to Custom Fields:** Go to your JIRA settings and locate the "Issues" section. Within this section, find and click on "Custom fields." This will take you to the custom fields administration page.
2. **Click "Create custom field":** On the custom fields page, click the "Create custom field" button. This will open a wizard that guides you through the creation process.
3. **Choose Field Type:** JIRA offers various field types, each designed for a specific kind of data. Some common types include:
    - **Text Field:** For capturing short text values.
    - **Textarea:** For capturing longer text values.
    - **Number Field:** For capturing numerical values.
    - **Date Picker:** For capturing date values.
    - **User Picker (single/multiple):** For selecting one or more users.
    - **Labels Field:** For adding labels to issues.
    - **Select List (single/multiple):** For creating a dropdown list of options.
    - **Checkbox:** For capturing yes/no values.
    - **URL Field:** For storing website URLs.
4. Select the field type that best suits the kind of information you want to capture.
5. **Name and Describe the Field:** Give your custom field a clear and descriptive name that indicates its purpose. Add a description to provide additional context or instructions for users.
6. **Configure Field Options (if applicable):** Some field types, like Select Lists, require you to define the available options. You can add, edit, or remove options as needed.
7. **Configure Field Behavior:** You can further customize the field's behavior by setting options like:
    - **Searchable:** Whether the field can be used for searching.
    - **Required:** Whether the field is mandatory for creating or updating issues.
    - **Default Value:** A pre-filled value that appears in the field when a new issue is created.
8. **Create the Field:** Click the "Create" button to finalize the custom field creation.

Editing and Deleting Custom Fields

To edit an existing custom field, navigate to the custom fields page, locate the field you want to modify, and click the "Edit" button next to it. You can then change the field's name, description, options, or behavior.

To delete a custom field, click the "Delete" button next to the field name. Note that deleting a custom field will remove all its associated data from your JIRA issues.

By mastering the management of custom fields, you can unlock a new level of flexibility and customization in JIRA, enabling you to track the information that is most valuable for your projects.

Managing Screens and Screen Schemes

While custom fields allow you to define the *types* of data you want to capture in JIRA, screens and screen schemes determine *how* that data is presented and interacted with. Let's delve into how you can manage these elements to tailor the user experience within JIRA:

Screens: Organizing Information

Screens act as the visual layout for displaying issue information. Each screen is a collection of fields arranged in a specific order. JIRA comes with default screens for different operations, such as creating, editing, or viewing an issue. However, you can create custom screens to control precisely which fields are visible and how they are organized.

Screen Schemes: Mapping Screens to Operations

Screen schemes define the mapping between screens and issue operations. They determine which screen is displayed for each type of operation and issue. For example, you might want a simplified screen with only essential fields when creating a new issue, but a more detailed screen when viewing an existing issue. Screen schemes enable you to control this mapping based on the issue's current state and the user's role.

Creating and Editing Screens

1. **Go to Screens:** Navigate to the "Issues" section in your JIRA settings and click on "Screens." This will open the screen administration page.
2. **Create a New Screen (or Edit Existing):** Click the "Create screen" or "Edit" button for an existing screen.
3. **Add or Remove Fields:** Use the drag-and-drop interface to add fields from the available fields list to the screen layout. You can also remove fields by dragging them back to the list.
4. **Arrange Fields:** Drag and drop fields within the layout to arrange them in the desired order.
5. **Save the Screen:** Click the "Save" button to save your changes.

Creating and Managing Screen Schemes

1. **Go to Screen Schemes:** Navigate to the "Issues" section in your JIRA settings and click on "Screen schemes."
2. **Create a New Scheme (or Edit Existing):** Click the "Add screen scheme" or "Edit" button for an existing scheme.
3. **Associate Screens with Operations:** For each issue operation (Create, Edit, View, etc.) and issue type, select the appropriate screen from the dropdown menu.
4. **Save the Scheme:** Click the "Save" button to save your changes.

Example

Imagine you have a "Bug" issue type in your project. You can create a simplified "Create Issue" screen for this issue type, displaying only the "Summary," "Description," and "Priority" fields. Then, you can create a more detailed "View Issue" screen that includes additional fields like "Environment," "Steps to Reproduce," and "Root Cause." Finally, you would create a screen scheme that associates the "Create Issue" screen with the "Create Issue" operation for the "Bug" issue type, and the "View Issue" screen with the "View Issue" operation for the "Bug" issue type.

By mastering screens and screen schemes, you can tailor the JIRA user interface to match your specific workflows, making it easier for users to enter and view relevant information for each issue type and operation.

Advanced Field and Screen Customization

While basic field and screen customization allows for a good degree of tailoring, JIRA offers even more advanced options to refine your issue views and data collection processes. Let's explore some of these advanced techniques:

Field Configurations

Field configurations give you granular control over the visibility and behavior of fields across different issue types and projects. With field configurations, you can:

- **Hide or Show Fields:** Determine which fields are visible on specific issue types or projects. For example, you might want the "Story Points" field to be visible only for "Story" issue types.
- **Make Fields Required or Optional:** Control whether a field is mandatory or optional for specific issue types or projects. This ensures that essential information is always captured.
- **Set Field Defaults:** Define default values for fields, streamlining data entry by pre-filling information that is common to most issues.

Contextual Fields

Contextual fields allow you to display different fields based on the value of another field. This is useful when certain fields are only relevant in specific contexts. For instance, you might want to show a "Root Cause Analysis" field only when the "Issue Type" is set to "Bug."

Calculated Fields

Calculated fields automatically calculate values based on other fields in the issue. This can save time and reduce manual effort. For example, you could create a calculated field that automatically calculates the "Time to Resolution" by subtracting the "Created Date" from the "Resolved Date."

Conditional Fields

Conditional fields allow you to dynamically show or hide fields based on certain conditions. This declutters the issue view and ensures that users only see the relevant fields for their current context. For example, you could hide the "Deployment Date" field until the issue's status is changed to "Ready for Deployment."

Default Values

Setting default values for fields can save time and ensure consistency in data entry. For instance, you could set the default value for the "Assignee" field to the project lead or the default value for the "Priority" field to "Medium."

Field Layouts

Field layouts allow you to organize fields into tabs or sections on your screens. This can improve the readability and usability of the issue view, especially when dealing with a large number of fields. You can group related fields together, create separate tabs for different types of information, and even use collapsible sections to hide less frequently used fields.

By mastering these advanced field and screen customization techniques, you can create a JIRA experience that is tailored to your team's specific workflows and needs. This not only improves efficiency but also enhances the overall user experience, leading to increased adoption and satisfaction with JIRA.

Chapter Summary

In this chapter, we explored the powerful customization options available in JIRA for tailoring fields and screens to meet your specific project needs. We started by introducing the concept of fields, both system-defined and custom-defined, and how they are used to capture essential information about issues. We then delved into screens, explaining how they control the display and arrangement of fields on an issue, and how screen schemes associate different screens with various issue operations.

We provided step-by-step guides on managing custom fields, including creating, editing, and deleting them, emphasizing the importance of choosing the appropriate field type and configuring field behaviors. Similarly, we guided you through managing screens and screen schemes, explaining how to create, edit, and associate screens with different operations and issue types.

Finally, we ventured into advanced field and screen customization techniques, discussing field configurations, contextual fields, calculated fields, conditional fields, default values, and field layouts. These techniques allow you to fine-tune the visibility, behavior, and organization of fields, creating a JIRA environment that seamlessly aligns with your project workflows and enhances the user experience. By mastering these customization options, you can unlock the full potential of JIRA, making it a truly personalized and efficient tool for managing your projects.

Automation Rules and Triggers

Outline

- What is Automation in JIRA?
- Benefits of Automation
- Components of Automation Rules
- Creating Automation Rules
- Common Automation Use Cases
- Best Practices for Automation
- Chapter Summary

What is Automation in JIRA?

Automation in JIRA is a powerful feature that allows you to streamline your project management processes by creating rules that automatically perform actions based on specific triggers or conditions. In essence, it's like having a virtual assistant that works tirelessly in the background, taking care of repetitive and mundane tasks, so you and your team can focus on more strategic work.

Triggers, Conditions, and Actions: The Building Blocks of Automation

At the heart of JIRA automation lies the concept of rules. Each rule consists of three essential components:

1. **Triggers:** These are events that initiate the rule. Examples of triggers include:
    - **Issue created:** The rule triggers when a new issue is created.
    - **Issue updated:** The rule triggers when an existing issue is modified.
    - **Field value changed:** The rule triggers when a specific field value is changed.
    - **Scheduled:** The rule triggers at a specified time or interval.
2. **Conditions:** These are optional criteria that must be met for the rule to execute. You can use conditions to narrow down the scope of the rule and ensure that it only applies to specific scenarios. For example, you could create a condition that only applies to issues in a particular project or with a specific priority level.
3. **Actions:** These are the tasks that the rule performs when it's triggered and the conditions are met. JIRA offers a wide range of actions, such as:
    - **Assigning issues:** Automatically assign issues to specific users or groups.
    - **Transitioning issues:** Move issues through the workflow to different statuses.
    - **Adding comments:** Automatically add comments to issues.
    - **Sending notifications:** Notify users or groups about changes to issues.
    - **Updating fields:** Modify field values based on specific criteria.
    - **Creating sub-tasks:** Automatically generate sub-tasks for specific issues.
    - **Triggering webhooks:** Send data to external systems to trigger actions outside of JIRA.

The Power of Automation

By combining triggers, conditions, and actions, you can create powerful automation rules that streamline your JIRA workflows and eliminate manual effort. For example, you could create a rule that automatically assigns new issues to the appropriate team member based on the issue type, or a rule that sends a notification to the project manager whenever a high-priority issue is created.

Automation not only saves time and reduces errors, but it also ensures consistency in your processes and improves communication within your team. By automating repetitive tasks, you free up your team members to focus on more strategic work, leading to increased productivity and overall project success.

Benefits of Automation

JIRA automation is a game-changer when it comes to streamlining project management workflows. It's not just about eliminating mundane tasks; it's about unlocking a whole new level of efficiency, accuracy, and collaboration within your team. Here's how automation can transform your JIRA experience:

- **Efficiency:** Automation is a productivity powerhouse. It takes over repetitive, time-consuming tasks, such as assigning issues, updating fields, or sending notifications. This frees up your team to focus on more strategic and value-adding activities, saving valuable time and resources.
- **Accuracy:** Humans are prone to errors, especially when performing repetitive tasks. Automation eliminates the risk of human error by ensuring that processes are executed consistently and accurately every time. This leads to more reliable data and smoother workflows.
- **Consistency:** Automation ensures that tasks are performed in a standardized manner, adhering to predefined rules and conditions. This consistency promotes predictability and eliminates variations in how different team members might handle the same task, leading to more reliable outcomes.
- **Improved Collaboration:** Automation can significantly enhance team collaboration by keeping everyone informed and up-to-date. Automated notifications and updates ensure that team members are aware of changes to issues, assignments, or deadlines, facilitating smoother communication and coordination.
- **Enhanced Productivity:** By taking over mundane tasks, automation allows team members to focus on more complex and strategic work. This not only boosts individual productivity but also elevates the overall output of the team. It empowers your team to work smarter, not harder.

Consider a scenario where your team receives a high volume of support tickets daily. Manually assigning each ticket to the appropriate team member can be a time-consuming and error-prone process. However, with JIRA automation, you can create a rule that automatically assigns tickets based on keywords, request type, or other criteria. This not only saves time but also ensures that tickets are routed to the right people efficiently, leading to faster resolution times and happier customers.

Components of Automation Rules

JIRA automation rules are powerful tools that allow you to streamline your project management processes. Each rule consists of three main components: triggers, conditions, and actions. These components work together to define when and how an automation rule should execute.

Triggers: The Initiators of Automation

A trigger is an event that sets an automation rule into motion. It's the spark that ignites the automation process. JIRA offers a variety of triggers to choose from, allowing you to tailor your rules to specific events within your project. Here are some common triggers:

- **Issue Created:** This trigger fires when a new issue is created in JIRA. You can use it to automate tasks such as assigning the issue to a team member, adding labels, or sending notifications.
- **Issue Updated:** This trigger activates whenever an existing issue is modified. You can use it to perform actions based on specific field changes, such as transitioning the issue to a new status or updating other fields.
- **Field Value Changed:** This trigger is more specific than the "Issue Updated" trigger. It fires only when a particular field value is changed. For example, you could create a rule that triggers when the "Priority" field is changed to "High."

- **Scheduled:** This trigger allows you to schedule automation rules to run at specific times or intervals. This is useful for automating recurring tasks, such as sending daily status reports or cleaning up old issues.
- **Webhook Triggered:** This trigger is activated when JIRA receives a webhook from an external system. It enables you to integrate JIRA with other tools and automate actions based on events occurring in those external systems.

Conditions: The Gatekeepers of Automation

Conditions are optional but powerful components of automation rules. They act as gatekeepers, determining whether a rule should execute based on specific criteria. By defining conditions, you can fine-tune your rules to apply only to specific scenarios. Here are some common conditions:

- **Issue Type:** The type of issue (e.g., Task, Bug, Story).
- **Project:** The project the issue belongs to.
- **Status:** The current status of the issue.
- **Assignee:** The person or group assigned to the issue.
- **Field Values:** Specific values in certain fields (e.g., "Priority" is "High," "Due Date" is before a specific date).
- **JQL Query:** A more complex JQL query to filter issues based on multiple criteria.

Actions: The Workhorses of Automation

Actions are the tasks that the automation rule performs when it's triggered and the conditions (if any) are met. JIRA offers a wide range of actions to choose from, giving you the flexibility to automate various tasks. Here are some common actions:

- **Assign Issue:** Assigns the issue to a specific user or group.
- **Transition Issue:** Moves the issue to a different status in the workflow.
- **Edit Issue:** Updates the values of specific fields in the issue.
- **Comment on Issue:** Adds a comment to the issue.
- **Send Email:** Sends an email notification to specific users or groups.
- **Create Sub-task:** Creates a new sub-task linked to the parent issue.
- **Trigger Webhook:** Sends data to an external system to trigger an action.
- **Add the issue to the queue:** Adds the issue to a specific queue.

By combining triggers, conditions, and actions strategically, you can create sophisticated automation rules that streamline your JIRA workflows, reduce manual effort, and improve overall team productivity. The possibilities for automation are virtually limitless, and it's up to you to unleash their power to optimize your project management processes.

Creating Automation Rules

JIRA's automation features are accessible and intuitive, making it easy to create rules that suit your specific needs. Here's a step-by-step guide to get you started:

1. **Navigate to the "Automation" section:**
    - Go to your JIRA project.
    - Click on the "Project settings" gear icon, usually found in the sidebar or the project menu.
    - In the settings menu, locate and click on the "Automation" section. This will open the automation rules page.
2. **Click "Create rule":**
    - On the automation rules page, click the "Create rule" button. This will launch the rule creation wizard.
3. **Select a trigger from the available options:**

- The first step is to choose the event that will trigger your automation rule. JIRA offers a wide range of triggers, as discussed in the previous section.
- Select the trigger that best aligns with your desired automation scenario. For example, if you want a rule to run when an issue is created, choose the "Issue created" trigger.
4. **Define conditions (optional):**
    - Conditions allow you to specify the criteria that must be met for the rule to execute. You can add multiple conditions and combine them using logical operators (AND, OR).
    - If you don't need any conditions, you can skip this step.
5. **Choose the actions to be performed:**
    - This is where you specify the tasks you want JIRA to perform automatically when the rule is triggered and the conditions (if any) are met.
    - Select the desired actions from the available list, such as assigning the issue, transitioning it, adding comments, sending notifications, or updating fields.
    - Configure each action according to your requirements. For example, if you choose the "Assign issue" action, you'll need to specify the user or group to whom the issue should be assigned.
6. **Save the rule:**
    - After configuring the trigger, conditions (if any), and actions, review your rule to ensure it's correct.
    - Give your rule a descriptive name so you can easily identify it later.
    - Click the "Save" button to activate your automation rule.

Congratulations! You've just created your first JIRA automation rule. Now, whenever the specified trigger occurs and the conditions are met, JIRA will automatically execute the actions you've defined, streamlining your workflow and saving you valuable time and effort. Remember, you can always edit or delete your rules later if needed.

Common Automation Use Cases

The versatility of JIRA automation enables a wide range of use cases that can significantly streamline your project management processes. Let's explore some real-world examples of how automation rules can be applied to enhance efficiency and collaboration:

1. **Automatic Issue Assignment:**
    When a new issue is created, you can automate the assignment process based on various criteria:
    - **Issue Type:** Assign bugs to developers and feature requests to product managers.
    - **Component:** If your project has components (sub-sections of the project), assign issues to specific team members responsible for those components.
    - **Priority:** Assign high-priority issues to senior team members or escalate them to managers.
    - **Load Balancing:** Distribute issues evenly among team members to ensure a fair workload.
2. **Escalation and Notification:**
    Keep stakeholders informed and ensure timely action:
    - **Priority Change:** Send notifications to relevant parties when an issue's priority is raised to "Critical" or "Blocker."
    - **Approaching Deadlines:** Send reminders to assignees and stakeholders when an issue's due date is approaching or has passed.
    - **SLA Breaches:** Notify the support team or management when a service-level agreement (SLA) is breached.
3. **Workflow Automation:**
    Streamline the progression of issues through your workflow:
    - **Automatic Transitions:** When specific conditions are met, automatically transition issues to the next status (e.g., move an issue from "In Progress" to "In Review" when all subtasks are completed).
    - **Auto-Close Issues:** Close issues automatically after a certain period of inactivity.

4. **Field Updates:**
   Dynamically update fields based on events or conditions:
   - **Set Due Date:** Automatically set the due date based on the issue creation date and estimated time to completion.
   - **Calculate Time to Resolution:** When an issue is resolved, automatically calculate and update the time it took to resolve.
   - **Update Priority:** Automatically increase the priority of issues that remain unresolved after a certain period.
5. **Task Creation:**
   Generate recurring tasks or sub-tasks for efficient planning and execution:
   - **Daily Stand-up:** Create daily tasks for team members to report their progress in the daily scrum.
   - **Sprint Planning:** Create sub-tasks for user stories during sprint planning to break down the work into smaller, manageable tasks.
   - **Recurring Tasks:** Create recurring tasks for routine activities, such as weekly reports or monthly reviews.

These are just a few examples of how automation rules can be used to optimize your JIRA workflow. The possibilities are endless, and the more you explore JIRA's automation capabilities, the more you'll discover ways to tailor it to your unique needs and preferences.

Best Practices for Automation

While JIRA automation is a powerful tool, it's essential to wield it wisely to maximize its benefits and avoid potential pitfalls. Here are some best practices to keep in mind:

1. **Start Simple, Scale Gradually:**
   Don't try to automate everything at once. Begin with simple, straightforward rules that address the most repetitive and time-consuming tasks. As you gain more experience and confidence, you can gradually add more complex rules to automate more intricate processes. This approach allows you to learn the ropes, test your rules thoroughly, and avoid overwhelming your team with too much change at once.
2. **Document Your Rules:**
   Clear documentation is essential for maintaining and troubleshooting automation rules. For each rule, document the trigger, conditions, actions, and the purpose of the automation. This will help you and your team understand how the rule works, troubleshoot any issues, and make modifications as needed. You can use JIRA's built-in comment feature or create dedicated Confluence pages to document your automation rules.
3. **Test Thoroughly:**
   Before activating an automation rule, thoroughly test it in a non-production environment or with a limited set of issues. This helps you identify and fix any errors or unintended consequences before the rule impacts your live projects. Test different scenarios and edge cases to ensure the rule behaves as expected.
4. **Monitor for Errors:**
   Even with thorough testing, automation rules can sometimes encounter unexpected errors or behaviors. It's crucial to monitor your rules actively and track any errors or issues that arise. JIRA provides audit logs that can help you diagnose and troubleshoot problems with your automation rules.
5. **Use Automation Responsibly:**
   Automation is a powerful tool, but it's not a magic wand. Not every task needs to be automated, and over-automation can lead to rigidity and stifle creativity. Use automation strategically to tackle repetitive tasks and free up your team's time for more valuable activities. Remember, human judgment and decision-making are still essential in many aspects of project management.

By following these best practices, you can harness the power of JIRA automation to streamline your workflows, reduce errors, and improve overall team productivity.

Chapter Summary

In this chapter, we explored the transformative power of automation in JIRA, highlighting how it can revolutionize your project management workflows. We began by defining automation as the ability to create rules that automatically execute actions based on specific triggers and conditions. We then delved into the core components of automation rules, including triggers, conditions, and actions, explaining their individual roles and how they work together to create powerful automation scenarios.

We also explored the myriad benefits of using automation in JIRA, such as increased efficiency, accuracy, consistency, improved collaboration, and enhanced productivity. By automating repetitive and mundane tasks, you can free up valuable time and resources, allowing your team to focus on more strategic and value-adding activities.

To provide practical guidance, we outlined a step-by-step process for creating automation rules in JIRA, covering everything from selecting triggers and defining conditions to choosing and configuring actions. We then showcased several real-world use cases, demonstrating how automation rules can be applied to various scenarios, such as automatic issue assignment, escalation and notification, workflow automation, field updates, and task creation.

Finally, we concluded with best practices for JIRA automation, emphasizing the importance of starting simple, documenting your rules, testing thoroughly, monitoring for errors, and using automation responsibly. By adhering to these best practices, you can maximize the benefits of automation and create a more efficient, accurate, and collaborative JIRA environment.

Section E:
Advanced JIRA Topics

Integrating JIRA with Other Tools

Outline

- The Power of Integration
- JIRA Integration Options
- Integrating JIRA with Development Tools
- Integrating JIRA with Communication and Collaboration Tools
- Integrating JIRA with DevOps Tools
- Integrating JIRA with Other Business Tools
- Best Practices for JIRA Integration
- Chapter Summary

The Power of Integration

In today's fast-paced and interconnected world, teams rely on a diverse array of tools to get their work done. Developers use code repositories and IDEs, project managers rely on JIRA for tracking and planning, while marketing teams might use communication platforms like Slack or Microsoft Teams. Each tool serves a specific purpose, but when used in isolation, they can create silos of information and disrupt workflows.

This is where the power of integration comes in. Integrating JIRA with your other tools can break down these silos and create a more cohesive and efficient work environment. It allows information to flow seamlessly between different systems, automating repetitive tasks, reducing manual effort, and enhancing collaboration across teams.

Streamlining Workflows

Imagine a scenario where a developer commits code to a repository like Bitbucket. With JIRA integration, that commit can automatically trigger an update in the corresponding JIRA issue, linking the code changes to the relevant task. This eliminates the need for manual updates and ensures that everyone involved in the project has a clear view of the progress.

Similarly, when a customer raises a support ticket in your CRM system, an integrated JIRA workflow can automatically create a corresponding issue in JIRA, assign it to the appropriate team member, and notify them. This streamlines the support process, ensuring that customer issues are addressed promptly and efficiently.

Automating Processes

Integration can also automate repetitive tasks, saving valuable time and reducing the risk of human error. For example, you can set up a rule that automatically creates a new JIRA issue whenever a build fails in your CI/CD pipeline. This ensures that the issue is immediately logged and tracked, allowing the team to address it quickly.

Enhancing Collaboration

By connecting JIRA with communication and collaboration platforms, you can foster better communication and teamwork. For instance, you can configure JIRA to send notifications to Slack channels or Microsoft Teams whenever an issue is updated or a comment is added. This keeps everyone informed in real-time, encouraging discussion and collaboration around the issue.

Integrating JIRA with DevOps tools allows development, operations, and support teams to work together more seamlessly. For example, by integrating JIRA with monitoring and logging tools, you can get alerts within JIRA when a production issue occurs. This allows you to quickly create a JIRA issue, assign it to the relevant team, and track its resolution, ensuring a swift response to critical incidents.

A Cohesive and Efficient Work Environment

In conclusion, integrating JIRA with other tools can create a more cohesive and efficient work environment by:

- **Streamlining workflows:** Eliminate manual handoffs and automate repetitive tasks.
- **Improving visibility:** Provide a unified view of project data across different tools.
- **Enhancing collaboration:** Facilitate real-time communication and collaboration among team members.
- **Increasing productivity:** Free up time and resources by automating tasks and reducing manual effort.

In the following sections, we'll delve deeper into how you can integrate JIRA with various tools, including development environments, communication platforms, DevOps tools, and other business applications.

JIRA Integration Options

JIRA offers a multitude of integration options to connect with your existing toolchain, catering to various needs and technical expertise. Whether you're looking for quick and easy connections or require a more bespoke solution, JIRA has you covered.

Built-in Integrations

JIRA comes with native integrations for other Atlassian products, creating a seamless experience across their suite of tools:

- **Confluence:** This integration allows you to link JIRA issues directly to Confluence pages, making it easy to access relevant documentation and knowledge within the context of your project tasks.
- **Bitbucket:** By connecting JIRA to Bitbucket, you can link issues to code commits, branches, and pull requests, providing traceability and visibility into the development process.
- **Opsgenie:** This integration enables you to receive alerts and notifications from Opsgenie directly in JIRA, streamlining incident management and resolution.

Marketplace Apps

The Atlassian Marketplace is a treasure trove of third-party apps that extend JIRA's functionality. You can find apps for integrating with a wide range of popular tools, including:

- **Slack:** Get real-time notifications in Slack channels about JIRA issue updates, comments, and transitions.
- **GitHub:** Link JIRA issues to GitHub pull requests, commits, and branches, fostering collaboration between development and project management teams.

- **Jenkins:** Trigger Jenkins builds and deployments based on JIRA issue transitions, automating your continuous integration and delivery processes.
- **Microsoft Teams:** Similar to Slack, integrate JIRA with Microsoft Teams to receive notifications and collaborate on issues within the Teams environment.
- **Salesforce:** Connect JIRA to Salesforce to track customer feedback, support requests, and other CRM data within the context of your projects.
- **Zephyr/Xray:** Integrate with these test management tools to streamline test case creation, execution, and tracking.

These are just a few examples, and the Marketplace is constantly expanding with new and innovative apps.

REST APIs

For maximum flexibility and customization, JIRA offers robust REST APIs (Application Programming Interfaces). These APIs allow you to programmatically interact with JIRA data and functionalities, enabling you to build custom integrations with virtually any tool or system that supports REST API calls.

With JIRA's REST APIs, you can:

- **Create, update, and delete issues:** Automate issue creation and updates based on external events or data.
- **Fetch issue data:** Retrieve information about issues, projects, users, and other JIRA entities.
- **Trigger workflows:** Automatically transition issues through the workflow based on external events.
- **Create custom reports and dashboards:** Build customized reporting and visualization tools tailored to your specific needs.

While using REST APIs requires some technical expertise, it offers unparalleled flexibility in integrating JIRA with your existing systems and workflows.

By exploring these different integration options, you can tailor JIRA to seamlessly fit into your unique tech stack, maximizing its potential and creating a more cohesive and efficient work environment.

Integrating JIRA with Development Tools

Integrating JIRA with your development tools can significantly streamline your software development process and enhance collaboration between developers and project managers. By connecting these tools, you can create a seamless workflow where development activities are tightly integrated with project tracking and management.

Code Repositories (e.g., Bitbucket, GitHub)

Integrating JIRA with code repositories like Bitbucket or GitHub bridges the gap between project management and code development. By linking JIRA issues to code commits, pull requests, and branches, you can:

- **Improve Traceability:** Easily track which code changes are associated with specific issues, making it simpler to understand the context of code modifications and assess their impact on the project.
- **Enhance Collaboration:** Developers and project managers can communicate more effectively by referencing JIRA issues in commit messages or pull request descriptions. This ensures that everyone is on the same page and understands the purpose of each code change.
- **Automate Updates:** You can configure automation rules to automatically update JIRA issues when code is committed or pull requests are merged, reducing manual effort and ensuring data accuracy.

Integrated Development Environments (IDEs)

Integrating JIRA with your favorite IDE, such as IntelliJ IDEA, Visual Studio Code, or Eclipse, brings JIRA's functionality directly to your coding environment. This integration allows you to:

- **View and Update Issues:** Access and modify JIRA issues directly from your IDE, eliminating the need to switch between applications. This streamlines your workflow and saves you time.
- **Track Time:** Log time spent on tasks without leaving your IDE, providing accurate time tracking data.
- **Start Workflows:** Initiate workflows, such as moving an issue to "In Progress," directly from your IDE.

Continuous Integration/Continuous Delivery (CI/CD) Tools (e.g., Jenkins, Bamboo)

Integrating JIRA with CI/CD tools like Jenkins or Bamboo enables you to automate various aspects of your software delivery pipeline. You can configure JIRA to:

- **Trigger Builds:** Automatically trigger builds in your CI/CD pipeline when specific JIRA issue transitions occur (e.g., when an issue is moved to "Ready for Testing").
- **Run Tests:** Automatically execute tests associated with JIRA issues and report the results back to JIRA.
- **Deploy Code:** Automate deployments to different environments based on JIRA issue transitions, ensuring a smooth and efficient delivery process.
- **Update Issue Status:** Automatically update the status of JIRA issues based on the results of builds, tests, or deployments.

By integrating JIRA with your development tools, you create a powerful synergy that enhances visibility, collaboration, and automation throughout your software development lifecycle. This leads to faster delivery cycles, improved code quality, and ultimately, a more successful product.

Integrating JIRA with Communication and Collaboration Tools

Communication and collaboration are essential ingredients for successful project management. Integrating JIRA with popular communication and collaboration tools like Slack, Microsoft Teams, and email can significantly enhance teamwork and streamline communication within your projects.

Slack

Slack is a widely used communication platform that allows teams to communicate and collaborate in real time. Integrating JIRA with Slack brings JIRA notifications and updates directly into your Slack channels, enabling you to:

- **Stay Informed:** Receive instant notifications in Slack channels when new issues are created, issues are updated, comments are added, or when issues are assigned to you.
- **Collaborate in Context:** Discuss JIRA issues directly in Slack channels, eliminating the need to switch between applications. This fosters real-time collaboration and ensures that everyone is on the same page.
- **Create JIRA Issues from Slack:** Create new JIRA issues directly from Slack conversations, capturing ideas and feedback without disrupting your workflow.
- **Preview JIRA Issues:** Get a quick overview of JIRA issues within Slack, including summary, status, and assignee.

Microsoft Teams

Microsoft Teams is a comprehensive collaboration platform that combines chat, meetings, notes, and attachments. Integrating JIRA with Microsoft Teams allows you to:

- **Receive Notifications:** Get JIRA notifications directly in Teams channels, keeping you informed about project updates.
- **Share Project Information:** Easily share JIRA issues, boards, and reports with your team members in Teams.
- **Collaborate on Issues:** Discuss and collaborate on JIRA issues directly within Teams, eliminating the need to switch between applications.
- **Create JIRA Issues:** Create new JIRA issues from Teams conversations, capturing ideas and action items.

Email

While not as interactive as Slack or Microsoft Teams, email remains a crucial communication tool for many teams. JIRA allows you to configure email notifications to keep stakeholders informed about project progress. You can set up notifications for various events, such as:

- **Issue Creation:** Notify team members when a new issue is created.
- **Issue Updates:** Send updates when an issue's status changes, comments are added, or the issue is assigned to a different person.
- **Deadline Reminders:** Send reminders when an issue's due date is approaching or has passed.

By strategically integrating JIRA with your preferred communication and collaboration tools, you can break down information silos, foster better teamwork, and streamline communication within your projects. This ultimately leads to faster decision-making, improved productivity, and a more cohesive team environment.

Integrating JIRA with DevOps Tools

In the modern world of software development, DevOps practices play a pivotal role in ensuring smooth and efficient delivery of applications and services. JIRA, with its robust project management and issue tracking capabilities, can be integrated with various DevOps tools to further enhance collaboration, visibility, and automation across the entire software development lifecycle (SDLC).

Monitoring and Logging Tools (e.g., Splunk, Datadog)

Integrating JIRA with monitoring and logging tools such as Splunk or Datadog enables you to gain deeper insights into the health and performance of your applications and infrastructure. This integration allows you to:

- **Track System Logs:** JIRA can automatically ingest logs from your monitoring tools, creating a centralized repository of log data within JIRA. This makes it easier to search, filter, and analyze logs, aiding in troubleshooting and root cause analysis.
- **Monitor Performance Metrics:** By visualizing performance metrics like response times, error rates, and resource utilization directly within JIRA, you can proactively identify potential issues and take corrective action before they impact your users.
- **Create JIRA Issues from Alerts:** You can set up rules to automatically create JIRA issues when specific events or thresholds are detected in your monitoring tools. This ensures that issues are promptly addressed and tracked within your project management workflow.

Incident Management Tools (e.g., Opsgenie)

Opsgenie is a powerful incident management platform that helps teams respond to and resolve critical issues quickly. Integrating JIRA with Opsgenie streamlines incident management by:

- **Automatically Creating JIRA Issues:** When an alert is triggered in Opsgenie, an integrated workflow can automatically create a corresponding JIRA issue. This ensures that the issue is immediately logged, assigned, and tracked within your project management system.
- **Bi-Directional Synchronization:** Updates made in either JIRA or Opsgenie are automatically reflected in the other system. This ensures that everyone involved in incident resolution has access to the latest information.
- **Enhanced Communication:** Opsgenie can notify relevant team members through various channels (email, SMS, phone calls) when a JIRA issue is created or updated, ensuring that everyone is aware of critical incidents and their progress.

By integrating JIRA with DevOps tools like Splunk, Datadog, and Opsgenie, you can break down silos between development, operations, and support teams. This integration fosters collaboration, improves visibility into the entire SDLC, and enables faster incident response and resolution. As a result, you can deliver software more reliably, efficiently, and with greater confidence.

Integrating JIRA with Other Business Tools

JIRA's versatility extends beyond software development and DevOps. It can also be seamlessly integrated with a variety of other business tools, enhancing cross-functional collaboration and streamlining processes across your organization. Let's explore some common integrations:

Customer Relationship Management (CRM) Software (e.g., Salesforce)

Integrating JIRA with your CRM system, such as Salesforce, can create a unified view of customer interactions and feedback. This integration enables you to:

- **Link Customer Feedback to JIRA Issues:** When a customer reports an issue or provides feedback through your CRM system, an automated workflow can create a corresponding JIRA issue. This ensures that customer concerns are captured and addressed within your project management system.
- **Track Issue Resolution:** You can track the progress of customer-related issues in JIRA and update the CRM system with the resolution status, providing transparency to your customer service team.
- **Improve Customer Service:** By having a direct link between customer feedback and development tasks, you can address customer needs more effectively and deliver a better customer experience.

Test Management Tools (e.g., Zephyr, Xray)

Integrating JIRA with test management tools like Zephyr or Xray streamlines your quality assurance (QA) process. This integration allows you to:

- **Manage Test Cases:** Create, organize, and execute test cases directly within JIRA, leveraging its familiar interface and workflows.
- **Link Test Cases to Issues:** Associate test cases with specific JIRA issues, ensuring that testing efforts are aligned with development tasks.
- **Track Test Results:** Record test results in JIRA, including pass/fail status, defects found, and relevant attachments. This provides a comprehensive view of your testing progress and helps identify areas that need attention.

Document Management Systems (e.g., Confluence)

Integrating JIRA with a document management system like Confluence creates a knowledge hub for your projects. By linking JIRA issues to Confluence pages, you can:

- **Provide Context:** Add context to JIRA issues by linking them to relevant documentation in Confluence, such as project requirements, design specifications, or user guides.
- **Share Information:** Make it easy for team members to access relevant information within the context of their work.
- **Improve Collaboration:** Foster collaboration by allowing team members to comment and provide feedback on both JIRA issues and Confluence pages.

These are just a few examples of how JIRA can be integrated with other business tools. By exploring the various integration options available on the Atlassian Marketplace or building custom integrations using JIRA's REST APIs, you can connect JIRA to virtually any tool in your organization's technology stack. This creates a more unified and efficient work environment, breaking down silos between different teams and enabling seamless collaboration and data sharing.

Best Practices for JIRA Integration

Integrating JIRA with other tools can significantly enhance your team's productivity and streamline your workflows. However, it's important to approach integration strategically to ensure a smooth and successful implementation. Here are some best practices to keep in mind:

1. **Identify Key Integration Points:**
   Before diving into integrations, take the time to analyze your team's workflows and identify the key points where integration can add the most value. Consider which tools are most frequently used, which processes are the most time-consuming or error-prone, and where data silos exist. Focus on integrating those tools that will have the most significant impact on your team's efficiency and collaboration.
2. **Start Small:**
   Don't try to integrate with every tool at once. Begin with a few essential integrations that address your most critical pain points. This allows you to test the waters, assess the impact of the integrations, and fine-tune your processes before adding more complexity. Once you've successfully implemented a few core integrations, you can gradually expand your integration efforts.
3. **Test Thoroughly:**
   Before deploying any integration to your production environment, thoroughly test it in a non-production environment or with a limited set of data. This helps you identify and resolve any issues or conflicts before they impact your live workflows. Testing different scenarios and edge cases is crucial to ensure that the integration works as expected under various conditions.
4. **Monitor and Maintain:**
   Integrations are not a "set it and forget it" solution. Regularly monitor your integrations to ensure they are functioning correctly. Check for errors, inconsistencies, or performance issues. Keep your integrated tools and JIRA up to date with the latest versions to ensure compatibility and take advantage of new features or bug fixes. Be prepared to make adjustments or updates to your integrations as needed to accommodate changes in your workflows or toolsets.

By adhering to these best practices, you can maximize the benefits of JIRA integration while minimizing risks and disruptions. Remember, integration is a journey, not a destination. It requires ongoing attention and refinement to ensure that it continues to deliver value to your team and organization.

Chapter Summary

In this chapter, we explored the immense potential of integrating JIRA with other tools to create a more streamlined and efficient workflow. We discussed how integrating JIRA with development tools like code repositories, IDEs, and CI/CD tools can enhance collaboration, improve traceability, and automate key processes.

Furthermore, we highlighted the benefits of integrating JIRA with communication and collaboration tools like Slack, Microsoft Teams, and email. Such integrations enable real-time notifications, seamless communication, and efficient collaboration within the context of JIRA issues.

We also delved into the value of integrating JIRA with DevOps tools like monitoring systems and incident management platforms, showcasing how it can improve incident response, enhance system visibility, and foster collaboration between development, operations, and support teams.

Additionally, we explored how integrating JIRA with other business tools, such as CRM software, test management tools, and document management systems, can break down silos, provide context, and streamline processes across different departments.

Finally, we provided a set of best practices for successful JIRA integration, emphasizing the importance of identifying key integration points, starting small, testing thoroughly, and monitoring and maintaining your integrations to ensure ongoing success. By following these recommendations, you can unlock the full potential of JIRA integration and create a more cohesive and efficient work environment.

Using JIRA Query Language (JQL)

Outline

- Introduction to JQL
- Basic JQL Syntax and Structure
- JQL Operators
- JQL Functions
- Practical JQL Examples
- Tips and Tricks for Using JQL
- JQL Resources
- Chapter Summary

Introduction to JQL

JIRA Query Language (JQL) is a flexible and powerful tool that sits at the heart of JIRA's search capabilities. It's a structured language designed specifically for querying and filtering data within JIRA. Think of it as the language that allows you to "talk" to JIRA and ask it specific questions about your projects and issues.

While JIRA's basic search is sufficient for simple queries, JQL elevates your search capabilities to a whole new level. It enables you to construct complex and precise search queries, allowing you to pinpoint exactly the information you need. Whether you want to find all high-priority bugs assigned to a specific team member, identify issues that are overdue, or analyze trends in your project data, JQL can help you achieve your goals.

A Powerful Tool for Efficiency

Mastering JQL is a valuable skill for any JIRA user. It allows you to work more efficiently by quickly accessing the information you need. Instead of manually sifting through countless issues, you can use JQL to create targeted searches that deliver the exact results you're looking for.

JQL is not only about finding issues; it's also about understanding your data. By using JQL to analyze and filter your project data, you can gain valuable insights into your team's performance, identify areas for improvement, and make data-driven decisions that can positively impact your project's success.

In the following sections, we'll delve into the syntax and structure of JQL, explore its various operators and functions, and provide practical examples to demonstrate its versatility. By the end of this chapter, you'll be well-equipped to harness the power of JQL and become a JIRA search expert.

Basic JQL Syntax and Structure

JQL queries are essentially structured sentences that JIRA understands. They follow a clear syntax to specify your search criteria and retrieve the desired results. Let's break down the basic components of a JQL query:

- **Fields:** These are the attributes of JIRA issues that you want to search or filter by. Common examples include:
    - `project` (The project the issue belongs to)
    - `issuetype` (The type of issue, such as Task, Bug, or Story)
    - `status` (The current status of the issue, like To Do, In Progress, or Done)

- assignee (The person to whom the issue is assigned)
- reporter (The person who created the issue)
- summary (The title or short description of the issue)
- description (The detailed description of the issue)
- Many other fields, both system-defined and custom-defined, are available.
- **Operators:** These are symbols that define the relationship between a field and its value. Common operators include:
    - = (equals)
    - != (not equals)
    - \> (greater than)
    - < (less than)
    - \>= (greater than or equal to)
    - <= (less than or equal to)
    - IN (in a list of values)
    - NOT IN (not in a list of values)
    - ~ (contains)
    - !~ (doesn't contain)
- **Values:** These are the specific pieces of data you are searching for. Values can be text strings (enclosed in quotes), numbers, dates, or even the names of users or groups.

Putting it Together: A Basic JQL Example

Let's look at a simple JQL query:

project = "MyProject" AND assignee = currentUser()

This query can be broken down as follows:

- **Field:** project
- **Operator:** =
- **Value:** "MyProject" (the name of a specific project)
- **Logical Operator:** AND
- **Field:** assignee
- **Operator:** =
- **Function:** currentUser() (a function that returns the current user)

This query translates to: "Find all issues in the project 'MyProject' that are assigned to me (current user)."

By understanding this basic structure of JQL, you can start constructing your own queries to filter and retrieve specific information from JIRA. Remember, you can combine multiple fields, operators, and values to create complex queries that precisely target the data you need.

JQL Operators

JQL operators are the special symbols or words that define the relationships between fields and values within your search queries. They are the glue that holds your JQL statements together, allowing you to construct precise and meaningful searches.

Comparison Operators

Comparison operators are the most fundamental operators in JQL. They are used to compare the value of a field with a specified value. JIRA supports the following comparison operators:

- **= (Equals):** This operator checks if the field value is equal to the specified value. For example, `status = "Done"` finds all issues with the status "Done."
- **!= (Not Equals):** This operator checks if the field value is not equal to the specified value. For example, `assignee != currentUser()` finds all issues that are not assigned to the current user.
- **> (Greater Than):** This operator checks if the field value is greater than the specified value. It's typically used for numerical fields or dates. For example, `created > "2023-01-01"` finds all issues created after January 1st, 2023.
- **< (Less Than):** This operator checks if the field value is less than the specified value. It's also used for numerical fields or dates. For example, `duedate < endOfWeek()` finds all issues due before the end of the current week.
- **>= (Greater Than or Equal To):** This operator checks if the field value is greater than or equal to the specified value.
- **<= (Less Than or Equal To):** This operator checks if the field value is less than or equal to the specified value.

Here are some examples to illustrate the use of comparison operators:

```
project = "MyProject"
assignee != "John Doe"
priority > "Medium"
created >= "2023-01-01" AND created <= "2023-01-31"
```

By mastering comparison operators, you can construct JQL queries that pinpoint specific issues based on their attribute values, allowing you to narrow down your search and find exactly what you're looking for.

Logical Operators

Logical operators in JQL are your tools for combining multiple search criteria, allowing you to create more nuanced and powerful queries. They enable you to find issues that match a combination of conditions, either all of them, at least one of them, or specifically excluding certain conditions.

- **AND:** This operator requires that **all** specified conditions be true for an issue to be included in the search results. For example, the query `project = "Marketing Campaign" AND assignee = "Emily Davis"` will return only issues that are both in the "Marketing Campaign" project and assigned to Emily Davis.
- **OR:** This operator requires that **at least one** of the specified conditions be true for an issue to be included. For instance, `status = "To Do" OR status = "In Progress"` will find all issues that are either in the "To Do" or "In Progress" state.
- **NOT:** This operator **excludes** issues that match the specified condition. For example, `status != "Done"` will find all issues that are not in the "Done" status.

Practical Examples

Let's see how these logical operators can be used in practice:

```
project = "Website Redesign" AND (status = "In Progress" OR status = "In Review")
```

This query will return all issues in the "Website Redesign" project that are either "In Progress" or "In Review."

```
issuetype = Bug AND priority = "High" AND NOT assignee = currentUser()
```

This query will return all high-priority bugs that are not assigned to the person currently running the search.

By combining comparison operators with logical operators, you can create highly targeted queries that precisely match your search criteria, making JIRA an even more powerful tool for managing your work.

Other Operators

Beyond the fundamental comparison and logical operators, JQL offers additional operators that provide further flexibility and precision in your searches. Let's delve into a few of these operators and their use cases:

- **IN, NOT IN:** These operators allow you to check if a field's value belongs to (IN) or does not belong to (NOT IN) a specified list of values. For example:

  ```
  status IN ("To Do", "In Progress")
  assignee NOT IN (membersOf("Marketing Team"))
  ```

  The first query will find issues whose status is either "To Do" or "In Progress." The second query will find issues not assigned to any member of the "Marketing Team."

- **IS, IS NOT:** These operators are primarily used for checking the presence or absence of values in fields.

  ```
  assignee IS EMPTY
  due IS NOT EMPTY
  ```

  The first query will find issues that have not been assigned to anyone. The second query will find issues that have a due date set.

- **ORDER BY:** This operator allows you to sort the search results by one or more fields in either ascending or descending order.

  ```
  project = "ABC Project" ORDER BY priority DESC, duedate ASC
  ```

  This query will first sort the results by priority in descending order (highest priority first) and then by due date in ascending order (earliest due date first).

Understanding and utilizing these additional operators in conjunction with comparison and logical operators will significantly enhance your ability to craft complex and precise JQL queries. This will enable you to extract the exact information you need from JIRA's extensive database of issues, empowering you to make informed decisions and manage your projects more effectively.

JQL Functions

JQL functions elevate your search capabilities, enabling you to perform calculations, comparisons, and transformations on field values within your queries. These functions unlock a new level of flexibility and precision, allowing you to extract even more meaningful insights from your JIRA data. Let's delve into some of the most common and useful JQL functions:

- **currentUser():** This function dynamically returns the username of the user who is currently executing the JQL query. It's particularly useful for finding issues assigned to the current user or filtering activity based on the user's actions.
  Example: `assignee = currentUser()` (Finds all issues assigned to the current user)
- **membersOf("group name"):** This function returns a list of all users who belong to a specific group. You can use it to find issues assigned to members of a particular team or department.

Example: `assignee in membersOf("Development Team")` (Finds all issues assigned to members of the "Development Team")
- **startOfDay(), endOfDay():** These functions return the start and end timestamps of the current day, respectively. They are useful for finding issues created or updated on a specific day.
Example: `created >= startOfDay() AND created <= endOfDay()` (Finds all issues created today)
- **issueHistory():** This function allows you to search through the change history of issues. You can use it to find issues that have undergone specific changes, such as status transitions or field updates.
Example: `issueHistory() AND status CHANGED FROM "In Progress" TO "Done"` (Finds all issues that were transitioned from "In Progress" to "Done")
- **updatedBy():** This function returns the username of the person who last updated an issue. You can use it to find issues that were recently updated by a specific user.
Example: `updatedBy() = "John Doe"` (Finds all issues last updated by John Doe)
- **watchedBy():** This function returns a list of users who are watching an issue. You can use it to find issues that are being watched by specific users or groups.
Example: `watchedBy() in membersOf("Project Managers")` (Finds all issues watched by members of the "Project Managers" group)

These are just a few examples of the many JQL functions available in JIRA. By incorporating these functions into your queries, you can create highly targeted searches that provide valuable insights into your project data.

Practical JQL Examples

Let's dive into some practical JQL examples that showcase the versatility and power of this query language in real-world scenarios:

1. Finding all high-priority bugs assigned to a specific user:

`project = "MyProject" AND issuetype = Bug AND priority = "High" AND assignee = "John Doe"`

This query will return all issues in the "MyProject" project that are of type "Bug," have a "High" priority, and are assigned to the user "John Doe."

2. Identifying issues updated within the last week:

`updated >= startOfWeek(-1) AND updated <= endOfWeek(-1)`

This query will return all issues that were updated within the last week (excluding the current week). The `startOfWeek(-1)` and `endOfWeek(-1)` functions calculate the start and end dates of the previous week, respectively.

3. Retrieving tasks with specific labels or components:

`project = "MyProject" AND issuetype = Task AND (labels = "urgent" OR component = "Frontend")`

This query will return all tasks in the "MyProject" project that are either labeled as "urgent" or belong to the "Frontend" component.

4. Finding issues that are blocked or have unresolved dependencies:

```
issueFunction in linkedIssuesOf("status = Blocked") OR issueFunction in
hasLinkType("is blocked by")
```

This query will return all issues that are either linked to another issue that has the status "Blocked" or are linked to another issue with the link type "is blocked by."

Advanced Example: Combining Multiple Criteria

You can combine multiple criteria using logical operators to create more complex queries. For example, to find all high-priority bugs in "MyProject" that were updated in the last week and are not assigned to the current user:

```
project = "MyProject" AND issuetype = Bug AND priority = "High" AND updated >=
startOfWeek(-1) AND updated <= endOfWeek(-1) AND assignee != currentUser()
```

By understanding and utilizing these examples, you can craft JQL queries that precisely target the information you need, making your work in JIRA more efficient and productive. Remember, these are just a few examples, and the possibilities with JQL are vast. Experiment with different combinations of fields, operators, and functions to create queries that perfectly suit your specific needs.

Tips and Tricks for Using JQL

JQL is a powerful tool, but like any language, it takes practice to master. Here are some tips and tricks to help you optimize your JQL searches and become a JIRA query ninja:

- **Use Parentheses for Grouping and Clarity:**
  When constructing complex queries with multiple conditions, use parentheses to group clauses and control the order of operations. This makes your queries easier to read and understand, reducing the chance of errors. For example:

  ```
  (project = "Project A" OR project = "Project B") AND status = "In
  Progress"
  ```

- **Leverage Autocomplete and Syntax Highlighting:**
  JIRA's JQL editor provides helpful features like autocomplete and syntax highlighting. As you type your query, JIRA suggests fields, operators, and values, making it easier to construct valid queries. Syntax highlighting visually distinguishes different elements of the query, making it easier to spot errors.
- **Test Queries in Small Increments:**
  Instead of writing a complex query all at once, start with a simple query and gradually add more conditions. Test each increment to ensure it's returning the expected results. This makes it easier to identify and fix errors, rather than trying to debug a long and complicated query.
- **Refer to JQL Documentation:**
  JIRA provides comprehensive documentation on JQL, including a complete list of fields, operators, functions, and examples. Refer to this documentation whenever you need help or want to explore the full range of JQL's capabilities. You can find it online or within JIRA itself.

By incorporating these tips into your JQL workflow, you can write more efficient, accurate, and maintainable queries. With practice, you'll be able to quickly find the information you need and unlock the full potential of JIRA's search capabilities.

JQL Resources

As you continue your JQL learning journey, there are many resources available to help you deepen your understanding and refine your skills:

- **Atlassian's JQL Documentation:** The official JIRA documentation provided by Atlassian is your primary resource for comprehensive and authoritative information on JQL. It covers everything from basic syntax to advanced functions and operators. You can find it online on the Atlassian website.
- **Online JQL Tutorials and Forums:** The internet is brimming with tutorials, blog posts, and forum discussions on JQL. Many experienced JIRA users and administrators share their knowledge and tips online. Searching for "JQL tutorial" or "JQL examples" will lead you to a wealth of resources.
- **Community-Created JQL Cheat Sheets:** Many JIRA communities and forums have created handy JQL cheat sheets that summarize the most commonly used fields, operators, and functions. These cheat sheets can be a quick reference when you need a refresher or a starting point for building your queries.

By exploring these resources, you can continue to expand your JQL knowledge and expertise, unlocking new ways to leverage JIRA's powerful search capabilities. Remember, practice is key, so don't hesitate to experiment with different queries and explore the endless possibilities that JQL offers.

Chapter Summary

In this chapter, we delved into the power and versatility of JIRA Query Language (JQL), a fundamental tool for effectively searching and filtering information within JIRA. We began by introducing JQL and emphasizing its importance in improving efficiency and productivity. We then explored the basic syntax and structure of JQL, outlining the essential components of a query, including fields, operators, and values.

Building upon this foundation, we discussed various JQL operators, including comparison operators for comparing values, logical operators for combining multiple search criteria, and other operators like IN, NOT IN, IS, IS NOT, and ORDER BY. We also explored common JQL functions, such as currentUser(), membersOf(), startOfDay(), endOfDay(), issueHistory(), updatedBy(), and watchedBy(), and provided practical examples of how they can be used to create powerful queries.

To solidify your understanding, we presented real-world JQL examples showcasing how to find high-priority bugs, identify recently updated issues, retrieve tasks with specific labels, and find blocked or dependent issues. We also offered tips for optimizing your JQL searches, such as using parentheses, leveraging autocomplete, testing queries incrementally, and referring to JIRA's documentation.

Finally, we provided a list of resources, including Atlassian's JQL documentation, online tutorials and forums, and community-created cheat sheets, to further your knowledge and mastery of JQL. By utilizing these resources and practicing your JQL skills, you can unlock the full potential of JIRA's search capabilities and become a more proficient and effective JIRA user.

Best Practices for JIRA Administration

Outline

- Project Planning and Organization
- User and Permission Management
- Workflow Configuration
- Custom Field and Screen Management
- Performance Optimization
- Backup and Disaster Recovery
- Continuous Improvement
- Chapter Summary

Project Planning and Organization

A well-organized JIRA project is the foundation of successful project management. It ensures that everyone on the team understands the project's goals, the tasks that need to be done, and how those tasks relate to each other. This clarity is essential for effective collaboration and efficient execution.

Importance of Well-Defined Project Structure

A well-defined project structure helps you visualize the big picture and break down complex projects into smaller, more manageable pieces. This makes it easier to assign tasks, track progress, and identify dependencies between different work items.

Setting Clear Goals

Clear and specific goals are essential for guiding your project's direction and measuring its success. Goals should be SMART: Specific, Measurable, Achievable, Relevant, and Time-Bound. By defining clear goals, you provide a roadmap for your team and ensure that everyone is working towards a common objective.

Efficient Workflows

Workflows define the lifecycle of an issue, from its creation to its resolution. Efficient workflows streamline your processes, ensuring that work items move smoothly through the different stages of development. They also provide transparency into the status of each task, making it easier to track progress and identify bottlenecks.

Breaking Down Large Projects

Large projects can quickly become overwhelming if not properly organized. JIRA provides tools to break down large projects into smaller, more manageable components:

- **Epics:** Epics represent large bodies of work that can be broken down into smaller user stories. They provide a high-level overview of the project's goals and roadmap.
- **Stories:** Stories are user-focused descriptions of desired functionality. They are typically small enough to be completed in a single sprint.
- **Tasks:** Tasks are the smallest unit of work in JIRA. They represent the specific actions that need to be taken to complete a user story.

By breaking down your project into epics, stories, and tasks, you create a hierarchical structure that makes it easier to track progress, manage dependencies, and allocate resources effectively.

Consistent Naming Conventions, Labeling, and Prioritizing

Consistency is key to maintaining a well-organized JIRA project. By using consistent naming conventions for your issues, labels, and other project elements, you make it easier for team members to find and understand information.

Labeling is another powerful tool for organizing your issues. Labels are keywords or tags that you can apply to issues to categorize them, filter them, or highlight specific attributes. For example, you might use labels like "Bug," "Feature," "Priority," or "Component" to categorize your issues.

Prioritizing issues is essential for ensuring that your team focuses on the most important tasks first. JIRA allows you to set priority levels for issues (e.g., Highest, High, Medium, Low) or rank them numerically. This helps you to manage your backlog effectively and ensure that critical issues are addressed promptly.

By adhering to these best practices for project planning and organization, you can create a JIRA environment that is efficient, transparent, and conducive to collaboration.

User and Permission Management

In any JIRA environment, the ability to control who can access what data and perform which actions is paramount. Proper user and permission management is not just about convenience; it's about safeguarding sensitive information, maintaining data integrity, and ensuring the smooth operation of your projects.

The Importance of Control

Imagine a scenario where anyone could access and modify any JIRA issue, regardless of their role or responsibilities. This could lead to chaos, with unauthorized changes, accidental deletions, and potential data breaches. Effective user and permission management prevents such scenarios by:

- **Protecting Sensitive Information:** By restricting access to confidential data, you ensure that only authorized personnel can view or modify it. This is crucial for maintaining the privacy and security of your project information.
- **Preventing Unauthorized Actions:** By assigning appropriate permissions, you prevent users from performing actions they shouldn't, such as deleting issues, modifying workflows, or accessing confidential reports. This helps maintain the integrity of your data and processes.
- **Streamlining Collaboration:** Clear roles and permissions clarify who is responsible for what, reducing confusion and promoting efficient collaboration. When everyone knows their role and access levels, it fosters a more organized and productive work environment.

Strategies for Effective User and Permission Management

JIRA provides a range of tools and features to help you manage users and permissions effectively:

- **User Accounts:** Each person who uses JIRA needs a user account. These accounts contain personal information, such as name, email address, and password. You can create user accounts manually or import them in bulk from a CSV file. It's essential to keep user accounts up-to-date and deactivate or delete accounts for users who no longer need access.
- **Groups:** Groups are collections of users who share common characteristics or roles. By organizing users into groups, you can simplify permission management. Instead of assigning permissions to individual users, you can grant them to groups, making it easier to manage access for multiple users at once.
- **Project Roles:** Project roles are predefined sets of permissions that define what actions users can perform within a project. JIRA comes with default project roles like Administrator, Developer, and User, but you can also create custom roles to tailor permissions to your specific needs.

- **Permission Schemes:** Permission schemes are collections of project roles and their associated permissions. Each project is linked to a permission scheme, which determines what actions users with different roles can perform within that project.

The Principle of Least Privilege

A fundamental principle in security is the "principle of least privilege." This means granting users only the minimum permissions necessary to perform their tasks. By adhering to this principle, you can minimize the risk of accidental or intentional misuse of JIRA, ensuring that your data and processes remain secure.

Workflow Configuration

Workflows in JIRA are the engines that drive your project processes. They define the lifecycle of an issue, outlining the steps it progresses through from creation to completion. By automating actions and enforcing rules, workflows ensure consistency, efficiency, and adherence to your team's unique practices.

The Crucial Role of Workflows

Workflows play a pivotal role in project management by:

- **Automating Processes:** Instead of manually moving issues through different stages, workflows automate transitions based on predefined criteria, saving time and reducing errors.
- **Enforcing Consistency:** Workflows ensure that every issue follows the same standardized process, promoting consistency and predictability in project execution.
- **Improving Visibility:** Workflows provide a clear visual representation of an issue's progress, allowing team members to track its status and identify bottlenecks.
- **Enhancing Collaboration:** By defining clear steps and responsibilities, workflows facilitate collaboration between team members and stakeholders.

Creating and Customizing Workflows

JIRA provides a user-friendly workflow editor that empowers you to create and customize workflows to match your specific project needs. Here's a simplified guide:

1. **Access the Workflow Editor:** Navigate to your project settings and find the "Workflows" section. Click on "Create workflow" to start from scratch or "Edit" to modify an existing workflow.
2. **Define Statuses:** Each workflow consists of multiple statuses, representing the different stages an issue can be in (e.g., "To Do," "In Progress," "In Review," "Done"). Add or remove statuses as needed, and provide meaningful names and descriptions for each.
3. **Create Transitions:** Transitions are the arrows that connect statuses, defining how issues move through the workflow. Create transitions between relevant statuses and name them accordingly (e.g., "Start Progress," "Submit for Review," "Approve").
4. **Set Conditions and Validators:** To add control and enforce business rules, you can add conditions (criteria that must be met before a transition is allowed) and validators (rules that validate input before a transition). For instance, you can create a condition that requires a certain field to be filled before an issue can move to "In Review."
5. **Add Post Functions:** Post functions are automated actions that occur after a transition. They can be used to assign issues, send notifications, update fields, or trigger external actions.

Recommended Workflow Practices

- **Keep It Simple:** Start with a basic workflow and gradually add complexity as needed.
- **Involve Your Team:** Collaborate with your team members to understand their process and ensure the workflow reflects their needs.

- **Document Your Workflow:** Create a clear and concise document that explains the purpose of each status, transition, condition, and validator. This will help onboard new team members and ensure everyone understands the process.

By mastering workflow configuration in JIRA, you can streamline your project management processes, automate repetitive tasks, and ensure that every issue progresses smoothly and consistently towards resolution.

Custom Field and Screen Management

JIRA's flexibility shines in its ability to be tailored to the specific needs of each project. Custom fields and screens empower administrators to capture unique data points and create intuitive user interfaces that simplify interactions for team members.

Importance of Customization

- **Tailored Data Collection:** Custom fields enable you to track data that is unique to your project, ensuring that no crucial information slips through the cracks. For instance, you might need a field to track customer priority levels or specific regulatory requirements that are relevant to your industry.
- **User-Friendly Interface:** By designing custom screens, you can present only the most relevant information to users, making it easier for them to interact with JIRA. A cluttered screen can lead to confusion and errors, while a well-designed screen enhances user experience and productivity.

Creating Custom Fields

1. **Access the Custom Fields Section:** In your project settings, navigate to the "Issues" section and select "Custom Fields."
2. **Choose a Field Type:** JIRA offers various field types, including text, number, date picker, user picker, select list, and more. Choose the type that best suits the kind of data you want to collect.
3. **Name and Describe Your Field:** Give your field a clear and descriptive name that reflects its purpose. Include a concise description to guide users on how to fill it out.
4. **Configure Field Options:** Depending on the field type, you may have additional options to configure. For example, if you're creating a select list, you'll need to define the available options.
5. **Associate with Screens:** Specify on which screens (create, edit, view) the new field should appear.

Designing Screens

1. **Go to Screens:** In the "Issues" section of your project settings, click on "Screens."
2. **Create or Edit a Screen:** Click "Create screen" for a new one or "Edit" for an existing screen.
3. **Add and Arrange Fields:** Drag and drop fields from the available list onto the screen layout. You can rearrange their order and group them into sections using the "Add Tab" option.
4. **Save the Screen:** Click "Save" to finalize your changes.

Managing Screen Schemes

Screen schemes control which screens are displayed for different issue operations and issue types. To manage screen schemes:

1. **Go to Screen Schemes:** In the "Issues" section of your project settings, click on "Screen schemes."
2. **Create or Edit a Scheme:** Click "Add screen scheme" or "Edit" for an existing scheme.
3. **Associate Screens:** For each issue operation and issue type, select the corresponding screen from the dropdown menus.
4. **Save the Scheme:** Click "Save" to finalize your changes.

Keeping it Simple

While customization is valuable, remember to keep your fields and screens simple and focused. Avoid overwhelming users with too many fields or complex layouts. Only include fields that are truly necessary and organize them in a logical and intuitive way.

Performance Optimization

As your JIRA instance grows, with increasing users, projects, and data, maintaining optimal performance becomes crucial. A sluggish JIRA can frustrate users, hinder productivity, and even impact business operations. In this section, we'll delve into the significance of JIRA performance optimization and provide practical tips for ensuring your JIRA instance runs smoothly.

Why Performance Matters

A high-performing JIRA instance offers several benefits:

- **Enhanced User Experience:** A responsive and snappy JIRA interface keeps users engaged and productive. Slow loading times and sluggish interactions can lead to frustration and decreased efficiency.
- **Improved Productivity:** When JIRA runs smoothly, teams can quickly access and update information, leading to faster decision-making and smoother workflows.
- **Cost Savings:** Performance issues can lead to increased resource consumption and higher infrastructure costs. Optimizing performance can help you save on these expenses.

Identifying and Resolving Performance Bottlenecks

JIRA performance bottlenecks can arise from various sources, including complex JQL queries, large attachments, excessive customizations, and inefficient workflows. Here are some tips for identifying and resolving common performance issues:

- **Optimize JQL Queries:** Complex or inefficient JQL queries can put a significant load on your JIRA instance. Review your saved filters and dashboards for queries that take a long time to execute. Simplify them by using appropriate filters, limiting the number of results, and avoiding unnecessary joins or calculations.
- **Manage Attachments:** Large attachments can consume significant storage space and slow down JIRA. Encourage users to compress attachments before uploading them and regularly review and delete old or unused attachments.
- **Archive Old Projects:** If you have projects that are no longer active, consider archiving them to reduce the amount of data JIRA needs to process. Archived projects are still accessible but won't impact the performance of your active projects.
- **Limit Customizations:** While customizations can be beneficial, excessive use of custom fields, workflows, or scripts can negatively impact performance. Review your customizations and remove any that are no longer necessary or are causing performance issues.
- **Monitor System Resources:** Keep an eye on your server's CPU usage, memory usage, and disk space to ensure that your JIRA instance has enough resources to function optimally. If you notice any resource constraints, consider upgrading your server or optimizing your JIRA configuration.

JIRA Performance Monitoring Tools

JIRA provides several built-in tools for monitoring and analyzing performance:

- **JIRA Health Check:** This tool provides a snapshot of your JIRA instance's health, including information on database connections, indexing, and memory usage.

- **Logging and Profiling:** Enable JIRA's logging and profiling features to gather detailed information about slow queries, performance bottlenecks, and other issues.
- **Third-Party Monitoring Tools:** Consider using third-party monitoring tools, such as New Relic or AppDynamics, to gain deeper insights into your JIRA performance.

By proactively monitoring your JIRA instance and utilizing the available tools, you can identify and address performance issues before they become major problems. This ensures that your JIRA remains a fast and responsive tool that supports your team's productivity.

Backup and Disaster Recovery

JIRA is a mission-critical tool for many organizations, serving as the central hub for project management and collaboration. Losing access to JIRA data due to unexpected events like hardware failures, software glitches, or natural disasters can have severe consequences for business continuity and productivity. Therefore, having a robust backup and disaster recovery plan in place is not just a best practice; it's a necessity.

The Importance of Backups

Regular backups are your insurance policy against data loss. They create snapshots of your JIRA data and configurations at specific points in time, allowing you to restore your system to a previous state in case of data corruption, accidental deletion, or other unforeseen events. Backups also provide a means to recover from ransomware attacks, ensuring that your valuable data is not held hostage.

Disaster Recovery Planning

A disaster recovery (DR) plan outlines the steps to be taken to restore your JIRA instance to a functional state in the event of a major outage or disaster. It encompasses not only data restoration but also infrastructure recovery, network connectivity, and user access. A well-prepared DR plan minimizes downtime, mitigates data loss, and ensures that your team can resume work quickly, even in the face of unexpected disruptions.

Backup Strategies

JIRA offers various backup strategies, each with its pros and cons:

- **JIRA Cloud Backups:** If you're using JIRA Cloud, Atlassian automatically backs up your data daily. These backups are stored in geographically diverse locations to ensure redundancy and resilience. However, you might have limited control over the backup frequency and retention period.
- **On-Premises Backups:** For JIRA Server or Data Center instances, you can set up on-premises backups. This involves creating backups of your JIRA data and configuration files and storing them on your own servers or storage devices. You have more control over the backup schedule and retention, but it requires additional infrastructure and management effort.
- **Third-Party Backup Solutions:** Several third-party backup solutions are available that integrate with JIRA and provide advanced features like automated backups, incremental backups, and granular restoration options. These solutions can offer more flexibility and control than native JIRA backups.

Testing Your Recovery Process

Creating backups is not enough; you also need to ensure that you can actually restore your JIRA instance from those backups. Regularly testing your recovery process is crucial to verify the integrity of your backups and identify any potential issues before a real disaster strikes.

Here are some key aspects to consider when testing your recovery process:

- **Recovery Time Objective (RTO):** This is the maximum amount of time you can afford for your JIRA instance to be down before it starts impacting your business.
- **Recovery Point Objective (RPO):** This is the maximum amount of data you can afford to lose in the event of a disaster.
- **Backup Validation:** Verify that your backups are complete and free of errors.
- **Restoration Testing:** Test restoring your JIRA instance from a backup in a controlled environment to ensure that the process works as expected.

By regularly testing your recovery process, you can fine-tune your DR plan and ensure that you're prepared to respond effectively to any unforeseen events that might threaten your JIRA data.

Continuous Improvement

JIRA administration is not a one-and-done task; it's an ongoing journey of learning, adapting, and refining your processes. To truly master JIRA administration, you need to embrace a mindset of continuous improvement. This means actively seeking feedback, staying up-to-date with the latest features, experimenting with new configurations, and learning from the JIRA community.

Gather Feedback

Your users are the ultimate judges of your JIRA instance's effectiveness. Regularly solicit feedback from them to identify pain points, usability issues, or areas where the system could be improved. This can be done through surveys, interviews, focus groups, or even casual conversations.

Stay Updated

JIRA is constantly evolving, with new features and enhancements being released regularly. Stay informed about these updates through Atlassian's documentation, blogs, webinars, and community forums. Experiment with new features in a test environment to see if they can benefit your team.

Experiment and Iterate

Don't be afraid to experiment with different configurations, workflows, and customizations. JIRA is a highly flexible platform, and what works for one team might not work for another. Continuously iterate and refine your JIRA setup to find the optimal configuration that aligns with your team's specific needs and processes.

Learn from the Community

The JIRA community is a vast and valuable resource. Connect with other JIRA administrators and users through online forums, discussion groups, and social media. Share your challenges, learn from others' experiences, and discover new ways to use JIRA. Participating in the community can be a great way to stay up-to-date with the latest trends and best practices.

Document Changes

Whenever you make changes to your JIRA configuration, document them thoroughly. This includes noting the changes made, the reasons behind them, the date they were implemented, and any potential impacts on users. This documentation will be invaluable for troubleshooting issues, reverting changes if necessary, and onboarding new administrators.

The Journey of Continuous Improvement

JIRA administration is not about achieving perfection; it's about continuous improvement. By embracing a mindset of learning and adaptation, you can create a JIRA environment that evolves with your team's needs, maximizes efficiency, and drives project success.

Chapter Summary

In this chapter, we delved into the realm of best practices for JIRA administration, emphasizing the importance of continuous improvement and optimization. We highlighted the significance of well-defined project structure, clear goals, and efficient workflows in ensuring successful project execution. We also stressed the critical role of user and permission management in maintaining data security and integrity, encouraging the use of groups, project roles, and the principle of least privilege.

Furthermore, we explored the art of workflow configuration, emphasizing the need to create customized workflows that align with specific project needs. We recommended using conditions, validators, and post-functions to streamline transitions and enforce business rules. Additionally, we discussed the benefits of customizing fields and screens to capture relevant project data and tailor the user interface, promoting user-friendliness and efficiency.

We then addressed the importance of performance optimization, offering tips for identifying and resolving bottlenecks, such as optimizing JQL queries, managing attachments, and archiving old projects. We encouraged administrators to leverage JIRA's built-in performance monitoring tools to proactively address performance issues.

Finally, we stressed the critical need for regular backups and a comprehensive disaster recovery plan to safeguard JIRA data and ensure business continuity. We discussed various backup strategies, including cloud backups, on-premises backups, and third-party solutions, along with the importance of regularly testing the recovery process.

By embracing these best practices and maintaining a mindset of continuous improvement, JIRA administrators can ensure that their JIRA instance remains a powerful and efficient tool that supports their teams in achieving project success.

Migrating and Upgrading JIRA Instances

Outline

- Introduction to JIRA Migration and Upgrades
- Planning Your Migration or Upgrade
- Preparing for Migration or Upgrade
- Executing the Migration or Upgrade
- Post-Migration or Upgrade Tasks
- Troubleshooting Migration or Upgrade Issues
- Chapter Summary

Introduction to JIRA Migration and Upgrades

While both migration and upgrade involve making significant changes to your JIRA instance, they serve distinct purposes and require different approaches. Understanding the difference between the two is crucial for choosing the right path for your organization's needs.

Migration

Migration refers to the process of moving your entire JIRA instance from one environment to another. This could involve:

- **Server to Cloud:** Moving your JIRA instance from a self-hosted server environment to Atlassian's cloud platform.
- **Cloud to Cloud:** Transferring your JIRA instance between different Atlassian cloud sites.
- **Server to Server:** Moving your JIRA instance between different self-hosted servers.

Migration is often driven by factors such as:

- **Cost Reduction:** Moving to JIRA Cloud can eliminate the need for maintaining your own hardware and infrastructure, potentially reducing costs.
- **Improved Scalability:** Cloud-based solutions offer better scalability, allowing you to easily adjust resources as your team or organization grows.
- **Simplified Maintenance:** Atlassian handles maintenance and upgrades for JIRA Cloud, freeing up your IT resources.
- **Enhanced Security:** Cloud providers often invest heavily in security measures, potentially offering better protection than self-hosted environments.

Upgrade

Upgrading, on the other hand, refers to updating your JIRA instance to a newer version of the software. This is typically done to:

- **Access New Features:** Newer JIRA versions often come with new features, enhancements, and bug fixes that can improve your productivity and user experience.
- **Improve Performance:** Upgrading can sometimes boost the performance of your JIRA instance, especially if you're running an older version.
- **Enhance Security:** Newer versions often include security patches and improvements that protect your data and system.
- **Maintain Compatibility:** Upgrading ensures that your JIRA instance remains compatible with other tools and integrations you might be using.

When to Migrate or Upgrade

The decision to migrate or upgrade your JIRA instance depends on your specific needs and circumstances. Here are some scenarios where you might consider each option:

- **Migration:**
  - You want to move from a self-hosted JIRA Server/Data Center to JIRA Cloud to reduce costs and simplify maintenance.
  - You need to consolidate multiple JIRA instances into a single cloud instance.
  - Your organization's data residency requirements necessitate a change in cloud providers.
- **Upgrade:**
  - You want to take advantage of new features and improvements in the latest JIRA version.
  - Your current JIRA version is no longer supported, and you need to upgrade to ensure security and compatibility.
  - You're experiencing performance issues with your current JIRA instance.

Both migration and upgrade can be complex processes, requiring careful planning and execution. In the following sections, we will delve into the specifics of planning and preparing for a migration or upgrade, as well as the steps involved in executing the process and post-migration/upgrade tasks.

Planning Your Migration or Upgrade

Embarking on a JIRA migration or upgrade is a significant undertaking that requires meticulous planning and preparation. A well-thought-out plan can mean the difference between a smooth transition and a disruptive experience. This section will guide you through the essential steps of creating a comprehensive plan for your JIRA migration or upgrade.

Defining Objectives

Before you begin, it's crucial to clearly define the objectives of your migration or upgrade. What are you hoping to achieve? Are you looking to reduce costs, improve performance, access new features, enhance security, or comply with new regulations? By articulating your goals upfront, you can align your efforts and make informed decisions throughout the process.

Assessing Your Current Environment

Take a comprehensive inventory of your existing JIRA setup. This includes:

- **Hardware:** Document the specifications of your current server infrastructure, including CPU, memory, storage, and operating system.
- **Software:** List all the JIRA versions, plugins, add-ons, and custom scripts you're using.
- **Customizations:** Document any customizations you've made to JIRA, such as custom fields, workflows, screens, or integrations.
- **Data:** Analyze the size and complexity of your JIRA data, including the number of issues, projects, users, and attachments.

This assessment will help you understand the scope of your migration or upgrade and identify any potential challenges or risks.

Choosing the Right Migration or Upgrade Path

JIRA offers several migration and upgrade paths. The right path for you depends on your current JIRA version, target version or environment, and specific requirements. Consult Atlassian's documentation or seek guidance from their support team to determine the most suitable path for your organization.

Creating a Timeline

Develop a realistic timeline for your migration or upgrade project. Consider the following factors:

- **Data Preparation:** Allocate time for cleaning up your data, removing unnecessary attachments, and archiving old projects.
- **Testing:** Schedule ample time for testing in a non-production environment to ensure that everything works as expected before deploying to production.
- **User Acceptance Testing (UAT):** Allow time for your users to test the new JIRA environment and provide feedback.
- **Deployment:** Schedule the actual migration or upgrade during a time of low usage to minimize disruption.
- **Post-Deployment Support:** Allocate resources for addressing any issues that arise after the deployment.

Communicating with Stakeholders

Communication is key throughout the migration or upgrade process. Keep all stakeholders informed about the project's progress, timelines, and any potential impacts on their work. This includes not only your IT team but also project managers, developers, testers, and end-users. Clearly communicate the benefits of the migration or upgrade to gain their support and buy-in.

By following these planning steps, you can lay a solid foundation for a successful JIRA migration or upgrade. Remember, thorough planning is an investment that pays off in the long run by minimizing risks, reducing downtime, and ensuring a smooth transition for your team.

Preparing for Migration or Upgrade

Thorough preparation is essential to ensure a successful JIRA migration or upgrade. By taking the necessary steps in advance, you can minimize downtime, prevent data loss, and avoid unexpected surprises during the process.

Backing Up Data

The most critical step in preparing for a JIRA migration or upgrade is creating a comprehensive backup of your JIRA data. This includes:

- **Issue Data:** All your issues, their fields, comments, history, and attachments.
- **Project Configuration:** Project settings, workflows, screens, fields, and issue types.
- **User Data:** User accounts, groups, roles, and permissions.
- **Global Configuration:** System settings, custom fields, and any other global configurations.

It's recommended to create multiple backups and store them in different locations to ensure redundancy. For JIRA Cloud, Atlassian automatically backs up your data daily, but you might want to create additional backups before the migration or upgrade. For JIRA Server/Data Center, use JIRA's built-in backup functionality or a third-party backup solution.

Testing Compatibility

If you're upgrading your JIRA instance or migrating to a newer version, it's crucial to check the compatibility of your plugins, add-ons, and custom scripts with the new JIRA version. Incompatible plugins can cause errors or unexpected behavior after the upgrade.

1. **Check the Atlassian Marketplace:** Visit the Atlassian Marketplace and check the compatibility of your plugins with the target JIRA version. Look for updates or newer versions of the plugins that are compatible.
2. **Test in a Staging Environment:** If possible, create a staging environment that mirrors your production environment. Install the new JIRA version and your plugins in the staging environment and thoroughly test their functionality.
3. **Contact Plugin Vendors:** If you encounter compatibility issues, contact the plugin vendors for support or guidance.

Updating Documentation

Ensure that your JIRA documentation is comprehensive and up-to-date. This includes:

- **User Guides:** Document how users interact with JIRA, including how to create and manage issues, use Agile boards, and generate reports.
- **Administration Guides:** Document your JIRA configuration, including custom fields, workflows, screens, and integrations.
- **Troubleshooting Guides:** Document common issues and their solutions.

Update your documentation to reflect any changes made during the preparation phase, such as changes to workflows or field configurations. This will help your team adapt to the new JIRA environment smoothly and reduce the learning curve after the migration or upgrade.

By diligently following these preparation steps, you can minimize risks and ensure a smooth and successful JIRA migration or upgrade. It's better to invest time in preparation now than to face unexpected problems later that could disrupt your work and jeopardize your data.

Executing the Migration or Upgrade

With meticulous planning and preparation complete, it's time to execute the JIRA migration or upgrade. The specific steps involved will vary depending on your chosen path (Server to Cloud, Cloud to Cloud, Server to Server) and the tools you're using. However, we'll outline the general process and highlight key considerations for each scenario.

Exporting Data (for Migration)

For migrations, you'll need to export your JIRA data and configuration from your existing instance. JIRA provides built-in tools for this purpose:

1. **Access the Administration Console:** Log in as a JIRA administrator and navigate to the administration console.
2. **System:** Go to the "System" section.
3. **Import & Export:** Choose "External System Import" then "Export."
4. **Select Data to Export:** Choose the specific data you want to export, such as projects, issues, users, or global configurations. You can export all data or select specific items based on your needs.
5. **Export Format:** Choose the appropriate export format. JIRA typically supports XML and JSON formats.
6. **Start Export:** Initiate the export process. This might take some time, depending on the size of your data.
7. **Download Export File:** Once the export is complete, download the generated file and store it in a secure location.

Installing and Configuring the New JIRA Instance

For migrations and upgrades, you'll need to set up the new JIRA instance.

- **Cloud Migration:** If you're migrating to JIRA Cloud, you don't need to install the software. Atlassian will provision a new cloud instance for you. You'll need to configure your site settings, users, and groups.
- **Server/Data Center Migration or Upgrade:** If you're migrating or upgrading a Server/Data Center instance, you'll need to install the new JIRA software on your server or data center. Follow Atlassian's documentation for detailed instructions on installation and configuration.

Importing Data (for Migration)

After setting up the new JIRA instance, import the exported data from your old instance.

1. **Access the Administration Console:** Log in as a JIRA administrator to the new instance.
2. **System:** Navigate to the "System" section.
3. **Import & Export:** Choose "External System Import" then "Import."
4. **Select Import Source and File:** Choose the import source (e.g., JIRA) and select the exported file you previously downloaded.
5. **Configure Import Settings:** Map the data fields and adjust any necessary settings.
6. **Start Import:** Initiate the import process. This might take a while, depending on the data size.

Applying Updates (for Upgrades)

If you're upgrading, apply the necessary updates to bring your JIRA instance to the new version. Follow Atlassian's upgrade guide for detailed instructions specific to your current and target versions.

Remember, thorough testing in a staging environment is crucial before applying any changes to your production instance. This allows you to identify and resolve any issues before they impact your users.

Post-Migration or Upgrade Tasks

Congratulations! You've successfully completed the technical aspects of your JIRA migration or upgrade. However, your work is not yet done. Several essential tasks remain to ensure a smooth transition for your users and the continued success of your JIRA instance.

Testing and Validation

Thorough testing is crucial after a migration or upgrade to verify that all JIRA functionalities are working correctly in the new environment. This involves:

- **Functional Testing:** Test all core JIRA features, such as creating and editing issues, transitioning issues through workflows, searching and filtering, using Agile boards, generating reports, and accessing any integrations or customizations.
- **Performance Testing:** Check the performance of your JIRA instance under different loads to ensure it can handle your expected user traffic and data volume.
- **User Acceptance Testing (UAT):** Involve a small group of users to test the new JIRA environment in a real-world scenario and provide feedback.

User Training

If your migration or upgrade introduces new features or changes to the JIRA interface, it's essential to provide comprehensive training to your users. This can be done through:

- **Training Sessions:** Conduct training sessions to walk users through the new features and changes.

- **Documentation:** Create user guides and documentation that explain how to use the new JIRA features.
- **Online Resources:** Provide links to online resources, such as Atlassian's documentation or community forums, where users can find additional information and support.

Monitoring and Troubleshooting

After the migration or upgrade, closely monitor your JIRA instance for any errors, performance issues, or unexpected behavior. Check your JIRA logs regularly for any error messages or warnings. Use JIRA's built-in monitoring tools or third-party monitoring solutions to track system performance and resource utilization.

Be prepared to troubleshoot any issues that arise. Consult Atlassian's documentation, community forums, or seek support from Atlassian's technical team if needed.

By diligently completing these post-migration or upgrade tasks, you can ensure that your JIRA instance is fully functional, your users are comfortable with the new environment, and your project management processes continue to run smoothly.

Troubleshooting Migration or Upgrade Issues

Even with careful planning and preparation, you might encounter some hiccups during or after a JIRA migration or upgrade. Don't panic! This section will equip you with tips and strategies to troubleshoot common issues that can arise.

Data Inconsistencies

Data inconsistencies can occur during the import/export process, resulting in missing or incorrect data in your new JIRA instance. Here's how to address them:

- **Review Logs:** Check JIRA's logs for error messages related to data import. These logs can provide clues about the cause of the inconsistencies.
- **Validate Data:** Compare your exported data with the data in the new instance to identify any discrepancies. You can use JQL queries or third-party tools to assist with this process.
- **Re-Import Data:** If you find missing or incorrect data, try re-importing the data, paying close attention to field mappings and import settings.
- **Manual Correction:** In some cases, you might need to manually correct data inconsistencies. This could involve editing issue fields, restoring deleted items, or fixing broken links.

Plugin Compatibility Issues

If you encounter issues with plugins or add-ons after an upgrade, try these solutions:

- **Update Plugins:** Check the Atlassian Marketplace for updates to your plugins. Newer versions might be compatible with the new JIRA version.
- **Disable or Uninstall Conflicting Plugins:** If a plugin is causing errors, try disabling it temporarily to see if the issue persists. If the problem is resolved, you might need to uninstall the plugin or contact the vendor for support.
- **Contact Atlassian Support:** If you're unable to resolve the issue on your own, contact Atlassian's support team for assistance.

Performance Problems

Performance issues can manifest as slow page loads, unresponsive UI elements, or sluggish search functionality. Here's how to troubleshoot them:

- **Check JIRA Logs:** Look for error messages related to performance issues, such as database connection errors, memory leaks, or excessive garbage collection.
- **Monitor Server Resources:** Use system monitoring tools to check CPU usage, memory usage, and disk space. If any of these resources are running low, it could be impacting JIRA performance.
- **Optimize JQL Queries:** Complex or inefficient JQL queries can cause performance problems. Review your saved filters and dashboards for queries that take a long time to execute.
- **Limit Customizations:** Excessive customizations, such as a large number of custom fields or complex workflows, can also affect performance. Evaluate your customizations and remove any that are not essential.
- **Contact Atlassian Support:** If you're unable to resolve performance issues on your own, contact Atlassian's support team for assistance.

Remember, patience and systematic troubleshooting are key to resolving migration or upgrade issues. Document all the steps you take and the errors you encounter to help you track your progress and communicate effectively with support teams if needed.

Chapter Summary

In this chapter, we explored the intricate process of migrating and upgrading JIRA instances, guiding you through the essential steps to ensure a successful transition. We emphasized the significance of meticulous planning, which involves defining clear objectives, assessing your current environment, choosing the right migration or upgrade path, creating a realistic timeline, and communicating effectively with stakeholders.

We then delved into the preparation phase, highlighting the critical need for comprehensive data backups, ensuring plugin compatibility, and updating documentation to reflect any changes. The execution phase was outlined in detail, covering data export, installation and configuration of the new JIRA instance, data import, and applying updates (for upgrades).

To ensure a seamless transition, we discussed post-migration or upgrade tasks, including thorough testing and validation, user training on new features or interface changes, and ongoing monitoring and troubleshooting. We also provided practical tips for addressing common issues that may arise during the process, such as data inconsistencies, plugin compatibility problems, and performance bottlenecks.

By following these comprehensive guidelines, you can confidently navigate the complexities of JIRA migration and upgrades, minimizing downtime, preserving data integrity, and ensuring a smooth transition for your team. This knowledge will empower you to keep your JIRA instance up-to-date and aligned with your evolving needs, unlocking its full potential for efficient project management and collaboration.

Section F:
Confluence for Documentation and Collaboration

Creating and Managing Spaces in Confluence

Outline

- Understanding Confluence Spaces
- Creating a New Space
- Space Permissions
- Organizing Spaces
- Chapter Summary

Understanding Confluence Spaces

In the realm of Confluence, spaces are the fundamental building blocks for organizing content and fostering collaboration. Think of them as virtual rooms where you can gather information, ideas, and people to work together towards a common goal. Each space serves as a dedicated hub for a specific team, project, or topic, providing a structured environment for knowledge sharing and collaborative work.

Spaces as Organizational Units

Spaces are designed to be flexible and adaptable to your team's specific needs. They can be tailored to accommodate various types of content, such as project plans, meeting notes, technical documentation, marketing materials, or even company-wide announcements. By creating separate spaces for different projects or teams, you can keep information organized and easily accessible to the relevant stakeholders.

Types of Spaces

Confluence offers several types of spaces to cater to different use cases:

- **Team Spaces:** These are designed for teams to collaborate on ongoing work. They typically contain meeting notes, project plans, team calendars, and other collaborative documents. Team spaces provide a centralized location for team members to communicate, share information, and track progress.
- **Project Spaces:** These spaces are focused on specific projects and contain all the relevant information, such as project goals, timelines, deliverables, and status updates. Project spaces help teams stay organized and aligned throughout the project lifecycle.
- **Knowledge Base Spaces:** These spaces are used to create and maintain a central repository of knowledge and information. They can contain how-to guides, tutorials, FAQs, and other resources that can be accessed by anyone in the organization. Knowledge base spaces promote knowledge sharing and reduce the need to reinvent the wheel.
- **Personal Spaces:** These are private spaces for individual users to organize their own notes, drafts, and personal projects. Personal spaces offer a secure and convenient place for users to store their work and ideas.

Confluence allows you to customize spaces to match your specific requirements. You can choose a space theme to give it a unique look and feel. You can also set permissions to control who can view, edit, and manage content within the space. This flexibility ensures that spaces can be tailored to the specific needs of each team or project.

By understanding the concept of spaces and the different types available, you can create a well-structured and organized Confluence environment that promotes collaboration, knowledge sharing, and efficient information management.

Creating a New Space

Creating a new space in Confluence is a straightforward process that empowers you to tailor a dedicated area for your team or project. Let's walk through the steps involved:

1. **Navigate to the Confluence Dashboard:** After logging into Confluence, you'll land on the dashboard, your central hub for accessing and managing your spaces.
2. **Click the "Create" Button or the "Spaces" Menu:** You'll typically find a prominent "Create" button on the dashboard or a "Spaces" menu in the navigation bar. Click either of these options to initiate the space creation process.
3. **Choose the Type of Space:** Confluence offers various space templates, each tailored for different purposes like team collaboration, project management, or knowledge bases. Choose the template that best aligns with your goals or select "Blank space" to start from scratch.
4. **Name Your Space and Provide a Description:** Give your space a clear, descriptive name that reflects its purpose (e.g., "Marketing Team Space" or "Project X Documentation"). Add a concise description to provide additional context about the space's content and goals.
5. **Select a Space Template (if applicable):** If you chose a space template in the previous step, you might be presented with different templates to choose from. Select the one that best suits your needs. If you opted for a blank space, you can skip this step.
6. **Customize Space Settings:** Confluence allows you to personalize your space. You can:
   - **Set Permissions:** Define who can view, edit, and manage content within the space.
   - **Choose a Theme:** Select a visually appealing theme that matches your brand or preferences.
   - **Add a Space Logo:** Upload a logo to represent your space.
   - **Configure Other Settings:** Customize additional settings like notifications, page restrictions, and space shortcuts.
7. **Invite Team Members to Collaborate:** Once your space is set up, invite your team members to join and start collaborating. You can add users individually or invite entire groups.

By following these steps, you can create a well-structured and personalized Confluence space that facilitates collaboration, knowledge sharing, and efficient information management. Your new space will serve as a central hub for your team or project, enabling you to work together seamlessly towards your goals.

Space Permissions

Space permissions are the bedrock of security and access control within Confluence. They determine who can view, edit, and manage content within a specific space. By carefully managing space permissions, you ensure that sensitive information is protected, collaboration is streamlined, and users only have access to the information and features they need.

The Importance of Space Permissions

Confluence spaces can contain various types of content, from confidential project plans to public knowledge base articles. Managing permissions ensures that:

- **Confidentiality is maintained:** Sensitive or proprietary information is only accessible to authorized individuals.
- **Collaboration is efficient:** Team members have the appropriate permissions to contribute and collaborate effectively.
- **Accountability is ensured:** Changes and updates are tracked, and users are held accountable for their actions.
- **Data integrity is preserved:** Unauthorized modifications or deletions are prevented.

Permission Levels in Confluence

Confluence offers several levels of permissions, each granting a different degree of access and control:

- **View:** This is the most basic level of permission. Users with "View" permission can only see the content within a space. They cannot edit, create, or delete pages.
- **Edit:** Users with "Edit" permission can create, edit, and delete content within a space. They can also comment on pages and participate in discussions.
- **Administer:** This is the highest level of permission. Users with "Administer" permission have full control over the space. They can manage permissions, change space settings, and perform administrative tasks.

Setting and Managing Space Permissions

To set and manage space permissions in Confluence:

1. **Access Space Settings:** Navigate to the space you want to manage and click on the "Space tools" menu in the sidebar. Then, select "Permissions."
2. **Add Users or Groups:**
   - To grant permissions to individual users, enter their names or email addresses in the "Add people" field.
   - To grant permissions to groups, enter the group names in the "Add groups" field.
   - You can choose to grant different permission levels (View, Edit, or Administer) to different users or groups.
3. **Grant or Revoke Permissions:**
   - To grant a permission, check the corresponding checkbox next to the user or group.
   - To revoke a permission, uncheck the checkbox.
4. **Save Changes:** Click the "Save" button to apply your changes.

Additional Tips

- **Use Groups:** It's generally more efficient to manage permissions through groups rather than individual users. This way, if you need to update permissions, you can simply modify the group's permissions, and the changes will apply to all members of the group.
- **Restrict "Administer" Permission:** The "Administer" permission should be granted judiciously, as it gives users complete control over the space. Typically, only space administrators or project leads should have this permission.
- **Review Permissions Regularly:** Periodically review space permissions to ensure they are up-to-date and reflect the current needs of your team or project.
- **Consider Nested Groups:** If you have a complex organizational structure, consider using nested groups (groups within groups) to simplify permission management.

By following these guidelines and best practices, you can effectively manage space permissions in Confluence, ensuring that your content is secure, your collaboration is efficient, and your users have the right level of access to contribute to your projects.

Organizing Spaces

A well-organized Confluence environment is essential for efficient knowledge management and collaboration. When spaces are structured logically and content is easy to find, teams can work more effectively and avoid wasting time searching for information. Here are some tips to help you organize your Confluence spaces:

- **Use a Clear Naming Convention:** Choose descriptive names for your spaces that accurately reflect their purpose or content. Avoid generic names like "Project A" or "Team Space." Instead, opt for names like "Marketing Team Projects" or "Product X Documentation." This makes it easier for users to identify relevant spaces and understand their contents at a glance.
- **Create a Space Hierarchy:** Organize your spaces into a hierarchical structure to create a logical flow and make it easier to navigate. You can create parent spaces that contain child spaces, creating a tree-like structure. For example, you could have a parent space called "Marketing" with child spaces for different marketing initiatives or campaigns.
- **Use Labels:** Labels are keywords or tags that you can add to spaces to categorize them and make them easier to find. For example, you could add labels like "Marketing," "Sales," "Engineering," or "HR" to your spaces. Users can then filter the space directory by labels to quickly find the spaces they need.
- **Regularly Review and Update Spaces:** As your team and projects evolve, it's important to periodically review and update your spaces. Ensure that the content is up-to-date, permissions are still relevant, and the space is still serving its intended purpose. Archive or delete spaces that are no longer needed.
- **Use the Space Directory:** The space directory is a centralized list of all the spaces in your Confluence instance. Encourage your users to explore the space directory to discover relevant spaces and content. You can customize the directory to highlight featured spaces or filter spaces by labels or categories.

By following these tips, you can create a well-organized and user-friendly Confluence environment. This will make it easier for your team members to find the information they need, collaborate effectively, and contribute to your organization's knowledge base.

Chapter Summary

In this chapter, we explored the fundamental concept of spaces within Confluence and how they serve as the backbone of organization and collaboration in the platform. We discussed the various types of spaces available, including team, project, knowledge base, and personal spaces, each catering to specific use cases and needs.

Furthermore, we provided a detailed guide on creating a new space, outlining the steps from navigating to the dashboard to customizing space settings and inviting team members. We emphasized the importance of choosing descriptive names and selecting appropriate space templates to streamline the process and ensure a clear purpose for each space.

Additionally, we delved into the critical aspect of space permissions, explaining how they control access and actions within a space. We discussed different permission levels like View, Edit, and Administer, and provided instructions on setting and managing these permissions for individual users and groups.

Lastly, we offered valuable tips on organizing spaces effectively. This included using clear naming conventions, creating space hierarchies, utilizing labels, regularly reviewing and updating spaces, and encouraging the use of the space directory. These best practices help establish a well-structured and user-friendly Confluence environment that fosters collaboration and knowledge sharing across the organization.

Building and Organizing Pages

Outline

- The Power of Confluence Pages
- Creating and Editing Pages
- Page Formatting
- Organizing Pages
- Chapter Summary

The Power of Confluence Pages

In Confluence, pages are the heart and soul of your knowledge base. They are the digital canvases where you create, organize, and share information with your team. Think of them as living documents that can be easily edited, updated, and collaborated on in real time.

More Than Just Text

Confluence pages are not limited to just text. They offer a rich multimedia experience, allowing you to embed various types of content to enhance your documentation and communication. Here are some examples:

- **Text:** This is the foundation of most Confluence pages. You can use the rich text editor to format text, add headings, create lists, and insert links.
- **Images:** Visuals are powerful tools for conveying information. You can easily add images to your pages to illustrate concepts, provide examples, or simply make your content more engaging.
- **Videos:** Embed videos from YouTube, Vimeo, or other sources to provide demonstrations, tutorials, or other types of video content.
- **Files and Documents:** Attach files to your pages, such as PDFs, spreadsheets, or presentations, to provide additional information or resources.
- **Code Snippets:** If you're documenting technical information, you can insert code snippets to make your content more precise and informative.
- **Drawings and Diagrams:** Use Confluence's built-in drawing tools or integrate with external diagramming tools to create visual representations of processes, workflows, or system architectures.

Collaborative Canvas

One of the most powerful aspects of Confluence pages is their collaborative nature. Multiple users can work on the same page simultaneously, making it easy to brainstorm ideas, gather feedback, and co-create content. The page history feature allows you to track changes and revert to previous versions if needed, ensuring that no valuable information is lost.

Documenting Knowledge

Confluence pages are ideal for documenting all types of knowledge, from project plans and meeting notes to technical specifications and user manuals. By creating and organizing pages within spaces, you can build a comprehensive knowledge base that is easily accessible to your team. This centralized repository of information promotes transparency, reduces duplication of effort, and ensures that everyone has access to the latest information.

In the following sections, we'll explore how to create and edit pages, format your content, and organize pages within spaces to create a well-structured and informative knowledge base for your team.

Creating and Editing Pages

Confluence makes it easy to create and edit pages to capture your team's knowledge and ideas. The process is simple and intuitive, whether you're starting from scratch or building upon a template.

Accessing Page Creation

You can create a new page in Confluence in a couple of ways:

- **From the Space Dashboard:** When you're in a specific space, click the "Create" button usually located at the top right of the dashboard.
- **From the Navigation Menu:** Click the "+" icon in the top navigation bar and select "Page."

Choosing a Page Template

Confluence offers a variety of page templates to jumpstart your content creation process. Some popular options include:

- **Blank Page:** This is a clean slate, allowing you to create any type of content you want.
- **Meeting Notes:** This template is structured for documenting meeting agendas, discussions, and action items.
- **Decision:** This template helps you outline a decision, its rationale, and any supporting information.
- **How-to:** This template guides you through creating step-by-step instructions or tutorials.
- **File List:** This template creates a list of attached files, making it easy to share and organize documents.

You can also find templates for product requirements, troubleshooting guides, and more. Choose the template that best fits your needs or start with a blank page and build from there.

Entering a Page Title and Adding Content

Once you've chosen a template (or a blank page), you'll be presented with the Confluence editor.

1. **Page Title:** Start by entering a clear and descriptive title for your page in the designated field at the top. This title should summarize the content of the page and make it easy for others to find.
2. **Rich Text Editor:** The main area of the page is the rich text editor, where you'll add your content. Confluence's editor is similar to a word processor, offering various formatting options.

Formatting and Adding Content

- **Text Formatting:** You can use the toolbar to format your text with bold, italic, underline, headings, lists, links, code blocks, and more.
- **Inserting Images and Tables:** Click the "+" icon in the toolbar to insert images, tables, or other types of content. You can upload images from your computer or embed them from the web. Tables can be created and customized to organize information effectively.
- **Adding Other Content:** Confluence supports a wide range of content types, including videos, files, code snippets, and more. You can embed videos from platforms like YouTube or Vimeo, attach files like PDFs or spreadsheets, or insert code snippets for technical documentation.

Editing Pages

Editing a Confluence page is as simple as creating one. Just click the "Edit" button at the top of the page to enter editing mode. You can then modify the content, add new sections, or rearrange elements as needed. When you're finished, click "Save" to publish your changes.

Remember to preview your page before publishing to ensure that the formatting and layout look as intended.

Page Formatting

Confluence's rich text editor offers a comprehensive set of formatting tools to help you create visually appealing and well-structured pages. Whether you're documenting a project plan, writing meeting notes, or creating a knowledge base article, these formatting options allow you to present your information in a clear and engaging manner.

Basic Formatting

The editor provides all the essential formatting tools you'd expect from a word processor:

- **Bold:** Emphasize important words or phrases.
- **Italic:** Highlight book titles, foreign words, or technical terms.
- **Underline:** Underline text for emphasis or to indicate a hyperlink.
- **Headings:** Organize your content with different levels of headings (H1, H2, H3, etc.).
- **Lists:** Create bulleted or numbered lists to present information in a structured way.
- **Links:** Insert hyperlinks to other Confluence pages, external websites, or files.
- **Code Blocks:** Format code snippets with syntax highlighting for better readability.

You can access these basic formatting options through the toolbar at the top of the editor or by using keyboard shortcuts.

Tables

Tables are excellent for organizing information in a structured format. Confluence allows you to create and customize tables by:

- **Inserting a table:** Choose the number of rows and columns you need.
- **Adding content:** Fill in the cells with text, numbers, or other data.
- **Formatting cells:** Merge or split cells, adjust column widths, and apply styles like bold or italic.
- **Adding headers:** Create header rows or columns for better organization.
- **Sorting data:** Sort the table by any column in ascending or descending order.

Images and Multimedia

Visuals can enhance the appeal and effectiveness of your Confluence pages. You can insert images, videos, and other multimedia content directly into your pages.

- **Images:** Upload images from your computer or embed them from the web. You can resize images, add captions, and create image galleries.
- **Videos:** Embed videos from popular platforms like YouTube and Vimeo to provide visual demonstrations or tutorials.
- **Other Multimedia:** Confluence supports various other multimedia formats, such as audio files and presentations.

Advanced Formatting

For more advanced formatting, Confluence offers additional features like:

- **Macros:** Macros are reusable snippets of code that you can insert into your pages to perform specific actions or display dynamic content. For example, the Table of Contents macro automatically generates a table of contents based on the headings in your page.
- **Emojis:** Add emojis to your text to convey emotions or add a touch of personality.
- **Code Block Macros:** Use special macros to display code snippets in various programming languages with syntax highlighting.
- **LaTeX:** If you need to include mathematical formulas or equations, you can use the LaTeX macro to render them beautifully.

By mastering these formatting options, you can create Confluence pages that are not only informative but also visually engaging and easy to read.

Organizing Pages

Organizing pages effectively is essential for maintaining a well-structured and easily navigable Confluence space. As your knowledge base grows, it's crucial to have a system in place to ensure that information is easy to find and access. Confluence offers several tools and techniques to help you organize your pages and keep your content tidy.

Page Hierarchy

Creating a hierarchical structure of pages is one of the most fundamental ways to organize content in Confluence. This involves establishing parent-child relationships between pages, where a parent page acts as a container for related child pages. This structure resembles a tree, with the main topic as the root and subtopics branching out from it.

To create a page hierarchy, you can simply create a new page and specify its parent page during the creation process. This will automatically nest the new page under its parent in the space's sidebar navigation. You can create multiple levels of hierarchy to organize your content in a logical and intuitive way.

Labels

Labels are keywords or tags that you can add to pages to categorize and classify them. They make it easier to find pages related to specific topics or projects. For example, you might label a page with "marketing," "product launch," or "Q2 goals." Users can then search or filter for pages based on these labels.

To add labels to a page, simply edit the page and enter the desired labels in the "Labels" field. You can add multiple labels to a single page, and you can also create custom labels to suit your needs.

Page Templates and Blueprints

Templates and blueprints are powerful tools for standardizing page formats and streamlining content creation. A template is a pre-formatted page that you can use as a starting point for new pages. For example, you might have a template for meeting notes, project plans, or product requirements documents.

Blueprints are more sophisticated than templates. They not only provide a pre-formatted structure but also guide users through the process of creating content. Blueprints can include instructions, checklists, and even automated workflows.

By using templates and blueprints, you ensure that your pages are consistent in terms of structure, formatting, and content. This makes it easier for users to consume and understand information, as well as contribute to the knowledge base.

Page Properties

Each Confluence page has a set of properties that you can use to manage its visibility, restrictions, and other settings. Some important page properties include:

- **Restrictions:** You can restrict access to a page to specific users or groups.
- **Labels:** Add labels to categorize the page.
- **Comments:** Enable or disable comments on the page.
- **Likes:** Allow users to like the page.
- **Attachments:** View and manage attachments associated with the page.

You can access and modify these properties by clicking the "Properties" button in the page view.

Archiving and Deleting Pages

If a page is no longer needed, you can either archive it or delete it. Archiving a page removes it from the space's navigation but keeps it accessible through search. Deleting a page permanently removes it from Confluence.

To archive or delete a page, click the "More actions" button in the page view and select "Archive" or "Delete," respectively.

Best Practices

Here are some additional tips for organizing your Confluence pages:

- **Use Clear and Descriptive Titles:** Choose titles that accurately reflect the content of the page. Avoid using vague or generic titles.
- **Keep Pages Concise and Focused:** Break down large pages into smaller, more manageable chunks. This makes it easier for users to find and digest information.
- **Use Links to Connect Related Pages:** Link related pages together to create a network of information. This makes it easier for users to navigate between pages and discover relevant content.
- **Create a Table of Contents:** If your page is long or complex, consider adding a table of contents to help users navigate it.
- **Regularly Review and Update Pages:** Ensure that your pages are up-to-date and accurate. Remove outdated or irrelevant information, and update links as needed.

By following these tips and utilizing Confluence's organization features, you can create a well-structured and user-friendly knowledge base that empowers your team to collaborate effectively and find the information they need quickly and easily.

Chapter Summary

In this chapter, we explored the art of building and organizing pages in Confluence, the essential building blocks of your collaborative workspace and knowledge repository. We began by highlighting the versatility of Confluence pages, which can house diverse content types like text, images, videos, files, and more. These pages serve as a collaborative canvas, enabling teams to co-create, share, and document knowledge seamlessly.

We then walked you through the steps of creating and editing pages, from accessing the page creation options to utilizing the rich text editor to craft your content. We discussed various formatting options, including basic formatting like bold, italics, headings, and lists, as well as more advanced features like tables, multimedia embedding, macros, and emojis.

Furthermore, we explored strategies for organizing pages within Confluence spaces. We emphasized the importance of creating a clear page hierarchy using parent-child relationships, employing labels for categorization, leveraging templates and blueprints for standardization, and utilizing page properties for managing visibility and restrictions. We also provided tips for maintaining an organized knowledge base, such as using descriptive titles, keeping pages concise, and linking related pages.

By mastering these page-building and organization techniques, you can transform your Confluence space into a well-structured, informative, and engaging knowledge hub that empowers your team to collaborate effectively and find the information they need effortlessly.

Using Templates and Blueprints

Outline

- What are Templates and Blueprints?
- Benefits of Using Templates and Blueprints
- Types of Templates and Blueprints in Confluence
- Creating and Customizing Templates
- Working with Blueprints
- Chapter Summary

What are Templates and Blueprints?

In the world of Confluence, templates and blueprints are your secret weapons for efficient and standardized content creation. They serve as pre-designed frameworks that streamline the process of building pages, ensuring consistency across your documentation, and saving you valuable time and effort.

Templates: Your Page's Starting Point

Think of templates as the foundation of your Confluence page. They provide a pre-built structure, complete with layout, formatting, and often even placeholder content. Instead of starting with a blank page, you can choose a template that aligns with the type of content you want to create, such as meeting notes, project plans, or how-to guides. This gives you a head start and eliminates the need to reinvent the wheel each time you create a new page.

Blueprints: Your Step-by-Step Guide

Blueprints take the concept of templates a step further. They not only provide a pre-designed structure but also guide you through a structured process for creating specific types of content. For instance, a project plan blueprint might prompt you to define project goals, timelines, deliverables, and responsibilities, ensuring that you don't miss any crucial details. This step-by-step approach not only streamlines content creation but also helps ensure that your pages are complete, accurate, and consistent with your team's standards.

Streamlining Content Creation and Ensuring Consistency

Both templates and blueprints share a common goal: to make content creation easier and more efficient. By providing a pre-defined structure, they eliminate the guesswork and allow you to focus on the actual content itself. They also help maintain consistency across your documentation, ensuring that all pages of a similar type follow the same format and style. This consistency makes it easier for users to navigate your Confluence space and find the information they need.

Imagine you're building a house. Templates are like prefabricated walls and floors that give you a head start, while blueprints are the detailed instructions that guide you through the entire construction process, ensuring that the finished house is structurally sound and meets your expectations.

By utilizing templates and blueprints in Confluence, you can create high-quality, standardized content quickly and easily. This not only saves you time but also improves the overall usability and effectiveness of your knowledge base.

Benefits of Using Templates and Blueprints

Templates and blueprints are not merely convenient shortcuts; they are powerful tools that can significantly enhance your team's collaboration and knowledge management in Confluence. Let's explore the key benefits they bring to the table:

1. **Standardization:**
   One of the primary advantages of templates and blueprints is their ability to enforce standardization across your documentation. When everyone uses the same template or blueprint for a specific type of content, it ensures consistency in structure, formatting, and information inclusion. This consistency makes your documentation more professional, easier to read and navigate, and less prone to errors or omissions.
2. **Efficiency:**
   Time is a valuable resource, and templates and blueprints are your time-saving allies. By providing a pre-built framework, they eliminate the need to start from scratch every time you create a new page. This significantly reduces the time and effort required for content creation, allowing you to focus on the actual information you need to convey.
3. **Improved Quality:**
   Templates and blueprints are designed with best practices in mind. They include essential sections, headings, and prompts that guide you through the content creation process. This ensures that you don't miss any crucial information and that your content is well-organized and logically structured. The result is higher quality documentation that is more informative and useful for your team.
4. **Reduced Errors:**
   Humans are prone to errors, especially when creating complex documents. Templates and blueprints minimize the risk of mistakes or omissions by providing a structured framework and guiding users through each step. They can include checklists, reminders, and even automated validation checks to ensure that all necessary information is captured and that the content adheres to your team's standards.
5. **Knowledge Sharing:**
   Templates and blueprints can encapsulate your team's collective knowledge and best practices. By using them, you ensure that this valuable information is not lost or forgotten. New team members can quickly learn how to create specific types of content, and existing team members can benefit from the accumulated wisdom embedded in the templates.

In summary, templates and blueprints are more than just pre-designed layouts; they are strategic tools for enhancing efficiency, quality, consistency, and knowledge sharing within your Confluence environment. By incorporating them into your workflow, you can empower your team to create better documentation, faster and with fewer errors.

Types of Templates and Blueprints in Confluence

Confluence offers a rich collection of templates and blueprints designed to cater to a wide range of use cases. These pre-built structures provide a solid foundation for your content, saving you time and effort while ensuring consistency and quality. Here are some of the most commonly used templates and blueprints:

- **Meeting Notes:** These templates are essential for documenting meetings efficiently. They typically include sections for the meeting agenda, attendees, discussion points, decisions made, action items, and next steps. By using a meeting notes template, you can ensure that all relevant information is captured and easily accessible for future reference.
- **Project Plans:** Project plan blueprints guide you through the process of creating a comprehensive plan for your project. They prompt you to define project goals, objectives, timelines, milestones, deliverables, resources, and risks. This structured approach helps ensure that you consider all aspects of your project and create a realistic plan for success.
- **Product Requirements:** These templates are invaluable for product managers and development teams. They help you document product features, user stories, acceptance criteria, and other

requirements in a clear and organized manner. This ensures that everyone involved in the project has a shared understanding of what needs to be built.
- **Knowledge Base Articles:** Knowledge base blueprints are designed to help you create informative and easy-to-follow guides, tutorials, and FAQs. They typically include sections for the purpose of the article, step-by-step instructions, troubleshooting tips, and related resources. By using a knowledge base blueprint, you can create high-quality documentation that empowers your users to find answers and solve problems on their own.
- **Decision Templates:** These templates provide a structured format for documenting decisions, their rationale, and potential impacts. They typically include sections for the problem statement, decision options, pros and cons, the final decision, and the next steps. Decision templates ensure that decisions are made thoughtfully and transparently, with all relevant information documented for future reference.
- **Status Reports:** Status report templates help you summarize the progress of your project, highlight achievements, and identify risks. They typically include sections for project overview, current status, completed tasks, upcoming tasks, risks and issues, and next steps. By using a status report template, you can keep stakeholders informed about the project's health and progress.

These are just a few examples of the many templates and blueprints available in Confluence. The platform also offers templates for marketing plans, release notes, product launch plans, and many other types of content. You can also find templates on the Atlassian Marketplace or create your own custom templates to meet your specific needs.

Creating and Customizing Templates

Confluence offers multiple avenues for creating and customizing templates, allowing you to tailor them precisely to your team's requirements. Whether you prefer to build from scratch, repurpose existing content, or leverage pre-built resources, Confluence provides the tools to make it happen.

Create from Scratch

For complete control over your template's structure and content, you can start with a blank page:

1. **Create a New Page:** Navigate to the desired space and click the "Create" button.
2. **Choose "Blank page":** Select the blank page option.
3. **Build Your Template:** Use the rich text editor to add text, headings, tables, images, and other content elements. Structure the page according to the layout you want for your template.
4. **Save as Template:** Once you've completed the design, click the "..." (more options) button and choose "Save as template."
5. **Name and Describe:** Give your template a clear and descriptive name, along with a brief description of its purpose.
6. **Save:** Click "Save" to add the template to your space's template library.

Use Existing Pages

If you have a well-structured page that could serve as a template, you can convert it directly:

1. **Open the Page:** Navigate to the page you want to convert.
2. **Save as Template:** Click the "..." (more options) button and choose "Save as template."
3. **Name and Describe:** Provide a suitable name and description for the template.
4. **Save:** Click "Save" to add the converted page to your template library.

Import Templates

Confluence boasts a vast library of pre-built templates you can import:

1. **Browse Templates:** Click the "Templates" option in the "Create" menu or the space dashboard.
2. **Select a Template:** Choose a template that aligns with your needs from the available categories.
3. **Customize:** Modify the imported template to match your specific requirements.

You can also import templates from external sources, such as files exported from other Confluence instances or custom-built templates.

Customizing Templates

Regardless of how you create your template, Confluence offers extensive customization options:

- **Add or Remove Content:** Modify the template by adding new sections, headings, or text. Remove any unnecessary elements.
- **Modify Formatting:** Change fonts, colors, and styles to match your branding or preferences.
- **Incorporate Macros:** Enhance your template's functionality with macros. For example, use the "Table of Contents" macro to automatically generate a table of contents, or the "Jira Issues" macro to display a list of related JIRA issues.

By creating and customizing templates, you empower your team to produce standardized, high-quality content quickly and easily. This not only saves time but also ensures that your documentation is consistent, professional, and user-friendly.

Working with Blueprints

Blueprints in Confluence elevate content creation by providing a structured, step-by-step approach to crafting specific types of documents. They act as interactive guides, prompting you for essential information and ensuring you don't miss any critical details.

Choosing a Blueprint

1. **Access Blueprints:** Click the "Create" button or the "+" icon in the top navigation bar and select "Page." Then, choose the "Blueprints" tab.
2. **Select a Blueprint:** Browse through the available blueprints and select the one that aligns with the type of content you want to create. Confluence offers blueprints for various purposes, such as project plans, meeting notes, knowledge base articles, and more.

Following the Blueprint

Once you've selected a blueprint, it will guide you through a series of steps:

1. **Answer Prompts:** The blueprint will ask you a series of questions related to the content you're creating. For example, a project plan blueprint might ask for the project name, goals, timelines, and deliverables.
2. **Fill in Information:** Provide the requested information in the designated fields. You can often include rich text, images, tables, and other multimedia elements.
3. **Follow Instructions:** The blueprint might offer additional instructions or tips to help you create comprehensive and well-structured content.

Reviewing and Publishing

After completing all the steps, the blueprint will generate a draft page based on your input.

1. **Review Content:** Carefully review the generated content to ensure it's accurate and complete. Make any necessary edits or additions.
2. **Publish Page:** Once you're satisfied with the content, click the "Publish" button to make the page live in your Confluence space.

Benefits of Blueprints

Using blueprints offers several advantages:

- **Structure and Guidance:** They provide a clear framework and step-by-step instructions, ensuring that your content is well-organized and comprehensive.
- **Time-Saving:** They automate the process of creating a basic structure, saving you time and effort.
- **Consistency:** They ensure that all pages created with the same blueprint follow a consistent format, making your knowledge base more user-friendly.
- **Knowledge Capture:** Blueprints can help capture and share knowledge within your team by incorporating best practices and standard procedures.

By leveraging blueprints, you can create high-quality content quickly and easily, even for complex documents. This empowers your team to document their work efficiently, share knowledge effectively, and collaborate seamlessly in Confluence.

Chapter Summary

In this chapter, we delved into the power of templates and blueprints in Confluence, highlighting their role in streamlining content creation and ensuring consistency throughout your knowledge base. We began by defining templates as pre-designed page layouts and blueprints as interactive guides for creating specific content types. We then explored the benefits of using these tools, emphasizing their ability to standardize formats, improve efficiency, enhance quality, reduce errors, and facilitate knowledge sharing.

Furthermore, we showcased various types of templates and blueprints commonly used in Confluence, including meeting notes, project plans, product requirements, knowledge base articles, decision templates, and status reports. We also provided step-by-step instructions on creating and customizing templates, offering options to start from scratch, convert existing pages, or import from Confluence's template library or external sources.

Lastly, we illustrated how to work with blueprints, outlining the process of choosing a blueprint, following its instructions, and reviewing and publishing the generated content. By mastering these tools and techniques, you can unlock a new level of efficiency and organization within your Confluence space, making it a valuable resource for your team's collaboration and knowledge management endeavors.

Collaborating with Team Members

Outline

- Real-Time Collaboration in Confluence
- Commenting and Annotations
- Tasks and Mentions
- Collaborative Editing
- Version History and Page Comparison
- Confluence Integrations for Collaboration
- Chapter Summary

Real-Time Collaboration in Confluence

In the realm of collaborative work, time is often of the essence. Confluence understands this and offers a powerful real-time collaboration feature that empowers multiple users to work together on the same page simultaneously, fostering efficiency and synergy within teams.

Imagine a team of content creators brainstorming ideas for a marketing campaign. With Confluence's real-time collaboration, they can all access the same page simultaneously, contribute their thoughts, build upon each other's ideas, and refine the campaign strategy in real time. There's no need to send files back and forth, wait for updates, or consolidate different versions.

How Real-Time Collaboration Works

When multiple users are editing the same page in Confluence, their changes are instantly visible to everyone else. You can see who else is on the page and where they are currently editing. This creates a sense of shared presence and allows for immediate feedback and discussion.

Confluence also handles simultaneous edits intelligently. If two people are editing the same paragraph at the same time, Confluence will create separate versions of the paragraph and present you with options to resolve the conflict. You can choose to accept one version, merge the changes, or manually edit the conflicting content.

Benefits of Real-Time Collaboration

Real-time collaboration in Confluence offers a multitude of benefits for teams:

- **Faster Decision-Making:** By enabling real-time discussions and feedback, decisions can be made faster and more effectively.
- **Improved Communication:** Team members can easily communicate and clarify their ideas, reducing misunderstandings and improving the overall quality of the work.
- **Increased Productivity:** Eliminating the need for back-and-forth communication and version control, real-time collaboration streamlines the content creation process and boosts productivity.
- **Enhanced Collaboration:** Real-time collaboration fosters a more collaborative and inclusive environment, where everyone can contribute their expertise and ideas.

By harnessing the power of real-time collaboration in Confluence, teams can work together more effectively, break down silos, and accelerate their progress toward shared goals.

Commenting and Annotations

Confluence's commenting and annotation features are powerful tools for fostering collaboration and providing feedback on documents. They allow team members to engage in discussions, ask questions, provide suggestions, and share their insights directly within the context of the content.

Commenting

Commenting is the cornerstone of collaborative feedback in Confluence. It enables users to leave comments on specific sections or paragraphs within a page. Comments can be used for various purposes, such as:

- **Providing feedback:** Offer suggestions, express opinions, or share constructive criticism on the content.
- **Asking questions:** Seek clarification on specific points or request additional information.
- **Engaging in discussions:** Discuss ideas, brainstorm solutions, or debate different viewpoints.

To add a comment, simply highlight the relevant text or section and click the "Comment" button that appears. You can then type your message in the comment box and click "Save."

Inline Comments

Inline comments are a specialized type of comment that allows you to provide feedback on specific words or phrases within a text. This is especially useful for highlighting typos, grammatical errors, or suggesting alternative wording. To add an inline comment, highlight the desired text and click the "Comment" button. The comment will appear directly next to the highlighted text.

Resolving Comments

Once a comment has been addressed or is no longer relevant, you can mark it as resolved. This helps declutter the page and indicates that the feedback has been taken into account. To resolve a comment, click the "Resolve" button next to the comment. Resolved comments are hidden by default but can be viewed by clicking the "Show resolved comments" link.

Threaded Conversations

Confluence supports threaded conversations within the comments section. This means you can reply to specific comments, creating a nested structure of discussions. This helps keep conversations organized and focused, making it easier to follow the flow of feedback and ideas.

By actively utilizing commenting and annotation features, you can foster a collaborative environment where team members can easily share their thoughts, provide feedback, and engage in meaningful discussions around your Confluence content. This not only improves the quality of your documentation but also strengthens communication and collaboration within your team.

Tasks and Mentions

Confluence's task and mention features add a layer of actionability and accountability to your collaborative efforts. They allow you to assign specific actions to team members, track their progress, and ensure everyone is aware of their responsibilities.

Tasks

Tasks are a powerful tool for delegating work and ensuring that action items don't get lost in the shuffle. You can create a task directly within a Confluence page, assigning it to a specific user and setting a due date. This turns a discussion or idea into a concrete action that someone is responsible for completing.

To create a task in Confluence:

1. Highlight the text or paragraph you want to turn into a task.
2. Click the "•••" (more actions) button that appears.
3. Select "Create task."
4. Fill in the task details, including the assignee and due date.
5. Click "Create" to save the task.

The assignee will receive a notification about the task, and it will appear in their JIRA task list. You can track the progress of tasks and mark them as complete when they are finished.

Mentions

Mentions are another handy feature for collaboration in Confluence. When you mention a user in a comment or task, they receive a notification, ensuring they are aware of the discussion or action required. This is particularly useful for drawing someone's attention to a specific question, request, or update.

To mention a user, simply type the "@" symbol followed by their name or username. Confluence will automatically suggest matching users as you type. Once you've selected the correct user, their name will be highlighted in the comment or task.

Benefits of Tasks and Mentions

By utilizing tasks and mentions, you can:

- **Increase Accountability:** Clearly assign responsibilities and track progress on action items.
- **Improve Communication:** Ensure that relevant team members are aware of discussions and tasks that require their attention.
- **Streamline Collaboration:** Facilitate a more efficient and organized workflow by directly assigning tasks and notifying stakeholders within the context of the Confluence page.

By incorporating tasks and mentions into your Confluence workflow, you can transform your pages into dynamic collaborative spaces where ideas are not only shared but also acted upon.

Collaborative Editing

Collaborative editing in Confluence enables seamless teamwork by allowing multiple users to work on the same page simultaneously. This real-time collaboration feature eliminates the need for version control hassles and promotes a more efficient and interactive editing experience.

Real-Time Updates

When multiple users are editing a Confluence page concurrently, their changes are instantly visible to everyone else. As you type, others on the page will see your additions and edits in real-time, just like a Google Doc. This instant feedback loop facilitates faster communication and ensures everyone is working from the latest version of the document.

Conflict Resolution

Confluence is designed to handle conflicts gracefully when multiple users edit the same section simultaneously. If two users modify the same paragraph or sentence at the same time, Confluence will create separate versions of the content and present you with options to resolve the conflict:

- **Accept One Version:** You can choose to accept either your version or the other user's version, discarding the other.
- **Merge Changes:** Confluence can often automatically merge changes if they don't directly conflict. For example, if one user adds a sentence and another user adds a different sentence in the same paragraph, Confluence can usually combine them seamlessly.

- **Manual Resolution:** If the changes are too complex to be automatically merged, Confluence will highlight the conflicting sections, allowing you to manually edit and resolve the conflict.

Additional Collaborative Editing Features

In addition to real-time updates and conflict resolution, Confluence offers other features that enhance collaborative editing:

- **Presence Indicators:** Confluence shows you who else is currently viewing or editing the page, along with their cursor position. This helps you coordinate your editing efforts and avoid accidentally overwriting each other's work.
- **Revision History:** Confluence keeps a detailed record of every change made to a page, including who made the change and when. This allows you to track the evolution of the document and revert to previous versions if needed.

By leveraging collaborative editing, your team can work together seamlessly on Confluence pages, promoting communication, accelerating decision-making, and ultimately improving the quality and efficiency of your documentation.

Version History and Page Comparison

Collaboration often involves making changes, revising ideas, and refining content. In this iterative process, it's crucial to have a way to track the evolution of your work and compare different versions. Confluence's version history and page comparison features provide this functionality, enabling your team to:

- **Maintain a Record of Changes:** Confluence automatically tracks every change made to a page, including the author, date, and time of each edit. This creates a comprehensive history of the page's development, allowing you to see how it has evolved over time.
- **Revert to Previous Versions:** If you make a mistake or need to undo changes, you can easily revert to a previous version of the page. This ensures that you can always recover from accidental deletions or unwanted modifications.
- **Track Individual Contributions:** Version history shows you who made each change, making it easy to identify individual contributions and track accountability.
- **Compare Changes:** The page comparison feature allows you to visually compare two different versions of a page side by side. This highlights the differences between the versions, making it easy to see what has been added, deleted, or modified.

Version History

To view a page's version history:

1. **Open the Page:** Go to the page you want to view the history of.
2. **Click "Page History":** Look for the "Page History" button in the page tools menu (usually located in the top right corner).
3. **Browse Versions:** You'll see a list of all the page's versions, with the most recent version at the top. Click on a version to view it.
4. **Restore a Version (Optional):** If you want to revert to a previous version, click the "Restore" button next to the desired version.

Page Comparison

To compare two versions of a page:

1. **Open Page History:** Go to the page's history as described above.

2. **Select Versions:** Select the two versions you want to compare by checking the boxes next to them.
3. **Click "Compare":** Click the "Compare" button to see the differences between the two versions. Confluence will highlight the changes, showing added content in green, deleted content in red, and modified content in blue.

Benefits of Version History and Page Comparison

- **Collaboration:** By tracking changes and comparing versions, team members can easily collaborate and understand the evolution of a document.
- **Error Recovery:** If mistakes are made, you can quickly revert to a previous version, ensuring data integrity.
- **Accountability:** Version history shows who made each change, promoting accountability and transparency.
- **Decision Tracking:** You can track the evolution of decisions and understand why certain changes were made.

By utilizing these features, you can leverage the power of collaboration while ensuring that your content remains accurate, reliable, and traceable.

Confluence Integrations for Collaboration

Confluence, in its essence, is a collaboration hub. However, its integration capabilities extend its collaborative power by seamlessly connecting it with other tools your team uses daily. This amplifies your team's efficiency and productivity, making collaboration more fluid and contextual.

Slack/Microsoft Teams Integration

By integrating Confluence with popular communication platforms like Slack or Microsoft Teams, you bring collaborative knowledge sharing directly into your team's conversations. This integration allows you to:

- **Receive Confluence Notifications:** Get real-time updates in your Slack channels or Microsoft Teams about page changes, new comments, mentions, or when someone shares a page with you.
- **Share and Preview Pages:** Easily share Confluence pages with your team members directly within Slack or Teams. The integration often provides a preview of the page content, allowing for quick reference without leaving the communication platform.
- **Collaborate on Documents:** Start discussions and provide feedback on Confluence pages within Slack or Teams, streamlining the review and approval process.
- **Search Confluence:** Find relevant Confluence pages directly from Slack or Teams using the integrated search functionality.

This integration bridges the gap between communication and knowledge sharing, ensuring that important information is readily accessible and discussions happen in the right context.

JIRA Integration

The integration between Confluence and JIRA is a powerful combination for Agile teams. By linking Confluence pages to JIRA issues, you create a seamless connection between project management and documentation. This integration enables:

- **Contextual Information:** Link relevant Confluence pages, such as product requirements or technical specifications, to JIRA issues. This provides developers with the necessary context and information to understand and complete tasks effectively.
- **Traceability:** Track the relationship between JIRA issues and Confluence pages, making it easy to see how decisions were made and how requirements evolved.

- **Collaborative Documentation:** Team members can collaborate on Confluence pages associated with JIRA issues, providing feedback, asking questions, and sharing insights.
- **Automated Updates:** You can set up automation rules to update Confluence pages based on JIRA issue transitions, ensuring that documentation stays in sync with the project's progress.

By integrating Confluence with JIRA, you bridge the gap between project management and knowledge sharing, creating a more cohesive and efficient workflow. This powerful combination enhances transparency, traceability, and collaboration, ultimately leading to better project outcomes.

Chapter Summary

In this chapter, we explored how Confluence fosters collaboration through its diverse features and integrations. We started by examining how real-time collaboration empowers teams to work on the same page simultaneously, enhancing efficiency and communication. Then we delved into commenting and annotations, discussing how these features facilitate feedback, discussions, and idea exchange directly within the context of the content.

Furthermore, we explored how tasks and mentions add a layer of actionability and accountability to collaboration, ensuring that responsibilities are assigned and progress is tracked. We also discussed the collaborative editing capabilities of Confluence, highlighting real-time updates and conflict resolution mechanisms. Additionally, we emphasized the importance of version history and page comparison for tracking changes and ensuring data integrity.

Lastly, we highlighted how Confluence integrations with tools like Slack, Microsoft Teams, and JIRA elevate collaboration to new heights. These integrations bring notifications, document sharing, and discussions into your preferred communication platforms, while the JIRA integration connects project management with documentation, fostering a seamless and transparent workflow.

By understanding and utilizing these collaborative features and integrations, you can unlock the full potential of Confluence as a powerful platform for teamwork and knowledge sharing, ultimately driving your projects towards success.

Section G:
Confluence Administration and Advanced Features

User and Permissions Management in Confluence

Outline

- Introduction to User and Permission Management in Confluence
- User Management in Confluence
- Permission Management in Confluence
- Best Practices for User and Permission Management
- Chapter Summary

Introduction to User and Permission Management in Confluence

In Confluence, safeguarding your valuable content while fostering a collaborative environment is paramount. This is where user and permission management comes into play. It serves as the gatekeeper of your knowledge base, ensuring that the right individuals have the right level of access to information and tools.

By effectively managing users and permissions, you can:

- **Protect sensitive information:** Prevent unauthorized access to confidential or proprietary content.
- **Facilitate collaboration:** Enable team members to contribute and share knowledge effectively.
- **Maintain data integrity:** Prevent accidental or malicious modifications or deletions of important documents.
- **Streamline workflows:** Ensure that users have the necessary access to complete their tasks without unnecessary hurdles.

User and permission management in Confluence encompasses several key aspects:

- **Adding and Managing Users:** This involves creating user accounts, organizing users into groups, and maintaining user profiles. It's essential to keep user information up-to-date and deactivate or remove accounts for users who no longer need access.
- **Assigning Permissions:** This involves granting or restricting access to specific spaces and pages based on user roles and responsibilities. Confluence offers different levels of permissions, ranging from view-only access to full administrative control.
- **Defining Access Levels:** You can fine-tune access by setting permissions at different levels: global (for the entire Confluence instance), space-level (for specific spaces), and page-level (for individual pages). This allows you to create a granular permission structure that aligns with your organization's needs.

By mastering user and permission management in Confluence, you can create a secure and collaborative environment where information is protected, and knowledge sharing is encouraged. This empowers your teams to work together efficiently, ensuring the success of your projects and initiatives. In the following sections, we'll delve deeper into the details of managing users, permissions, and access levels in Confluence.

User Management in Confluence

Effectively managing users in Confluence is essential for maintaining a well-organized and secure collaborative environment. Let's explore the various aspects of user management within Confluence.

Adding Users

There are two primary methods for adding users to Confluence:

1. **Manually Adding Users:**
    - Navigate to the "User Management" section in the Confluence administration console.
    - Click on the "Add users" button.
    - Enter the user's full name and email address (which will serve as their username).
    - Optionally, you can add the user to relevant groups and assign them permissions at this stage.
    - Click "Add" to create the new user account.
2. **Bulk Import of Users:**
    - If you have a large number of users to add, bulk import can save you time.
    - Prepare a CSV file with the required user information (name, email, groups).
    - In the "User Management" section, click on the "Bulk User Management" tab.
    - Select "Import users from CSV" and upload your file.
    - Follow the instructions to map the fields and complete the import process.

Editing User Profiles

To modify a user's details or preferences:

1. Go to the "User Management" section.
2. Search for and select the user you want to edit.
3. Click on the "Edit profile" button.
4. Modify the desired fields, such as the user's name, email address, or profile picture.
5. Click "Update" to save the changes.

Managing User Groups

User groups in Confluence help you organize users and streamline permission management. You can create groups based on teams, departments, or roles, and then assign permissions to the group rather than individual users.

- To create a new group, go to the "Groups" tab in the User Management section and click "Create group."
- To add or remove users from a group, search for the group and use the "Add members" or "Remove members" functions.

Deactivating and Reactivating Users

If a user is no longer active, you can deactivate their account:

1. Go to the "User Management" section.
2. Locate the user and click the "Deactivate" button.
3. Confirm the deactivation. The user will lose access to Confluence, but their content and data will be preserved.

To reactivate a deactivated user, follow the same steps and click the "Reactivate" button.

Deleting Users

Deleting a user account should be a last resort, as it permanently removes the user's profile, contributions, and history from Confluence. Before deleting a user, consider exporting their content or transferring ownership of their pages.

1. Go to the "User Management" section.
2. Locate the user and click the "Delete" button.
3. Confirm the deletion. This action is irreversible.

By implementing these user management practices, you can ensure that your Confluence environment is well-organized, secure, and conducive to collaboration.

Permission Management in Confluence

In Confluence, permissions act as the gatekeepers, determining who can access what content and what actions they can perform within the platform. Confluence offers a hierarchical permission structure, ranging from global permissions that apply to the entire instance to more granular permissions at the space and page levels. Understanding these different permission levels is crucial for maintaining a secure and collaborative environment.

Global Permissions

Global permissions are the highest level of permissions in Confluence. They apply to all spaces within the Confluence instance, regardless of individual space settings. These permissions are typically granted to system administrators or users with elevated privileges.

The default groups that come with global permissions are:

- **confluence-administrators:** This group has full administrative access to Confluence. They can manage users, groups, global permissions, system settings, and all content across the instance.
- **confluence-users:** This group includes all authenticated users in Confluence. They have basic permissions to view and create content, but their access to specific spaces or pages may be further restricted by space-level or page-level permissions.

Managing Global Permissions

To manage global permissions in Confluence:

1. Navigate to the "Administration" console.
2. Go to the "Global Permissions" section.
3. Here, you'll see a list of all the global permissions available, along with the groups or users who have been granted those permissions.
4. To modify global permissions, click the "Edit Permissions" button next to the desired permission.
5. You can then add or remove users or groups from the permission, effectively granting or revoking their access.

It's important to exercise caution when modifying global permissions, as they can have a significant impact on the entire Confluence instance. Ensure that you thoroughly understand the implications of each permission before making any changes.

Next, we'll delve into space-level permissions, which offer a more granular way to control access to specific spaces within your Confluence instance.

Space Permissions

Space permissions in Confluence determine who can access and perform actions within a specific space and its content. They offer a more granular level of control compared to global permissions, allowing you to tailor access for individual spaces based on the needs of your teams or projects.

There are three main permission levels for spaces:

- **View:** Users with this permission can see the space and its contents but cannot edit or modify anything. This is ideal for stakeholders who need to be informed but not actively contribute.
- **Edit:** Users with this permission can view and modify the space and its contents, including creating and editing pages. This is typically granted to team members actively working on projects or contributing to documentation.
- **Administer:** Users with this permission have full control over the space. They can manage users and permissions, configure space settings (like themes or restrictions), and perform other administrative tasks. This level is usually reserved for space administrators or project leads.

Managing Space Permissions

To add or remove users and groups from a space and assign permission levels:

1. **Access Space Permissions:** Navigate to the space you want to manage. Click the "Space tools" menu (usually a gear icon) in the sidebar and select "Permissions."
2. **Add or Remove Users/Groups:**
    - Click the "Add people or groups" button.
    - Start typing the name of the user or group you want to add. Confluence will suggest matching results.
    - Select the desired user or group and click "Add."
    - To remove a user or group, click the "x" next to their name.
3. **Assign Permission Levels:**
    - Once a user or group is added, you'll see a dropdown menu next to their name.
    - Select the appropriate permission level: "View," "Edit," or "Administer."
    - If you have custom permission schemes, you might see additional roles or permissions.
4. **Save Changes:** Click the "Save" button to apply your changes.

Remember, you can also set more specific page restrictions to control access at the individual page level, which will be discussed in a later section.

Page Restrictions

While space permissions govern access to an entire space, page restrictions offer a more granular level of control. They allow you to define specific access rules for individual pages within a space. This is particularly useful when you have sensitive information that only a subset of users should be able to see or edit.

For instance, you might have a space for project documentation that is generally accessible to the entire team. However, there might be a confidential budget document within that space that should only be viewed by the project manager and finance team. In such a scenario, you can apply page restrictions to the budget document, ensuring that only authorized personnel can access it.

How to Restrict Page Access

To restrict page access, follow these steps:

1. **Open the Page:** Navigate to the page you want to restrict.

2. **Click "Restrictions":** In the page tools menu (usually located in the top right corner), click on "Restrictions." This will open the page restrictions dialog.
3. **Add Restrictions:** Click the "Add restrictions" button.
4. **Select Users or Groups:** Choose the specific users or groups that you want to grant or restrict access to the page. You can also use predefined groups like "Space Administrators" or "Logged-in Users."
5. **Choose Permission Level:** Select the desired permission level for each user or group. You can typically choose between "View," "Edit," or "No Access."
6. **Save Restrictions:** Click "Apply" to save the page restrictions.

The restricted page will now only be accessible to the users or groups you've specified with the corresponding permission levels. Other users will either be denied access or see a message indicating that the page is restricted.

Key Considerations

When applying page restrictions, keep in mind the following:

- **Page Hierarchy:** Page restrictions are inherited by child pages. This means that if you restrict access to a parent page, all its child pages will also be restricted.
- **Space Permissions:** Page restrictions override space permissions. If a user has "View" permission for the space but "No Access" restriction for a specific page, they won't be able to view that page.
- **Exceptions:** You can create exceptions to page restrictions for specific users or groups. This allows you to grant access to certain individuals even if they don't belong to the groups with the required permissions.

By utilizing page restrictions effectively, you can ensure that your sensitive content remains confidential while still promoting collaboration and knowledge sharing within your Confluence space.

Best Practices for User and Permission Management

Effective user and permission management in Confluence is an ongoing process that requires careful planning and continuous attention. By following these best practices, you can create a secure, collaborative, and efficient environment for your team:

1. **Plan Your Permission Structure:** Before creating users or assigning permissions, take the time to map out your organization's hierarchy and project requirements. Identify the different roles within your organization and the types of access each role needs. This will help you create a clear and logical permission structure that is easy to understand and manage.
2. **Use Groups for Efficiency:** Groups are a powerful tool for managing permissions in Confluence. By organizing users into groups, you can assign permissions to entire groups rather than individual users, saving you time and effort. For example, you could create groups for different teams, departments, or roles and then assign permissions accordingly.
3. **Apply the Principle of Least Privilege:** This fundamental security principle states that users should only be granted the minimum permissions necessary to fulfill their roles. Avoid giving users excessive permissions, as this can increase the risk of accidental or intentional misuse of Confluence. Regularly review user permissions and revoke any unnecessary access.
4. **Regularly Review Permissions:** People's roles and responsibilities change over time, so it's crucial to review and update permissions regularly. Conduct periodic audits of your user accounts and groups to ensure that everyone has the appropriate access levels. This helps maintain security and prevents unauthorized access to sensitive information.
5. **Document Your Processes:** Create clear and concise documentation that outlines your user and permission management procedures. This should include instructions on how to create and manage user accounts, assign permissions, create and manage groups, and handle deactivation

and deletion of users. This documentation will be invaluable for new administrators and will help maintain consistency in your permission management practices.

By following these best practices, you can create a well-structured and secure Confluence environment that promotes collaboration and knowledge sharing while protecting sensitive information. Remember, user and permission management is an ongoing process that requires continuous attention to ensure the optimal functioning of your Confluence instance.

Chapter Summary

In this chapter, we delved into the intricacies of user and permission management in Confluence, a critical aspect of ensuring a secure and collaborative knowledge-sharing environment. We emphasized the importance of controlling access to content to protect sensitive information, facilitate collaboration, maintain data integrity, and streamline workflows.

The chapter provided a comprehensive guide on user management, encompassing adding new users, editing user profiles, managing user groups, deactivating or reactivating users, and deleting users when necessary. We also explored the various permission levels in Confluence, including global permissions, space permissions, and page restrictions. Understanding these permissions is crucial for controlling access to content at different levels, from the entire Confluence instance to individual pages.

Finally, we outlined best practices for user and permission management, including planning a clear permission structure, utilizing groups for efficiency, applying the principle of least privilege, regularly reviewing permissions, and documenting processes. By adhering to these best practices, you can establish a robust and scalable user and permission management system that fosters collaboration while safeguarding your valuable knowledge base in Confluence.

Integrating Confluence with JIRA

Outline

- The Power of JIRA and Confluence Integration
- Methods for Integrating JIRA with Confluence
- Linking JIRA Issues to Confluence Pages
- Displaying JIRA Information in Confluence
- Using Confluence Macros for JIRA
- Best Practices for JIRA and Confluence Integration
- Chapter Summary

The Power of JIRA and Confluence Integration

Integrating JIRA and Confluence creates a powerful synergy that elevates both project management and knowledge sharing. While JIRA excels at tracking tasks, issues, and project progress, Confluence provides a collaborative workspace for documentation, knowledge management, and team communication. By integrating these two platforms, you bridge the gap between action and information, creating a more cohesive and efficient workflow.

This integration transforms the way teams work together by:

- **Providing Context for Development Tasks:** By linking JIRA issues to Confluence pages, developers gain immediate access to relevant documentation, requirements, and specifications. This eliminates the need to search for information in disparate locations, saving time and reducing context switching.
- **Tracking Decisions and Rationale:** Confluence pages can be used to document decisions, discussions, and the rationale behind them. By linking these pages to JIRA issues, you create a traceable record of how decisions were made and how they impact the project.
- **Centralizing Project-Related Information:** Integrating JIRA and Confluence creates a central repository for all project-related information. Teams can easily access project plans, meeting notes, technical documentation, and other resources, fostering transparency and ensuring everyone is on the same page.
- **Improving Collaboration:** By linking JIRA issues to Confluence pages, team members can collaborate more effectively. They can comment on pages, ask questions, and provide feedback directly within the context of the relevant tasks, fostering better communication and knowledge sharing.

Consider a scenario where your team is developing a new software feature. The product manager creates a Confluence page outlining the requirements and acceptance criteria for the feature. Developers can then link this page to the corresponding JIRA issue, ensuring that they have a clear understanding of what needs to be built. As they work on the task, they can add comments to the Confluence page to ask questions, raise concerns, or share updates. This collaborative approach ensures that everyone is aligned on the requirements and that the final product meets the expectations of the stakeholders.

In essence, integrating JIRA and Confluence transforms these two individual tools into a unified platform for project management and collaboration. It creates a seamless flow of information, promotes transparency, and empowers teams to work together more effectively. In the following sections, we'll explore the different methods and tools available for integrating JIRA and Confluence, and how you can leverage them to maximize the benefits of this powerful integration.

Methods for Integrating JIRA with Confluence

JIRA and Confluence offer seamless integration through two primary methods: application links and Confluence macros. These methods enable you to connect your JIRA projects with your Confluence knowledge base, creating a unified platform for project management and documentation.

Application Links: The Foundation of Integration

Application links are the backbone of JIRA and Confluence integration. They establish a secure connection between your JIRA and Confluence instances, enabling them to communicate and share data. Once you've established an application link, you can:

- **Link JIRA issues to Confluence pages:** Embed JIRA issue keys or URLs in Confluence pages to provide context and traceability.
- **Display JIRA information in Confluence:** Use macros to embed JIRA charts, reports, and issue lists directly into Confluence pages.
- **Synchronize data between JIRA and Confluence:** Keep project information up-to-date by automatically syncing data between the two platforms.

To create an application link, you'll need administrator access to both your JIRA and Confluence instances. The process involves configuring the connection settings, authentication credentials, and data sharing options. Detailed instructions can be found in the Atlassian documentation.

Confluence Macros for JIRA: Enhancing Content with JIRA Data

Confluence macros are powerful tools that allow you to embed dynamic content from various sources, including JIRA, directly into your Confluence pages. JIRA-specific macros provide a convenient way to display relevant JIRA information within your documentation, such as:

- **Jira Issues Macro:** This macro allows you to display a list of JIRA issues based on JQL queries or project/filter selections.
- **Jira Chart Macro:** This macro enables you to embed charts from JIRA dashboards or reports directly into Confluence pages.
- **Jira Issue/Filter Macro:** This macro lets you display detailed information about a single JIRA issue or a filtered list of issues.
- **Jira Road Map Macro:** This macro displays a visual timeline of JIRA versions and associated issues, providing a roadmap for your project.

These macros offer a flexible and customizable way to integrate JIRA data into your Confluence pages, enhancing the context and relevance of your documentation.

By leveraging application links and Confluence macros, you can seamlessly integrate JIRA and Confluence, creating a unified platform where project management and knowledge sharing work in harmony.

Linking JIRA Issues to Confluence Pages

Linking JIRA issues to Confluence pages is a fundamental aspect of integrating these two platforms. It creates a bridge between your project management tasks and the documentation that supports them, providing valuable context and traceability. Confluence offers two primary methods for linking JIRA issues: direct linking and using macros.

Direct Linking

Direct linking is the simplest way to connect a JIRA issue to a Confluence page. You can do this by inserting the JIRA issue key or the full URL of the issue into your Confluence page.

1. **Issue Key:** Simply type the issue key (e.g., PROJ-123) directly into your Confluence page. Confluence will automatically recognize it as a JIRA issue link and format it accordingly.
2. **URL:** Copy the full URL of the JIRA issue and paste it into your Confluence page. Confluence will convert it into a clickable link.

Using Macros

Confluence macros offer a more sophisticated way to display JIRA information within your pages. The "Jira Issues" macro, in particular, is designed for this purpose. Here's how to use it:

1. **Insert Macro:**
   - Click the "+" icon in the Confluence editor toolbar and select "Jira Issue/Filter."
   - Alternatively, type "{" followed by "jira" to trigger the macro browser.
2. **Configure Macro:**
   - Choose whether to display a single issue or a filtered list of issues.
   - If displaying a single issue, enter the issue key.
   - If displaying a list of issues, construct a JQL query to filter the results or select a saved filter.
   - Customize the display options, such as columns to show and the number of results to display.
3. **Insert Macro:**
   - Click "Insert" to add the macro to your page.

The macro will then dynamically display the JIRA information within your Confluence page. You can also use other JIRA macros, such as the "Jira Chart" macro, to embed charts and graphs from JIRA dashboards into your Confluence pages.

By linking JIRA issues to Confluence pages, you create a seamless connection between your project management and documentation efforts. This enhances collaboration, improves traceability, and provides valuable context for your work.

Displaying JIRA Information in Confluence

In addition to linking to JIRA issues, Confluence allows you to embed JIRA information directly into your pages. This creates a dynamic and up-to-date view of your project data, enhancing the context and relevance of your documentation. Confluence offers several powerful macros for this purpose.

Jira Issues Macro

The Jira Issues macro is a versatile tool that enables you to display a list of JIRA issues on your Confluence page. You can filter the issues based on various criteria, such as project, issue type, status, assignee, or even a custom JQL query. This macro is particularly useful for:

- **Creating project status reports:** Show the current status of all open issues in a project.
- **Tracking team progress:** Display a list of tasks assigned to a specific team member.
- **Highlighting priority issues:** Show a list of high-priority bugs that need immediate attention.
- **Creating knowledge base articles:** Embed a list of related issues in a knowledge base article to provide additional context.

To use the Jira Issues macro:

1. **Insert Macro:** Type "/jira" in the Confluence editor and select the "Jira Issues" macro.
2. **Configure Macro:**

- **Choose your JIRA site:** Select the JIRA instance you want to connect to.
- **Choose display options:** Select how you want to filter the issues (by project, JQL query, etc.).
- **Customize display:** Choose the columns you want to display (e.g., issue key, summary, status, assignee).
3. **Insert Macro:** Click "Insert" to add the macro to your page.

Jira Chart Macro

The Jira Chart macro allows you to embed charts and graphs from your JIRA dashboards or reports directly into Confluence pages. This can be a powerful way to visualize project data and communicate progress to stakeholders.

To use the Jira Chart macro:

1. **Insert Macro:** Type "/jira" in the Confluence editor and select the "Jira Chart" macro.
2. **Configure Macro:**
   - **Choose your JIRA site:** Select the JIRA instance you want to connect to.
   - **Choose chart type:** Select the type of chart you want to embed (e.g., pie chart, bar chart, line chart).
   - **Configure chart data:** Choose the data source for the chart, such as a JIRA dashboard or a saved filter.
3. **Insert Macro:** Click "Insert" to add the macro to your page.

Jira Issue/Filter Macro

The Jira Issue/Filter macro provides a detailed view of a single JIRA issue or a filtered list of issues. It displays all the relevant information about the issue(s), including the summary, description, status, assignee, comments, and attachments. This is a great way to provide in-depth context within a Confluence page.

To use the Jira Issue/Filter macro:

1. **Insert Macro:** Type "/jira" in the Confluence editor and select the "Jira Issue/Filter" macro.
2. **Configure Macro:**
   - **Choose your JIRA site:** Select the JIRA instance you want to connect to.
   - **Enter issue key or filter:** Enter the issue key of a single issue or create a JQL query to filter the results.
   - **Customize display:** Choose which fields you want to display (e.g., summary, description, comments).
3. **Insert Macro:** Click "Insert" to add the macro to your page.

By incorporating these JIRA macros into your Confluence pages, you can create a more interactive and informative knowledge base, seamlessly integrating your project management data with your documentation and collaboration efforts.

Using Confluence Macros for JIRA

Confluence offers several other macros that can significantly enhance your JIRA integration and enrich your project documentation.

Jira Road Map Macro

The Jira Road Map macro is a visual powerhouse, providing a bird's-eye view of your project's timeline and progress. It displays a timeline of JIRA versions (or releases) and their associated issues, allowing you to track your project's evolution over time.

With the Jira Road Map macro, you can:

- **Visualize Release Schedules:** See the planned release dates for your JIRA versions and track their progress toward completion.
- **Identify Dependencies:** Easily spot dependencies between different versions or releases, helping you prioritize your work and avoid bottlenecks.
- **Communicate Progress:** Share your project roadmap with stakeholders to keep them informed about upcoming features and releases.
- **Track Issues:** See which issues are associated with each version or release, making it easy to understand the scope of each release and monitor its progress.

To use the Jira Road Map macro:

1. **Insert Macro:** Type "/jira" in the Confluence editor and select the "Jira Road Map" macro.
2. **Configure Macro:**
   - **Choose your JIRA site:** Select the JIRA instance you want to connect to.
   - **Choose project or filter:** Select the project or JQL filter to display in the roadmap.
   - **Customize display:** Choose which fields you want to display (e.g., version name, release date, issue summary).
3. **Insert Macro:** Click "Insert" to add the macro to your page.

Jira Report Blueprint

The Jira Report Blueprint is a powerful tool for creating comprehensive reports in Confluence based on JIRA data. It guides you through a step-by-step process to generate reports that aggregate and visualize data from your JIRA projects.

With the Jira Report Blueprint, you can:

- **Create Custom Reports:** Tailor reports to your specific needs, including charts, graphs, tables, and other visualizations.
- **Track Key Metrics:** Monitor project progress, team performance, and other important metrics.
- **Identify Trends and Patterns:** Analyze data over time to identify trends, bottlenecks, and areas for improvement.
- **Share Insights:** Share reports with stakeholders to keep them informed and facilitate data-driven decision-making.

To use the Jira Report Blueprint:

1. **Create a New Page:** Click the "Create" button or the "+" icon in the top navigation bar and select "Page."
2. **Choose "Jira Report":** Select the Jira Report blueprint from the list of available blueprints.
3. **Follow the Blueprint:** The blueprint will guide you through the process of selecting a JIRA project or filter, choosing the data you want to display, and customizing the report's layout and appearance.
4. **Publish Your Report:** Once you're satisfied with your report, click "Publish" to share it with your team or stakeholders.

By utilizing these additional JIRA macros, you can enhance your project documentation in Confluence with dynamic and informative visualizations of JIRA data. These macros provide a powerful way to communicate project progress, track key metrics, and foster data-driven decision-making.

Best Practices for JIRA and Confluence Integration

Integrating JIRA and Confluence can be a game-changer for your team's collaboration and productivity. However, to maximize the benefits of this integration, it's essential to follow some best practices:

1. **Establish Clear Links:**
   Always link JIRA issues to relevant Confluence pages and vice versa. This creates a bidirectional connection, allowing you to easily navigate between project tasks and their associated documentation. Use consistent linking practices, such as always linking from the JIRA issue to the Confluence page, to avoid confusion and maintain a clear information hierarchy.
2. **Use Labels and Categories:**
   Labels and categories are powerful tools for organizing and cross-referencing information in both JIRA and Confluence. Use them consistently to categorize issues and pages by project, team, topic, or any other relevant criteria. This makes it easier to find related information and ensures that everyone is working from the same context.
3. **Keep Information Up-to-date:**
   Stale information is of little value. Ensure that both your JIRA issues and Confluence pages are regularly updated to reflect the latest project developments. Encourage team members to update issue statuses, add comments, and revise documentation as needed. Consider setting up automatic updates to ensure that changes in one system are reflected in the other.
4. **Leverage Automation:**
   JIRA and Confluence offer powerful automation capabilities that can streamline your integration efforts. Explore options like automatically creating Confluence pages from JIRA issues or updating issue statuses based on page content. Automation can save you time, reduce manual effort, and ensure consistency across your project data.
5. **Use the Right Macro for the Right Job:**
   Confluence offers a variety of JIRA macros, each designed for a specific purpose. Choose the appropriate macro based on the type of information you want to display. For example:
   - **Jira Issues Macro:** To display a list of JIRA issues.
   - **Jira Chart Macro:** To embed charts and graphs from JIRA.
   - **Jira Issue/Filter Macro:** To show details of a single issue or a filtered list.
   - **Jira Road Map Macro:** To visualize project timelines and releases.

By following these best practices, you can ensure that your JIRA and Confluence integration is seamless, efficient, and delivers maximum value to your team. It's a powerful combination that can revolutionize the way you manage projects, document knowledge, and collaborate with your team members.

Chapter Summary

In this chapter, we delved into the power of integrating JIRA and Confluence, two cornerstone tools in the Atlassian suite, to create a seamless and comprehensive project management and documentation environment. We highlighted how this integration bridges the gap between project tasks and their corresponding documentation, enhancing collaboration, traceability, and overall project visibility.

We explored two primary methods for integrating JIRA and Confluence: application links, which establish a secure connection between the two platforms, and Confluence macros for JIRA, which enable embedding JIRA data directly into Confluence pages.

Furthermore, we demonstrated how to create direct links between JIRA issues and Confluence pages, either using issue keys or URLs, or through the Jira Issues macro for displaying lists of relevant issues. We also discussed various other JIRA macros, such as the Jira Chart macro for embedding JIRA charts and the Jira Issue/Filter macro for showcasing specific issue details. Additionally, we highlighted the Jira Road Map macro for visualizing project timelines and the Jira Report Blueprint for creating comprehensive reports in Confluence.

To ensure successful integration, we outlined best practices, including establishing clear links, utilizing labels and categories for cross-referencing, keeping information up-to-date, leveraging automation, and choosing the right macro for the desired data presentation.

By implementing these integration techniques and best practices, you can unlock the full potential of JIRA and Confluence, creating a cohesive and efficient ecosystem that fosters collaboration, streamlines workflows, and enhances knowledge sharing throughout your projects.

Advanced Formatting and Macros

Outline

- Text Formatting in Confluence
- Working with Tables
- Using Macros
- Other Advanced Formatting Options
- Chapter Summary

Text Formatting in Confluence

Confluence's rich text editor makes it easy to format your content and enhance its readability. It provides a variety of text formatting options similar to those found in word processors, allowing you to emphasize key points, structure your content, and add visual interest to your pages.

Basic Formatting

Here are some of the basic formatting options you can use in Confluence:

- **Bold:** Used to emphasize important words or phrases. Select the text you want to bold and click the "B" icon in the toolbar, or use the keyboard shortcut `Ctrl+B` (or Cmd+B on Mac).
  Example: **This is important information.**
- **Italic:** Used to highlight book titles, foreign words, technical terms, or to indicate emphasis. Select the text and click the "I" icon or use the shortcut `Ctrl+I` (or Cmd+I on Mac).
  Example: This product is the *crème de la crème*.
- **Underline:** Used sparingly for emphasis or to indicate a hyperlink (though Confluence automatically formats hyperlinks as underlined). Select the text and click the "U" icon or use the shortcut `Ctrl+U` (or Cmd+U on Mac).
  Example: <u>This section is still under development.</u>
- **Headings:** Used to organize your content into sections and subsections. There are six heading levels available (Heading 1 to Heading 6). Select the text and choose the desired heading level from the "Styles" dropdown menu.

  Example:

Heading 1

Heading 2

Heading 3

Heading 4

Heading 5

Heading 6

- **Lists:** Used to present information in a structured format. You can create either bulleted or numbered lists. Click the "List" icon in the toolbar to choose the list type.
  Example:

- Item 1
- Item 2
- Item 3

- **Links:** Used to connect to other Confluence pages, external websites, or files. Highlight the text you want to turn into a link, click the "Link" icon, and enter the URL or search for the page you want to link to.
Example: Visit the Atlassian website - https://www.atlassian.com/ for more information.
- **Code Blocks:** Used to display code snippets in a formatted way with syntax highlighting. Click the "Code" icon in the toolbar or use the backticks (``) to enclose your code.

Example:

```
def hello_world():
    print("Hello, world!")
```

By mastering these basic formatting options, you can create well-structured, easy-to-read Confluence pages that effectively communicate your ideas and information.

Working with Tables

Tables are indispensable tools for organizing and presenting data in a structured format within your Confluence pages. They enhance readability and make it easier for users to grasp complex information at a glance. Confluence's table functionality offers a range of features for creating and customizing tables to suit your specific needs.

Creating a Table

There are multiple ways to create a table in Confluence:

- **Insert Menu:** Click the "+" icon in the editor toolbar and select "Table." Choose the desired number of rows and columns, and Confluence will insert a blank table for you.
- **Slash Command:** Type "/table" in the editor and press Enter. This will open a dialog where you can specify the number of rows and columns.
- **Markdown:** If you're familiar with Markdown syntax, you can create a simple table using pipes (|) and dashes (-).

Adding and Deleting Rows and Columns

- **Adding:** Right-click on a row or column header and choose "Insert row above/below" or "Insert column left/right."
- **Deleting:** Right-click on a row or column header and choose "Delete row" or "Delete column."

Merging and Splitting Cells

- **Merging:** Select the cells you want to merge, right-click, and choose "Merge cells."
- **Splitting:** Select the merged cell you want to split, right-click, and choose "Split cell."

Basic Formatting

Confluence allows you to apply basic formatting to table elements to enhance their appearance and clarity:

- **Text formatting:** Apply bold, italic, underline, or other text formatting options to individual cells or the entire table.
- **Alignment:** Align text within cells to the left, center, or right.

- **Background color:** Change the background color of cells or the entire table to visually distinguish different sections.
- **Borders:** Customize the style and thickness of cell borders.

Example

Here's an example of a simple table in Confluence:

Feature	Description	Status
User Login	Implement user login functionality.	In Progress
Password Reset	Allow users to reset their passwords.	Done
Account Profile	Create user profile pages.	To Do

By mastering these table functionalities, you can effectively organize and present data within your Confluence pages, making your content more informative and easier to comprehend.

Using Macros

While Confluence's rich text editor provides a wide range of formatting options, macros take customization and functionality to the next level. Essentially, macros are reusable pieces of code that extend Confluence's capabilities, allowing you to automate tasks, create dynamic content, and enhance the appearance of your pages.

What are Macros?

Think of macros as building blocks that you can insert into your pages to achieve specific results. They can range from simple formatting enhancements, like adding a table of contents or inserting a status indicator, to more complex functionalities, like displaying a dynamic chart of JIRA data or integrating with external systems.

Types of Macros

Confluence offers two main types of macros:

1. **Built-in Macros:** These are macros that come pre-installed with Confluence. They provide a wide range of functionality, including:
   - Formatting macros (e.g., Table of Contents, Expand, Status)
   - Content macros (e.g., Gallery, Chart, Jira Issues)
   - Layout macros (e.g., Section, Column, Sidebar)
   - Other macros for specific tasks (e.g., Draw.io Diagram, Excerpt, Page Properties Report)
2. **Marketplace Macros:** The Atlassian Marketplace is a vast repository of third-party macros that you can install to extend Confluence's capabilities even further. These macros can offer specialized functionality, such as integration with other tools, advanced charting options, or custom workflow automation.

How to Use Macros

Using macros is straightforward:

1. **Insert Macro:** Click the "+" icon in the editor toolbar or type "/" to open the macro browser.
2. **Select a Macro:** Browse or search for the macro you want to use.

3. **Configure Macro:** Fill in the required fields and options to customize the macro's behavior and appearance.
4. **Insert Macro:** Click "Insert" to add the macro to your page.

The Benefits of Using Macros

Macros offer several key benefits:

- **Automation:** Automate repetitive tasks, such as creating reports or updating content.
- **Dynamic Content:** Embed dynamic content, such as charts or live data feeds, that automatically updates.
- **Improved Presentation:** Enhance the look and feel of your pages with visual elements and interactive features.
- **Increased Functionality:** Extend Confluence's capabilities with specialized macros for specific tasks.
- **Simplified Content Creation:** Save time and effort by reusing pre-built macros instead of creating content from scratch.

By mastering macros, you can unlock the full potential of Confluence, making it a more powerful and versatile tool for your team's collaboration and knowledge management needs.

Commonly Used Macros

Confluence offers a wide array of macros to enhance your pages' functionality and visual appeal. Here's a look at some of the most popular ones:

- **Table of Contents:** This macro automatically generates a table of contents for your page, making it easier for readers to navigate long documents. It extracts headings and subheadings from your content and creates a clickable list that allows users to jump to specific sections.
- **Code Block:** Ideal for technical documentation, this macro lets you display code snippets with proper syntax highlighting. You can choose from various programming languages, ensuring that your code is presented clearly and professionally.
- **Draw.io Diagram:** Integrate the popular diagramming tool draw.io directly into Confluence. This macro allows you to create and embed various types of diagrams, such as flowcharts, network diagrams, and UML diagrams, directly within your pages.
- **Jira Issues:** This macro brings JIRA data into Confluence, allowing you to display lists of issues, single issue details, or even JIRA charts. You can filter the results based on project, issue type, status, or custom JQL queries.
- **Status:** This macro is a visual indicator that conveys the current state of a page or section. It's perfect for signaling whether content is a draft, in progress, under review, or completed. You can customize the appearance of the status indicator (e.g., color, icon) to match your needs.

These are just a few examples of the many useful macros available in Confluence. The Atlassian Marketplace offers a wide selection of additional macros, including integrations with other tools, advanced formatting options, and custom content types. By exploring and utilizing these macros, you can elevate your Confluence pages from simple documents to interactive and engaging knowledge resources.

Creating Custom Macros

While Confluence's built-in and marketplace macros cater to a wide range of needs, you might encounter situations where you require a highly specialized or tailored functionality. In such cases, Confluence allows you to create custom macros using web technologies like HTML, CSS, and JavaScript.

Creating custom macros is an advanced feature that requires knowledge of web development. It involves writing code to define the macro's behavior, appearance, and interaction with Confluence. You can create macros that perform complex calculations, fetch data from external sources, or even integrate with other applications.

The process of creating a custom macro typically involves the following steps:

1. **Define the Macro:** Determine the macro's purpose, functionality, and the parameters it will accept.
2. **Write the Macro Code:** Develop the HTML, CSS, and JavaScript code to implement the macro's functionality and style its appearance.
3. **Test and Debug:** Thoroughly test the macro to ensure it works as expected and doesn't conflict with other Confluence features.
4. **Deploy the Macro:** Once tested, deploy the macro to your Confluence instance, making it available for use in your pages.

While creating custom macros offers great flexibility, it's important to note that it's not for everyone. It requires a certain level of technical expertise and understanding of web development principles. However, if you have the necessary skills, custom macros can be a powerful tool for extending Confluence's capabilities and tailoring it to your specific needs.

Tip: If you're not comfortable with coding, you can often find pre-built macros in the Atlassian Marketplace or seek assistance from a developer to create a custom macro for you.

Other Advanced Formatting Options

Beyond the basic text formatting and macros, Confluence provides a range of advanced formatting options that empower you to further enhance the visual appeal and functionality of your pages. Let's explore some of these options:

Emojis: Adding Personality and Flair

Emojis have become a ubiquitous part of modern communication, and Confluence allows you to incorporate them into your pages. They can be used to express emotions, add visual cues, or simply make your content more engaging. To insert an emoji, type a colon (":") followed by the emoji's name (e.g., "●"). Confluence will suggest matching emojis as you type.

LaTeX: Rendering Mathematical Formulas

If your documentation involves mathematical formulas or equations, Confluence's LaTeX support is invaluable. LaTeX is a typesetting system that excels at rendering complex mathematical notation. By enclosing your LaTeX code within the appropriate delimiters, you can create beautifully formatted equations that are easy to read and understand.

Layouts: Organizing Content with Structure

Layouts allow you to arrange content on your page in a visually appealing and organized manner. Confluence offers various layout options, such as columns, sections, and sidebars. You can use these layouts to create distinct sections within your page, highlight specific content, or simply break up long blocks of text.

Custom Styles: Tailoring the Look and Feel

If you want to create a unique visual identity for your Confluence pages, custom stylesheets are the way to go. By writing CSS code, you can define specific styles for your text, headings, tables, and other elements. This allows you to create a consistent look and feel across your pages, aligning with your organization's branding or your personal preferences.

HTML and CSS: Unleashing Advanced Customization

For the most adventurous users, Confluence allows you to directly embed HTML and CSS code within your pages. This opens up a world of possibilities for customization, allowing you to create complex layouts, interactive elements, and dynamic content that goes beyond the capabilities of Confluence's built-in features. However, this requires knowledge of HTML and CSS, so it's best suited for users with web development experience.

By experimenting with these advanced formatting options, you can take your Confluence pages to the next level, creating visually stunning and highly functional documentation that effectively communicates your ideas and information.

Chapter Summary

In this chapter, we explored the advanced formatting and macro features available in Confluence, allowing you to elevate your documentation to new heights of clarity and engagement. We began by discussing basic text formatting options like bold, italic, underline, headings, lists, links, and code blocks, providing you with the tools to structure and emphasize your content effectively.

We then delved into working with tables, explaining how to create, customize, and format them to organize data in a clear and visually appealing manner.

Macros, as reusable snippets of code, were introduced as a powerful way to extend Confluence's functionality. We discussed their benefits, including automation, dynamic content generation, and improved presentation. We also highlighted commonly used macros like Table of Contents, Code Block, Draw.io Diagram, Jira Issues, and Status, showcasing their practical applications in enhancing your pages.

For those seeking more advanced customization, we briefly touched upon the process of creating custom macros using HTML, CSS, and JavaScript. This option opens up a world of possibilities but requires technical expertise.

Finally, we explored other advanced formatting options like emojis, LaTeX for mathematical formulas, layouts, custom stylesheets, and direct HTML/CSS embedding. These features allow you to tailor the appearance and functionality of your Confluence pages to your specific needs and preferences. By mastering these advanced formatting and macro techniques, you can create compelling and informative Confluence pages that effectively communicate your message and engage your audience.

Best Practices for Confluence Administration

Outline

- Space Management and Organization
- Content Creation and Curation
- User and Permission Management
- Search and Navigation
- Performance Optimization
- Security and Compliance
- Continuous Improvement and Adaptation
- Chapter Summary

Space Management and Organization

In a Confluence instance, spaces are the foundation of organization. Just as a well-organized physical workspace promotes productivity and efficiency, a well-structured Confluence environment facilitates knowledge sharing and collaboration. Let's delve into the best practices for space management and organization.

The Importance of a Well-Structured Space Hierarchy

A space hierarchy provides a logical structure to your Confluence content. It involves organizing spaces into parent-child relationships, creating a tree-like structure where broader topics or departments are represented as parent spaces, and more specific projects or sub-topics are nested as child spaces.

This hierarchical organization brings several benefits:

- **Ease of Navigation:** Users can easily navigate through the space directory, drilling down from broad categories to specific areas of interest.
- **Content Discoverability:** Related pages are grouped together, making it easier for users to discover relevant information.
- **Permission Management:** You can assign permissions at the parent space level, which automatically applies to all child spaces, simplifying permission administration.

Clear Naming Conventions for Spaces and Pages

Choosing clear and descriptive names for your spaces and pages is crucial for usability. Avoid generic names like "Project A" or "Team Space." Instead, opt for names that accurately reflect the purpose or content of the space or page. For example, "Marketing Team Projects" or "Product X Documentation" are more informative and easier to understand.

Consistent naming conventions also help maintain a sense of order and make it easier for users to locate specific spaces or pages. Consider establishing guidelines for naming spaces and pages based on your organization's structure or project naming conventions.

Archiving or Deleting Obsolete Content

Over time, some Confluence spaces or pages may become obsolete or irrelevant. It's essential to regularly review your content and archive or delete outdated information. This keeps your Confluence instance clean, improves search results, and prevents users from accessing outdated or incorrect information.

Archiving a space or page removes it from the navigation but keeps it accessible through search. This is useful if you might need to refer to the content in the future. Deleting a space or page permanently removes it from Confluence. Only delete content that you are sure you will never need again.

User-Friendly Space Homepages

The homepage of a space is the first impression users get of its content. A well-designed homepage can guide users to the most relevant information and encourage them to explore further. Here are some tips for creating user-friendly space homepages:

- **Clear Purpose:** State the purpose of the space clearly and concisely.
- **Navigation Aids:** Provide a table of contents, quick links, or other navigation aids to help users find what they need.
- **Featured Content:** Highlight important pages or announcements.
- **Visual Appeal:** Use images, banners, or other visual elements to make the homepage more engaging.

By following these best practices for space management and organization, you can create a well-structured, easy-to-navigate, and user-friendly Confluence environment that fosters collaboration and knowledge sharing.

Content Creation and Curation

The heart of Confluence lies in its content – the pages, documents, and knowledge that teams create and share. High-quality content that is relevant, up-to-date, and easy to find is essential for effective collaboration and knowledge management. This section delves into the best practices for creating, curating, and organizing content within Confluence.

High-Quality, Relevant, and Up-to-date Content

Confluence serves as a central repository of your team's collective knowledge, so the quality and relevance of its content directly impact its effectiveness. Stale or inaccurate information can mislead users, hinder decision-making, and waste time. Therefore, it's crucial to:

- **Create High-Quality Content:** When creating new pages or documents, focus on clarity, accuracy, and completeness. Use proper formatting, structure your content logically, and include all relevant information. Consider using visuals like images, diagrams, and videos to enhance understanding.
- **Keep Content Relevant:** Regularly review and update your content to ensure it remains relevant and aligned with your team's current goals and priorities. Remove outdated information or mark it as archived to avoid confusion.
- **Encourage User Contributions:** Confluence thrives on collaboration. Encourage your team members to contribute their knowledge and expertise by creating new pages, editing existing ones, and sharing their insights through comments and discussions.

Maintaining Content Quality through Reviews and Updates

To maintain the quality of your Confluence content:

- **Establish a Review Process:** Implement a review process where content is reviewed by peers or subject matter experts before it's published. This helps identify errors, inconsistencies, or areas that need improvement.
- **Regularly Update Content:** Schedule regular reviews of your most important pages to ensure they are up-to-date and accurate. Assign ownership of specific pages to team members responsible for keeping them current.

- **Use Version History:** Confluence's version history feature allows you to track changes and revert to previous versions if needed, ensuring that you can always recover from mistakes or accidental deletions.

Templates and Blueprints for Consistency and Efficiency

Templates and blueprints are invaluable tools for ensuring consistency and efficiency in content creation. They provide pre-designed structures and guidelines, making it easier for users to create new pages that adhere to your organization's standards.

- **Templates:** Offer pre-formatted layouts for common types of documents, such as meeting notes, project plans, or how-to guides.
- **Blueprints:** Provide step-by-step instructions and prompts to guide users through the creation of more complex documents, ensuring that all essential information is captured.

By utilizing templates and blueprints, you can streamline the content creation process, reduce errors, and ensure that all your documentation follows a consistent format.

Effective Use of Labels, Categories, and Metadata

Organizing your Confluence content is crucial for easy retrieval and discoverability. Confluence offers several tools to help you categorize and organize your pages:

- **Labels:** Keywords or tags that you can apply to pages to categorize them by topic, project, or other relevant criteria.
- **Categories:** Broader classifications for grouping related spaces and pages.
- **Metadata:** Additional information about a page, such as author, creation date, or last updated date.

By effectively using labels, categories, and metadata, you can create a well-structured and easily searchable knowledge base. Users can then find the information they need quickly and efficiently, contributing to a more collaborative and productive work environment.

User and Permission Management

Effective user and permission management is crucial for maintaining a secure and organized Confluence environment. By carefully controlling access to spaces and pages, you ensure that sensitive information remains confidential while fostering collaboration among authorized individuals.

Managing Users and Groups

Confluence allows you to add users individually or import them in bulk from a CSV file. Once users are added, you can organize them into groups based on their roles, departments, or projects. Groups provide a convenient way to manage permissions for multiple users at once.

To create a custom user group:

1. Navigate to the "User Management" section in the Confluence administration console.
2. Click the "Groups" tab and then click "Add Group."
3. Enter a name and description for the group.
4. Add users to the group by typing their names or email addresses.

Assigning Space and Page Permissions

Confluence offers a flexible permission system that allows you to grant or restrict access to spaces and pages at various levels:

- **Space Permissions:** Control who can view, edit, and administer a space. You can grant these permissions to individual users, groups, or even anonymous users.
- **Page Restrictions:** Restrict access to specific pages within a space. This is useful for protecting sensitive information or ensuring that only authorized personnel can edit certain documents.

To manage space permissions:

1. Go to the space you want to manage and click "Space tools" > "Permissions."
2. Add users or groups and select the appropriate permission level (view, edit, or administer).

To manage page restrictions:

1. Open the page you want to restrict.
2. Click the "•••" icon and select "Restrictions."
3. Add users or groups and choose the desired restriction type (view, edit, or no access).

Regularly Review and Update Permissions

As your team and projects evolve, so do user roles and responsibilities. It's essential to regularly review and update permissions to ensure they are still relevant and accurate. This helps maintain security and prevents unauthorized access to sensitive information.

Consider conducting periodic audits of your user accounts and groups to identify any inactive or unauthorized users. Remove or deactivate accounts that are no longer needed and update group memberships as roles change.

By diligently managing users, groups, and permissions, you can create a Confluence environment that is both secure and collaborative, empowering your teams to work effectively and share knowledge without compromising data integrity.

Search and Navigation

Efficient search and navigation are crucial for making Confluence a truly valuable resource for your team. When users can easily find the information they need, it fosters productivity, collaboration, and knowledge sharing. Let's explore the tools and techniques that can elevate your Confluence navigation experience.

Optimizing Search Results

Confluence's search functionality is powerful, but it can be fine-tuned to deliver even more relevant results. Here are some tips:

- **Use Specific Keywords:** Be as specific as possible in your search queries. Instead of searching for "project," try searching for "Project X timeline" or "Project X meeting notes."
- **Use Quotation Marks for Exact Phrases:** Enclose phrases in quotation marks to search for the exact word combination (e.g., "marketing strategy").
- **Use Boolean Operators:** Combine search terms with AND, OR, or NOT to refine your search (e.g., "marketing AND strategy").
- **Use Wildcards:** Use the asterisk (*) wildcard to match any number of characters (e.g., "market* plan" to find "marketing plan" or "marketplace strategy").
- **Search Within Specific Spaces or Pages:** Narrow down your search by specifying the space or page you want to search within.

Creating Custom Search Filters

Custom search filters allow you to save frequently used search queries with specific criteria. This saves time and ensures consistency in your search results. To create a custom filter:

1. Perform a search using the desired criteria.
2. Click the "Save as" button next to the search bar.
3. Name your filter and optionally add a description.

Using Labels and Categories

As discussed earlier, labels and categories are valuable tools for organizing and classifying content. By applying relevant labels and categories to your pages, you make it easier for users to find them through search or browsing.

Breadcrumbs and Page Tree Macros

Confluence provides visual aids to help users understand their location within the space hierarchy:

- **Breadcrumbs:** These are navigational links at the top of a page that show the path from the space homepage to the current page.
- **Page Tree Macro:** This macro displays a tree-like structure of the pages within a space, allowing users to visualize the hierarchy and navigate to other pages easily.

Other Navigation Aids

Confluence offers additional navigation aids, such as:

- **Space Homepages:** Design your space homepages to serve as a starting point for users. Include links to important pages, recent updates, and a table of contents.
- **Recently Viewed:** Confluence tracks the pages you've recently visited, making it easy to return to them.
- **Starred Pages:** You can mark frequently used pages as favorites for quick access.

By implementing these search and navigation best practices, you can create a user-friendly Confluence environment where information is easy to find and access, ultimately promoting collaboration and knowledge sharing.

Performance Optimization

Confluence, like any software, can experience performance issues that slow down page loads, affect search functionality, or cause other disruptions. Understanding the factors that contribute to these issues and implementing optimization techniques can ensure a smooth and responsive user experience.

Factors Affecting Confluence Performance

- **Large Attachments:** Uploading numerous or large attachments (images, videos, documents) can consume significant storage space and increase page load times. This is especially true if you're using Confluence Server or Data Center, where storage limitations might be more pronounced.
- **Excessive Customizations:** Confluence allows extensive customization through themes, plugins, and user macros. However, excessive use of these can add overhead to the system and lead to performance degradation.
- **Outdated Plugins:** Plugins that haven't been updated in a while might not be optimized for newer Confluence versions, potentially causing compatibility issues and performance bottlenecks.
- **Server Resources:** The available server resources (CPU, memory, disk space) also play a significant role in Confluence's performance. Insufficient resources can lead to slowdowns and delays, especially during peak usage.
- **Database Performance:** The database used by Confluence (PostgreSQL or MySQL) can also become a bottleneck if it's not properly tuned or if it's experiencing heavy loads.

Tips for Optimizing Performance

To ensure optimal Confluence performance, consider the following tips:

- **Manage Attachments:**
    - **Compress Images:** Before uploading images, compress them to reduce their file size without compromising quality.
    - **Remove Unused Attachments:** Regularly review and delete attachments that are no longer needed.
    - **External Storage:** If you have a large number of attachments, consider using an external storage solution like AWS S3 or Azure Blob Storage.
- **Limit Customizations:**
    - **Review Themes and Plugins:** Disable or uninstall themes or plugins that you don't use or that are causing performance problems.
    - **Use Macros Judiciously:** Be mindful of the number and complexity of macros used on a page, as they can impact loading times.
- **Monitor Performance:**
    - **Confluence Monitoring:** Utilize Confluence's built-in monitoring tools to track performance metrics like page load times, database queries, and memory usage.
    - **Third-Party Monitoring:** Consider using external monitoring tools like New Relic or AppDynamics for more in-depth performance analysis.

By actively monitoring and optimizing your Confluence instance, you can ensure that it remains a responsive and reliable platform for your team's collaboration and knowledge-sharing needs.

Security and Compliance

Confluence often houses critical company information, from project plans and technical documentation to sensitive business strategies and financial data. Therefore, ensuring the security and compliance of your Confluence instance is of paramount importance. This involves implementing robust measures to protect sensitive information, control user access, and monitor activity to meet regulatory and organizational requirements.

Protecting Sensitive Information

Not all information in Confluence needs to be accessible to everyone. You can safeguard sensitive content by employing:

- **Page Restrictions:** Utilize page restrictions to control who can view and edit specific pages. Restrict access to confidential documents to authorized personnel only.
- **Space Permissions:** Manage space permissions to limit access to entire spaces based on user roles and responsibilities.
- **Encryption:** Ensure that sensitive data is encrypted both in transit (while being transferred over the network) and at rest (when stored in the database). Confluence supports SSL/TLS encryption for data in transit and offers encryption options for data at rest.

Managing User Access

Control over who can access your Confluence instance and what they can do is vital. Implement the following measures:

- **Strong Password Policies:** Enforce strong password requirements, such as minimum length, complexity (uppercase, lowercase, numbers, symbols), and regular password changes. This makes it harder for unauthorized users to guess or crack passwords.

- **Two-Factor Authentication (2FA):** Enable 2FA to add an extra layer of security to user logins. This requires users to provide a second authentication factor, such as a code from their phone, in addition to their password.
- **User Provisioning and Deprovisioning:** Automate the process of creating and deactivating user accounts to ensure timely access and prevent unauthorized access by former employees.

Audit Logs

Confluence audit logs provide a detailed record of user activity and changes to content. By reviewing these logs, you can:

- **Track Changes:** See who made which changes to pages, when those changes were made, and what the changes were.
- **Detect Unauthorized Activity:** Identify any suspicious activity or unauthorized access attempts.
- **Meet Compliance Requirements:** Many industries have regulatory requirements for data retention and auditing. Audit logs can help you demonstrate compliance with these regulations.

Additional Security Measures

Consider implementing additional security measures to further protect your Confluence instance:

- **Regular Security Updates:** Keep your Confluence software and plugins up-to-date to address any security vulnerabilities.
- **Security Training:** Educate your users about security best practices, such as avoiding phishing scams and using strong passwords.
- **Vulnerability Scanning:** Regularly scan your Confluence instance for vulnerabilities using automated tools.
- **Incident Response Plan:** Develop a plan for responding to security incidents, such as data breaches or unauthorized access.

By implementing these security and compliance measures, you can safeguard your Confluence data, protect sensitive information, and ensure that your team can collaborate with confidence, knowing that their work is secure.

Continuous Improvement and Adaptation

Confluence administration isn't a one-time setup; it's an ongoing journey of refining and adapting to evolving needs. By consistently evaluating your Confluence environment and implementing improvements, you can ensure that it remains a valuable and effective tool for your team.

Gather User Feedback

Your users are the lifeblood of your Confluence instance. Their feedback is invaluable for understanding what's working well and what needs improvement. Regularly solicit feedback through surveys, polls, or informal discussions. Ask about their experience with search, navigation, content organization, and any pain points they encounter.

Monitor Usage Statistics

Confluence provides various analytics and usage statistics that can offer valuable insights into how your team is using the platform. Analyze these statistics to identify popular pages, usage trends, and areas where users might be struggling. This data can guide your improvement efforts and help you prioritize changes.

Stay Updated with the Latest Features and Best Practices

Confluence is constantly evolving, with new features and enhancements being released regularly. Stay informed about these updates by reading Atlassian's documentation, blogs, and release notes. Participate in webinars or training sessions to learn about new features and best practices. Consider joining Confluence user groups or online communities to exchange ideas and learn from other administrators.

Adapt to Changing Needs

As your team grows, projects evolve, and goals shift, your Confluence setup should adapt accordingly. Regularly review your space hierarchy, page organization, and permission structure to ensure they still align with your current needs. Be open to experimenting with new workflows, templates, and macros to optimize your Confluence experience.

Example: Continuous Improvement in Action

Imagine your team is using Confluence to document a large project. After gathering feedback, you discover that users are struggling to find relevant information due to a lack of clear organization. To address this, you decide to:

1. **Restructure Space Hierarchy:** Create a more logical hierarchy of spaces, grouping related pages together under parent spaces.
2. **Update Page Titles and Descriptions:** Ensure that page titles and descriptions are clear and informative, making it easier for users to understand the content at a glance.
3. **Use Labels and Categories:** Apply relevant labels and categories to pages to enable easier filtering and search.
4. **Create a Space Homepage:** Design a user-friendly homepage that guides users to the most important pages and resources.
5. **Offer Training:** Provide training sessions or create a user guide to help team members understand the new space structure and navigation aids.

By taking these steps, you've significantly improved the usability and effectiveness of your Confluence space, making it a more valuable resource for your team.

Remember, continuous improvement is an ongoing journey. By staying vigilant and adaptable, you can ensure that your Confluence instance remains a valuable asset that empowers your team to collaborate effectively and achieve their goals.

Chapter Summary

In this chapter, we delved into the realm of best practices for Confluence administration, emphasizing the importance of continuous evaluation and improvement of your Confluence setup. We highlighted various key areas where administrators can focus their efforts to optimize the user experience and maximize the value of the platform.

We began by discussing the significance of space management and organization, stressing the need for a well-structured hierarchy and clear naming conventions for spaces and pages. We also provided strategies for archiving or deleting obsolete content and creating user-friendly space homepages that guide users to relevant information.

Next, we emphasized the importance of high-quality, relevant, and up-to-date content within Confluence. We discussed how to encourage user contributions and maintain content quality through reviews and updates. We also recommended using templates and blueprints to ensure consistency and efficiency in content creation, as well as leveraging labels, categories, and metadata for effective organization and retrieval of information.

We also explored strategies for user and permission management, highlighting the importance of creating custom user groups, assigning space and page permissions, and regularly reviewing and updating permissions to reflect changing team roles and responsibilities.

Furthermore, we discussed the importance of search and navigation in Confluence, providing tips for optimizing search results, creating custom search filters, and utilizing labels, categories, breadcrumbs, and page tree macros to enhance content discoverability.

We addressed performance optimization by identifying factors that can affect Confluence performance, such as large attachments, excessive customizations, and outdated plugins. We offered tips for managing attachments, limiting customizations, and monitoring performance to ensure a smooth and responsive user experience.

Lastly, we emphasized the significance of security and compliance in Confluence administration. We discussed strategies for protecting sensitive information, managing user access, and implementing security measures like password policies, two-factor authentication, data encryption, and audit logs.

By adhering to these best practices and remaining committed to continuous improvement and adaptation, Confluence administrators can ensure that their instance remains a valuable and effective tool for collaboration, knowledge sharing, and documentation within their organizations.

Section H:
Real-World Examples and Case Studies

Setting Up a Project from Scratch

Outline

- Project Planning and Preparation
- Creating the JIRA Project
- Configuring the Project
- Setting up the Confluence Space
- Chapter Summary

Project Planning and Preparation

Before embarking on the journey of setting up your project in JIRA and Confluence, it's crucial to lay a solid foundation through meticulous project planning and preparation. This preliminary phase sets the stage for success by ensuring that everyone involved has a clear understanding of the project's objectives, scope, and path to completion.

Defining Project Goals and Objectives

At the heart of any successful project lies a clear vision of what you want to achieve. Start by defining your project goals and objectives in detail. What problem are you trying to solve, or what opportunity are you pursuing? What are the desired outcomes or benefits you expect to realize? Clearly articulate these goals to provide a guiding light for the entire project team.

Identifying Stakeholders

Every project has stakeholders, individuals or groups who have a vested interest in the project's outcome. Identify all the key stakeholders, including project sponsors, end-users, team members, and any other relevant parties. Understand their needs, expectations, and concerns. Establishing clear communication channels with stakeholders is essential for gathering feedback, managing expectations, and ensuring their buy-in throughout the project.

Establishing Timelines and Milestones

Develop a realistic timeline for your project, outlining key milestones and deadlines. Break down the project into smaller phases or stages, each with its own set of deliverables and target dates. This timeline will serve as a roadmap for your project, helping you track progress and identify potential delays early on.

Defining Deliverables

Clearly define the deliverables for each phase of the project. What specific products, services, or outcomes do you expect to produce? Specify the quality standards, acceptance criteria, and any other relevant details for each deliverable. This clarity ensures that everyone understands what is expected and helps prevent scope creep, where the project's scope expands uncontrollably.

Establishing Communication Channels

Effective communication is the lifeblood of any project. Establish clear and regular communication channels to keep everyone informed and aligned. This could include weekly status meetings, email updates, or dedicated Slack channels. Make sure that team members have easy access to relevant information and that there are open channels for feedback and collaboration.

Gathering Requirements and Defining User Stories

A critical aspect of project planning is gathering requirements from stakeholders. What are their needs and expectations for the final product or service? Use techniques like interviews, surveys, or workshops to gather comprehensive requirements. Once you have a clear understanding of the requirements, translate them into user stories. User stories are short, simple descriptions of desired functionality from the end user's perspective. They provide a valuable framework for prioritizing and planning your work.

Establishing a Project Roadmap

A project roadmap is a high-level visual representation of your project's timeline, milestones, and key deliverables. It serves as a communication tool for stakeholders and a guide for the project team. The roadmap should be flexible and adaptable, allowing you to adjust your plans as new information or challenges arise.

Emphasizing Collaboration

Throughout the planning and preparation phase, emphasize the importance of collaboration among team members. Encourage open communication, feedback, and brainstorming sessions. A collaborative approach fosters a sense of shared ownership and commitment, increasing the likelihood of project success.

By investing time and effort in thorough project planning and preparation, you lay a solid foundation for your JIRA and Confluence implementation. This ensures that your tools are aligned with your project goals, your team is clear on their responsibilities, and you have a roadmap to guide you through the project lifecycle.

Creating the JIRA Project

With a solid project plan in place, you're ready to bring your project to life within JIRA. Let's walk through the steps of creating a new JIRA project from scratch.

1. **Access the JIRA project creation page:** After logging into your JIRA instance, you'll usually find a prominent "Create project" button or link. It might be located on your dashboard, in the top navigation bar, or in the project sidebar. Click on it to initiate the project creation process.
2. **Choose a project template:** JIRA offers a variety of project templates designed for different methodologies and use cases. The most common options include:
    - **Scrum:** Ideal for Agile software development teams that work in sprints and follow the Scrum framework.
    - **Kanban:** Suitable for teams that prefer a continuous flow of work and visualize their workflow on a Kanban board.
    - **Bug tracking:** Designed specifically for tracking and resolving software bugs or defects.
    - **Other templates:** JIRA might offer additional templates for various project types, such as content management, task management, or service desk.
3. Select the template that best aligns with your project's methodology and goals. You can always customize the template further to fit your specific needs.
4. **Name the project and define the project key:**

- **Project Name:** Give your project a clear and descriptive name that reflects its purpose. This will make it easy for you and your team members to identify the project in JIRA.
- **Project Key:** The project key is a unique short code that will be used to identify your project throughout JIRA (e.g., "MKT" for a marketing project or "WEB" for a website development project). It's often used as a prefix for issue keys (e.g., MKT-123).

5. **Invite team members (if applicable):**
   - If you have team members who need to access the project immediately, you can invite them during the project creation process. Enter their email addresses in the "Invite team members" field, and they will receive an invitation to join the project.
   - You can also assign initial project roles to the invited members based on their responsibilities.

Once you've completed these steps, click the "Create" or "Submit" button to create your new JIRA project. You will then be taken to your newly created project's dashboard, where you can start configuring the project further and adding content.

Configuring the Project

Now that your JIRA project is created, it's time to tailor it to your specific requirements. This involves configuring various aspects of the project to align with your team's workflow, data collection needs, and visual preferences.

Issue Types

Issue types are the building blocks of your project, representing different types of work items. While JIRA offers default issue types like Task, Bug, Story, and Epic, you can create custom issue types to better reflect your specific needs. For example, if you're working on a marketing project, you might create issue types like "Campaign," "Social Media Post," or "Content Review."

To create custom issue types:

1. Navigate to your project settings and click on "Issue types."
2. Click "Add issue type" and choose whether to create a new issue type from scratch or copy an existing one.
3. Give your issue type a name and description.
4. Choose an icon to represent the issue type (optional).
5. Save the new issue type.

Workflows

Workflows define the lifecycle of an issue, outlining the steps it goes through from creation to completion. Each issue type can have its own workflow. You can customize workflows by adding or removing statuses, defining transitions between statuses, and setting conditions for when transitions are allowed.

To configure workflows:

1. Go to your project settings and click on "Workflows."
2. Select the workflow you want to edit or create a new one.
3. Use the workflow editor to add, remove, or reorder statuses.
4. Define transitions between statuses and specify conditions (if needed).
5. Save the workflow.

Screens and Fields

Screens determine which fields are displayed when creating or editing an issue. JIRA provides default screens, but you can customize them by adding or removing fields. You can also create custom fields to capture specific data points relevant to your project.

To customize screens and fields:

1. Go to your project settings and click on "Screens" or "Fields."
2. Create new screens or fields, or edit existing ones.
3. For screens, drag and drop fields to arrange them in the desired order.
4. Save your changes.

Components and Versions

Components are used to break down a project into smaller, more manageable parts. They can represent different functional areas, modules, or teams. Versions are used to track releases or iterations of your product.

To add components and versions:

1. Go to your project settings and click on "Components" or "Versions."
2. Add new components or versions and provide relevant details.

Boards

Boards are visual representations of your project's workflow. JIRA supports two main types of boards: Scrum boards and Kanban boards. Scrum boards are ideal for projects that follow the Scrum methodology, while Kanban boards are suitable for projects that prioritize continuous flow.

To create a board:

1. Go to your project and click on "Boards."
2. Choose the type of board you want to create (Scrum or Kanban).
3. Configure the board settings, such as columns, swimlanes, and quick filters.

By carefully configuring your JIRA project, you can create a tailored environment that perfectly aligns with your team's needs and working style.

Setting up the Confluence Space

After establishing your project in JIRA, the next step is to create a corresponding Confluence space where you can document your project, collaborate on ideas, and share knowledge with your team.

Creating a Space

1. **Access the Space Creation Page:** From your Confluence dashboard, click the "Create" button or the "Spaces" menu in the navigation bar.
2. **Choose a Space Type:** Confluence offers several space types:
   - **Team Space:** Ideal for general team collaboration and communication.
   - **Project Space:** Designed for project-specific documentation, meeting notes, and plans.
   - **Knowledge Base Space:** Suitable for creating and organizing knowledge base articles, how-to guides, and FAQs.
   - **Personal Space:** Private space for individual use.
3. **Name Your Space:** Give your space a clear and descriptive name that reflects the project's purpose. For example, "Project X Documentation" or "Marketing Team Space for Project X."

4. **Configure Space Settings:** You can customize the look and feel of your space by choosing a theme and adding a logo. You can also set permissions to control who can view and edit the space's content.

Organizing Pages

Once your space is created, start organizing your project documentation:

- **Create a Hierarchical Structure:** Use parent-child relationships to create a logical hierarchy of pages. For example, you might have a top-level page for "Project Overview" with child pages for "Project Plan," "Meeting Notes," "Technical Documentation," etc.
- **Use Templates and Blueprints:** Leverage templates for common document types like meeting notes, project plans, and status reports. Blueprints can guide you through creating more complex documents, ensuring you capture all necessary information.
- **Link to JIRA Issues:** Integrate your Confluence space with your JIRA project by linking relevant pages to JIRA issues. This allows for easy access to project context and ensures that documentation is always up-to-date.

Managing Permissions

Control access to your Confluence space by setting permissions:

1. **Go to Space Settings:** Navigate to your space and click on "Space tools" > "Permissions."
2. **Add Users/Groups:** Click "Add people or groups" to grant access to specific users or groups.
3. **Assign Permissions:** Choose the appropriate permission level (view, edit, or administer) for each user or group.

By following these steps, you can create a well-organized Confluence space that serves as a central hub for your project documentation and collaboration.

Chapter Summary

In this chapter, we explored the practical steps involved in setting up a new project from scratch using JIRA and Confluence. We emphasized the importance of thorough project planning and preparation, highlighting key elements such as defining project goals, identifying stakeholders, establishing timelines and deliverables, and creating a project roadmap.

We then provided a step-by-step guide on how to create a new JIRA project, selecting the appropriate template and configuring essential elements like issue types, workflows, screens, fields, components, versions, and boards.

Furthermore, we walked you through the process of setting up a corresponding Confluence space for your project, including choosing the space type, naming it, organizing pages in a hierarchical structure, using templates and blueprints, and managing space permissions. By following these steps, you can create a comprehensive and well-organized environment where your team can effectively collaborate, track progress, and document their work throughout the project lifecycle.

Real-World Use Cases for JIRA

Outline

- JIRA in Software Development
- JIRA for Marketing Teams
- JIRA in HR and Recruitment
- JIRA for IT Service Management
- JIRA in Education
- JIRA for Nonprofits
- Cross-Functional Collaboration with JIRA
- Chapter Summary

JIRA in Software Development

JIRA has become a staple in the software development world, streamlining the entire Software Development Life Cycle (SDLC) from ideation to deployment and maintenance. Its flexibility and robust features make it a versatile tool that adapts to various software development methodologies and team structures.

Agile Project Management

JIRA's Agile capabilities are a cornerstone of its success in the software development domain. The platform seamlessly supports both Scrum and Kanban methodologies, providing teams with the necessary tools to plan, execute, and track their work effectively.

- **Scrum Boards:** These visual boards offer a clear overview of sprints, allowing teams to easily manage their backlog, prioritize user stories, assign tasks, and track progress in real time. The drag-and-drop interface makes it simple to move tasks through different stages of the workflow, such as "To Do," "In Progress," and "Done." Additionally, features like sprint reports and burndown charts provide valuable insights into team velocity and sprint progress.
- **Kanban Boards:** For teams that prefer a continuous flow approach, JIRA's Kanban boards visualize the workflow and limit work in progress (WIP) to ensure smooth and steady progress. The ability to customize columns and swimlanes allows teams to tailor the board to their specific process, while visual cues like card colors and labels facilitate quick identification of issue types and priorities.

Bug Tracking and Issue Management

JIRA's core strength lies in its comprehensive issue tracking capabilities. Teams can easily create, assign, prioritize, and track issues throughout their lifecycle. These issues can represent bugs, tasks, feature requests, or any other work item that needs to be addressed. JIRA's customizable workflows ensure that issues follow a defined process, from identification and investigation to resolution and closure.

Release Planning

JIRA goes beyond individual sprints by facilitating effective release planning. Teams can create versions (representing releases) and associate them with specific issues or epics. This allows them to plan and track the progress of features and fixes targeted for each release. The release hub in JIRA provides a consolidated view of all versions, their associated issues, and their planned release dates, ensuring that everyone is aligned on the release schedule and the scope of work.

Examples of JIRA in Software Development

To illustrate how software development teams utilize JIRA, let's consider some real-world examples:

- A Scrum team uses JIRA to manage their two-week sprints. They create a sprint backlog during sprint planning, assign tasks to team members, and track their progress on the Scrum board. They use JIRA's reporting features to generate burndown charts and velocity charts to monitor their performance and identify areas for improvement.
- A development team uses JIRA to track and resolve bugs. They create a separate project for bug tracking and use JIRA's issue linking feature to link bugs to the relevant user stories or features. They also use JIRA's automation features to trigger notifications and escalate critical bugs to the appropriate team members.
- A product manager uses JIRA to plan and manage the release of a new software version. They create a version in JIRA and associate it with the relevant issues and epics. They use the release hub to track the progress of the release and communicate the release date to stakeholders.

These are just a few examples of how JIRA can be leveraged in software development. Its flexibility and extensive feature set make it an indispensable tool for teams of all sizes and methodologies. By mastering JIRA, software development teams can streamline their workflows, improve collaboration, and deliver high-quality software faster and more efficiently.

JIRA for Marketing Teams

JIRA's adaptability extends beyond software development, making it a valuable asset for marketing teams as well. By leveraging JIRA's versatile features, marketing teams can streamline their processes, improve collaboration, and drive successful campaigns.

Campaign Management

JIRA provides a structured framework for managing marketing campaigns from inception to completion. By creating JIRA projects for each campaign, teams can:

- **Plan and Organize:** Outline campaign goals, target audience, messaging, channels, and timelines.
- **Track Tasks and Deadlines:** Create and assign tasks for various campaign activities, such as creating content, designing assets, launching ads, and analyzing results. JIRA's issue tracking features help monitor progress and ensure deadlines are met.
- **Collaborate Effectively:** Facilitate communication and collaboration among team members by centralizing campaign information, discussions, and updates within JIRA.
- **Measure Results:** Utilize JIRA's reporting features to track campaign performance, measure key metrics, and identify areas for improvement.

Content Creation and Approval

JIRA can streamline the often complex process of content creation and approval. By creating custom workflows and issue types, marketing teams can:

- **Manage Content Pipeline:** Track the status of each content piece (e.g., blog post, social media graphic, video) as it moves through the stages of drafting, review, editing, approval, and publication.
- **Assign Tasks and Responsibilities:** Clearly define who is responsible for each stage of the content creation process, ensuring accountability and smooth collaboration.
- **Automate Approvals:** Set up automation rules to notify relevant stakeholders when content is ready for review and approval, eliminating manual follow-ups.
- **Maintain Version Control:** Track changes and revisions to content, ensuring that everyone is working with the latest version.

Event Planning

JIRA's project management capabilities are ideal for organizing and managing events, whether it's a small webinar or a large-scale product launch. Teams can:

- **Create Task Lists:** Break down event planning into manageable tasks, such as booking venues, coordinating logistics, creating marketing materials, and managing registration.
- **Assign Responsibilities:** Assign tasks to team members and track their progress to ensure everything gets done on time.
- **Schedule and Track Deadlines:** Use JIRA's calendar view or timeline to visualize event timelines and deadlines, ensuring a well-coordinated execution.
- **Manage Resources:** Track budget, equipment, and other resources needed for the event, preventing overspending or resource shortages.

Real-World Examples

Here are some specific examples of how marketing teams utilize JIRA:

- **Social Media Campaigns:** Create JIRA issues for each social media post, track their performance, and analyze engagement metrics.
- **Content Calendars:** Manage editorial calendars in JIRA, tracking the progress of articles, blog posts, and other content pieces.
- **Webinar Execution:** Create tasks for webinar planning, promotion, execution, and follow-up, ensuring a smooth and successful event.
- **Product Launch:** Use JIRA to coordinate the various activities involved in a product launch, from marketing and PR to sales and customer support.

By embracing JIRA's versatility, marketing teams can transform their operations, improve collaboration, and achieve greater efficiency and success in their campaigns, content creation, and event planning endeavors.

JIRA in HR and Recruitment

JIRA's flexibility and customizability make it a valuable tool for HR and recruitment teams, allowing them to streamline processes, enhance collaboration, and improve the overall employee experience.

Recruitment Management

JIRA can transform the often chaotic recruitment process into a well-organized and efficient workflow. Here's how:

- **Job Openings Tracking:** Create JIRA issues to represent job openings. Track the status of each opening, from posting the job to filling the position. This allows for easy monitoring of the recruitment pipeline and identification of any bottlenecks.
- **Candidate Application Management:** Use JIRA to store and manage candidate applications. Create custom fields to track essential information, such as resume, cover letter, and references. Easily filter and sort candidates based on qualifications and experience.
- **Interview Scheduling:** Schedule and track interviews using JIRA's calendar view or by linking JIRA issues to calendar events. This ensures that interviews are well-organized and no candidate falls through the cracks.

Real-World Example: A recruitment team uses JIRA to manage their hiring process. They create a JIRA project for each job opening, with issue types like "Candidate Application" and "Interview." They use custom fields to track candidate information and create a Kanban board to visualize the recruitment pipeline.

Onboarding and Training

JIRA can streamline the onboarding process and facilitate employee training and development. Here's how:

- **Onboarding Checklists:** Create JIRA issues to represent onboarding tasks, such as setting up email accounts, providing access to systems, and scheduling orientation sessions. Use checklists within the issues to track the completion of each task.
- **Training Progress Tracking:** Create JIRA projects for different training programs and track employee progress through custom workflows. This allows you to monitor who has completed which training modules and identify any areas where additional support might be needed.
- **Performance Reviews:** Use JIRA to schedule and track performance reviews, set goals, and document feedback. This creates a centralized record of employee performance and facilitates ongoing development discussions.

Real-World Example: An HR team uses JIRA to manage employee onboarding. They create a JIRA project for each new hire, with issue types like "Onboarding Task" and "Training Module." They use checklists to track the completion of onboarding tasks and create reports to monitor the overall onboarding progress.

Employee Help Desk

JIRA Service Management (JSM) is a powerful tool for providing IT support and service management within your organization. It enables employees to submit help desk tickets, request services, and track the status of their requests. HR teams can leverage JSM to:

- **Manage Employee Inquiries:** Employees can easily submit questions or issues related to HR policies, benefits, payroll, or other HR-related matters.
- **Track and Resolve Requests:** HR teams can use JIRA's issue tracking features to assign and track requests, ensuring timely resolution.
- **Create a Knowledge Base:** JSM's knowledge base functionality allows HR teams to create articles and FAQs to address common employee questions, reducing the need for repetitive inquiries.

Real-World Example: An HR team uses JIRA Service Management to create an employee self-service portal. Employees can submit various requests, such as leave requests, benefits enrollment, or IT support tickets. The HR team uses JIRA workflows and SLAs to ensure timely resolution of requests and improve employee satisfaction.

By harnessing the power of JIRA for HR and recruitment, organizations can streamline their processes, improve communication, and enhance the overall employee experience. JIRA's flexibility and customization options make it a valuable asset for managing the entire employee lifecycle, from recruitment and onboarding to training and development.

JIRA for IT Service Management

JIRA Service Management (JSM), previously known as JIRA Service Desk, is a powerful solution designed to streamline and enhance IT service management (ITSM) processes. It empowers IT teams to efficiently handle incidents, manage changes, and address underlying problems, ultimately improving the overall IT service delivery and user satisfaction.

Incident Management

JSM provides a structured framework for managing IT incidents, which are unplanned disruptions or reductions in the quality of IT services. With JSM, IT teams can:

- **Log Incidents:** Users can easily submit incident reports through a user-friendly portal, providing details about the issue they are facing.
- **Prioritize and Assign Incidents:** IT teams can prioritize incidents based on urgency and impact, and assign them to the appropriate technicians for resolution.
- **Track Progress:** JIRA's issue tracking features allow teams to monitor the progress of incidents, ensuring timely resolution and keeping stakeholders informed.
- **Automate Workflows:** JSM enables the creation of automated workflows to streamline incident response and resolution processes, reducing manual effort and improving efficiency.

Change Management

JSM also supports change management, which involves planning, implementing, and tracking changes to IT systems and infrastructure. With JSM, IT teams can:

- **Create Change Requests:** Users can submit change requests through the portal, providing details about the desired change and its potential impact.
- **Assess and Approve Changes:** IT teams can assess the risks and benefits of proposed changes and seek approval from relevant stakeholders.
- **Implement and Track Changes:** Once approved, changes can be implemented, and their progress tracked within JIRA. This ensures that changes are implemented safely and effectively.
- **Communicate Changes:** JSM can be configured to notify stakeholders about the status of change requests and their implementation, ensuring transparency and minimizing disruption.

Problem Management

JSM includes tools for problem management, which focuses on identifying and addressing the root causes of recurring incidents. This proactive approach aims to prevent future incidents and improve the overall stability of IT services. With JSM, IT teams can:

- **Link Incidents to Problems:** When multiple incidents share a common root cause, they can be linked to a problem issue in JIRA. This helps track the investigation and resolution of the underlying problem.
- **Analyze Trends:** JSM's reporting features can help identify patterns and trends in incidents, pointing to potential problems that need further investigation.
- **Implement Solutions:** Once a problem is identified, JSM can be used to track the implementation of solutions and monitor their effectiveness.

Real-World Examples

Here's how IT teams are using JIRA Service Management:

- **Managing Support Tickets:** A large enterprise uses JSM to manage thousands of incoming support tickets each month, ensuring timely resolution and providing a centralized view of all IT issues.
- **Automating Incident Response:** A software company uses JSM to automate incident response workflows, reducing manual effort and ensuring faster resolution times.
- **Creating a Knowledge Base:** A university IT department uses JSM to build a knowledge base of solutions for common problems, empowering users to self-resolve issues and reducing the burden on the help desk.

By implementing JIRA Service Management, IT teams can transform their service delivery processes, improve customer satisfaction, and ensure that IT services remain reliable and efficient.

JIRA in Education

While traditionally associated with software development, JIRA's versatility extends to the educational realm. It offers a structured framework that can be adapted to various educational contexts, from course management and student project tracking to research collaboration.

Course Management

JIRA can serve as a powerful tool for organizing course materials, assignments, and grading. Educators can create JIRA projects for each course, with issues representing individual lessons, assignments, or quizzes.

- **Organizing Course Materials:** Instructors can attach lecture notes, presentations, and other course materials to JIRA issues, creating a centralized repository for students to access resources.
- **Managing Assignments:** Create JIRA issues for assignments, specifying due dates, grading criteria, and submission instructions. Students can submit their assignments directly through JIRA, and instructors can track submissions and provide feedback within the platform.
- **Grading and Feedback:** Utilize JIRA's custom fields to record grades and provide detailed feedback to students. This streamlines the grading process and ensures that feedback is easily accessible to students.

Student Project Tracking

JIRA can be a valuable asset for students working on group projects or individual assignments. By creating JIRA projects for their projects, students can:

- **Define Tasks:** Break down project requirements into smaller tasks and assign them to team members.
- **Track Progress:** Monitor the progress of each task and the overall project timeline.
- **Collaborate Effectively:** Utilize JIRA's commenting and notification features to communicate with team members, share updates, and discuss challenges.
- **Manage Deadlines:** Ensure timely completion of tasks by setting deadlines and receiving reminders in JIRA.

Research Collaboration

In the realm of research, collaboration is key. JIRA can facilitate collaboration among researchers on joint projects by:

- **Centralizing Information:** Create a JIRA project to store research data, notes, and findings in one place, accessible to all team members.
- **Tracking Experiments:** Create JIRA issues to track the progress of individual experiments, including hypothesis, methodology, results, and conclusions.
- **Managing Publications:** Use JIRA to manage the publication process, tracking manuscript drafts, revisions, and submissions to journals or conferences.
- **Coordinating Tasks:** Assign tasks to team members, track their progress, and ensure that everyone is working towards the common research goals.

JIRA's flexibility allows it to be tailored to the specific needs of educational institutions and research teams. By leveraging its features for task management, collaboration, and documentation, JIRA can empower educators, students, and researchers to achieve their goals more efficiently and effectively.

JIRA for Nonprofits

JIRA's adaptability extends to the nonprofit sector, providing valuable tools for organizations to manage projects, volunteers, and fundraising efforts efficiently. By leveraging JIRA's capabilities, nonprofits can streamline their operations, improve collaboration, and maximize their impact.

Project Management

Nonprofits often undertake diverse projects, such as community outreach programs, advocacy campaigns, or fundraising events. JIRA's project management features can be instrumental in ensuring these projects are well-organized and successfully executed.

- **Planning and Tracking:** Nonprofits can create JIRA projects for each initiative, defining goals, milestones, and tasks. They can assign tasks to team members, track progress, and visualize timelines to ensure that projects stay on track.
- **Resource Allocation:** JIRA helps nonprofits allocate resources effectively, whether it's assigning volunteers to specific tasks or allocating budget to different project phases. This ensures that resources are utilized optimally to achieve the organization's goals.
- **Donation Tracking:** Nonprofits can utilize JIRA to track donations, including donor information, donation amounts, and payment methods. This allows for better transparency and accountability in managing funds.

Volunteer Management

Volunteers are the backbone of many nonprofit organizations. JIRA can help streamline volunteer management by:

- **Recruitment and Onboarding:** Create JIRA issues to track volunteer applications, schedule interviews, and manage onboarding processes. This ensures a smooth and efficient onboarding experience for new volunteers.
- **Task Assignment and Tracking:** Assign tasks to volunteers based on their skills and interests. Track their progress using JIRA's issue tracking features to ensure that tasks are completed and deadlines are met.
- **Communication and Collaboration:** Use JIRA's commenting and notification features to communicate with volunteers, provide feedback, and foster collaboration among team members.

Fundraising Campaigns

Fundraising is a critical activity for nonprofits. JIRA can help plan and execute fundraising campaigns effectively by:

- **Campaign Planning:** Create a JIRA project for each campaign, outlining goals, timelines, and strategies.
- **Task Management:** Break down the campaign into smaller tasks, such as creating marketing materials, organizing events, and soliciting donations. Assign tasks to team members and track their progress.
- **Goal Tracking:** Use JIRA's reporting features to track donations, monitor progress towards fundraising goals, and analyze campaign performance.
- **Donor Management:** Track donor information and communication history within JIRA, facilitating personalized engagement and follow-up.

By leveraging JIRA's versatility, nonprofits can streamline their operations, enhance collaboration, and achieve their mission more effectively. Whether it's managing projects, volunteers, or fundraising campaigns, JIRA provides a powerful and adaptable platform to support the work of organizations dedicated to making a positive impact on the world.

Cross-Functional Collaboration with JIRA

In today's dynamic business landscape, successful organizations thrive on cross-functional collaboration. Teams from different departments need to work together seamlessly to achieve common goals. JIRA, with its versatile features and flexible workflows, serves as an ideal platform for fostering this collaboration.

A Centralized Hub for Collaboration

JIRA acts as a central hub where teams from diverse departments can come together to plan, track, and manage their work collaboratively. By creating projects that involve multiple teams, you can break down silos and promote cross-functional communication and coordination.

Flexible Workflows for Diverse Teams

JIRA's customizable workflows can be tailored to the specific needs of each team or department. This ensures that everyone can follow their own established processes while still maintaining visibility and transparency across the entire organization. For example, a marketing team might have a workflow for content creation and approval, while a development team might have a separate workflow for bug tracking and feature development.

Issue Linking for Seamless Collaboration

JIRA's issue linking feature enables teams to connect related issues, even across different projects. This is particularly valuable for cross-functional collaboration. For instance, a marketing team can link a "Launch New Product" task to a development team's "Implement Product Feature" task. This creates a clear link between marketing and development activities, ensuring alignment and coordination.

Reporting for Organizational Insight

JIRA's reporting capabilities provide a comprehensive view of project progress and team performance across the organization. You can create cross-project reports and dashboards that aggregate data from different teams, allowing you to identify bottlenecks, track overall progress, and measure the impact of cross-functional initiatives.

Real-World Examples

Here are some examples of how JIRA can foster cross-functional collaboration:

- **Marketing and Development:** Marketing teams can use JIRA to submit feature requests and track their progress, while development teams can update the status of these requests and provide feedback within JIRA.
- **HR and IT:** HR teams can use JIRA to track onboarding tasks for new employees, while IT teams can create and manage tickets for hardware requests or software installations.
- **Sales and Customer Support:** Sales teams can use JIRA to log customer feedback or feature requests, which can then be prioritized and addressed by the development team.

By providing a centralized platform for communication, coordination, and knowledge sharing, JIRA empowers teams to work together seamlessly, regardless of their department or location. This cross-functional collaboration not only streamlines workflows but also fosters a culture of transparency and accountability, leading to improved efficiency, innovation, and overall organizational success.

Chapter Summary

In this chapter, we explored the diverse real-world applications of JIRA across various industries and functions. We highlighted how JIRA's flexibility and robust features make it a valuable asset for teams beyond software development.

We delved into how JIRA can be used for campaign management, content creation, and event planning in marketing, showcasing examples of tracking social media campaigns, managing content calendars, and coordinating webinars or product launches.

Furthermore, we discussed how JIRA can streamline HR and recruitment processes, including tracking job openings, managing candidate applications, scheduling interviews, creating onboarding checklists, tracking training progress, and managing performance reviews. We also explored how JIRA Service Management can be used to create employee help desks and manage IT support requests.

We then highlighted JIRA's applicability in education, from organizing course materials and assignments to tracking student projects and facilitating research collaboration. We also discussed how nonprofits can utilize JIRA for project management, volunteer management, and fundraising campaigns.

Finally, we emphasized the power of JIRA as a central hub for cross-functional collaboration. By connecting teams from different departments, JIRA fosters communication, coordination, and knowledge sharing, ultimately driving organizational efficiency and success.

By showcasing these diverse use cases, we aim to demonstrate the wide-ranging potential of JIRA as a versatile tool that can adapt to the unique needs of various teams and organizations. Whether you're in software development, marketing, HR, IT, education, or the nonprofit sector, JIRA can be tailored to streamline your processes, improve collaboration, and achieve your goals more effectively.

Real-World Use Cases for Confluence

Outline:

- Confluence in Software Development
- Confluence for Marketing and Sales Teams
- Confluence in HR and Operations
- Confluence for IT and Support Teams
- Confluence for Education and Research
- Confluence for Personal Use
- Chapter Summary

Confluence in Software Development

Confluence plays a crucial role throughout the software development lifecycle (SDLC), acting as a central repository for information and a collaborative platform for teams. It streamlines communication, enhances documentation, and promotes knowledge sharing, ultimately contributing to the success of software projects.

Requirement Gathering and Documentation

In the initial phases of a software project, Confluence serves as a collaborative workspace where product managers, designers, and stakeholders can gather and document requirements. Teams can create dedicated spaces for each project and utilize various page types to capture different aspects of the requirements:

- **Product Requirements Pages:** Clearly articulate the overall goals, objectives, and scope of the project.
- **User Story Pages:** Capture user stories in a standardized format, including the user role, desired action, and benefit.
- **Acceptance Criteria Pages:** Define the specific conditions that must be met for a user story to be considered complete and accepted.

By documenting requirements in Confluence, teams ensure that everyone has a shared understanding of what needs to be built, minimizing misunderstandings and rework later in the development process.

Technical Documentation

As the project moves into the design and development phases, Confluence becomes a repository for technical documentation. Teams can create and maintain comprehensive documentation for various aspects of the software, including:

- **Design Documents:** Outline the system architecture, data models, user interface designs, and other technical specifications.
- **API Specifications:** Document the application programming interfaces (APIs) that the software exposes, including endpoints, request/response formats, and authentication mechanisms.
- **Deployment Guides:** Provide step-by-step instructions on how to deploy and configure the software in different environments.

Confluence's rich text editor and powerful formatting options make it easy to create professional-looking technical documentation that is easy to understand and follow.

Knowledge Sharing

Confluence fosters knowledge sharing and collaboration among team members throughout the SDLC. Teams can use Confluence to:

- **Share Best Practices:** Document coding standards, design patterns, and other best practices to ensure consistency and quality across the codebase.
- **Create How-to Guides:** Provide step-by-step instructions on how to perform specific tasks or use particular tools.
- **Document Troubleshooting Tips:** Share solutions to common problems and known issues to help team members quickly resolve issues.
- **Collaborate on Code Reviews:** Use Confluence's commenting and annotation features to review code, provide feedback, and suggest improvements.

Examples of Confluence in Software Development

- **Product Roadmaps:** Create and share product roadmaps that outline the project's vision, goals, and release timeline.
- **Sprint Planning and Retrospectives:** Document sprint planning meetings and retrospective sessions to capture decisions, action items, and lessons learned.
- **Technical Knowledge Base:** Maintain a central repository of technical documentation, including design documents, API specifications, deployment guides, and troubleshooting tips.

By integrating Confluence into their software development workflow, teams can improve communication, collaboration, and knowledge sharing, ultimately leading to faster development cycles, higher quality software, and increased team productivity.

Confluence for Marketing and Sales Teams

Confluence extends its utility beyond technical teams, proving to be a valuable asset for marketing and sales teams. Its collaborative nature and versatile features empower these teams to streamline their processes, centralize information, and improve communication, ultimately leading to more effective marketing campaigns and successful sales outcomes.

Marketing Campaign Planning

Confluence acts as a central hub for planning and organizing marketing campaigns. Teams can create dedicated spaces for each campaign, where they can collaborate on:

- **Defining Goals:** Clearly articulate the campaign's objectives, whether it's increasing brand awareness, generating leads, or driving sales.
- **Identifying Target Audiences:** Document detailed buyer personas to understand the needs, interests, and pain points of the target audience.
- **Crafting Messaging:** Develop compelling messaging that resonates with the target audience and aligns with the campaign goals.
- **Choosing Channels:** Determine the most effective marketing channels to reach the target audience, whether it's social media, email marketing, content marketing, or paid advertising.
- **Creating a Timeline:** Outline the campaign timeline, including key milestones and deadlines for each activity.

Real-World Example: A marketing team uses Confluence to create a comprehensive marketing plan for a new product launch. The plan includes detailed information about the target audience, messaging, channels, budget, and timeline. Team members can easily access and collaborate on the plan within Confluence, ensuring everyone is aligned and working towards the same goals.

Sales Enablement

Confluence serves as a powerful tool for sales enablement, providing sales teams with the knowledge and resources they need to close deals. Some common use cases include:

- **Sales Playbooks:** Create detailed playbooks that outline sales strategies, objection handling techniques, and best practices for closing deals.
- **Competitive Battlecards:** Develop battlecards that compare your product or service with competitors, highlighting your unique selling points and addressing potential objections.
- **Product Information Sheets:** Create comprehensive product information sheets that provide detailed descriptions, features, benefits, and use cases of your products or services.

Real-World Example: A sales team uses Confluence to store and share sales playbooks, battlecards, and product information sheets. They can easily access these resources during sales calls or meetings, ensuring they have the most up-to-date information at their fingertips.

Customer-Facing Documentation

Confluence can also be used to create customer-facing documentation, such as:

- **User Guides:** Provide step-by-step instructions on how to use your product or service.
- **Product Manuals:** Offer detailed information about product features, specifications, and troubleshooting tips.
- **Knowledge Base Articles:** Create a library of self-service articles that address common customer questions and issues.

Real-World Example: A software company uses Confluence to host their customer knowledge base. Customers can easily search for and access articles that help them troubleshoot problems, understand features, and get the most out of the product.

Additional Use Cases

Here are some additional examples of how marketing and sales teams utilize Confluence:

- **Creating marketing plans and content calendars.**
- **Sharing customer feedback and success stories.**
- **Collaborating on sales proposals and presentations.**
- **Tracking lead generation and conversion metrics.**
- **Managing partner and affiliate relationships.**

By leveraging Confluence's collaborative features and versatile content creation tools, marketing and sales teams can improve communication, streamline their processes, and ultimately drive greater success in their efforts.

Confluence in HR and Operations

Confluence proves to be a valuable asset for HR and operations teams, streamlining their processes, centralizing information, and fostering collaboration. Its versatility and collaborative features empower these teams to manage onboarding, document policies and procedures, and create an internal company intranet, ultimately contributing to a more efficient and organized workplace.

Onboarding and Training

Confluence provides a comprehensive platform for onboarding new employees, ensuring a smooth and successful transition into their roles. Teams can create and share:

- **Onboarding Guides:** Create step-by-step guides that outline the onboarding process, including company culture, policies, procedures, and benefits.

- **Training Materials:** Develop and share training materials, such as presentations, videos, and job aids, to help new employees learn the necessary skills and knowledge.
- **Employee Handbooks:** Create and maintain employee handbooks that provide comprehensive information about company policies, benefits, and expectations.

Real-World Example: An HR team uses Confluence to create an onboarding guide for new software engineers. The guide includes information about the company culture, the engineering team, the software development lifecycle, and the tools and technologies used by the team.

Policy and Procedure Documentation

Confluence serves as a central repository for documenting and managing company policies and procedures. Teams can create dedicated spaces for different categories of policies, such as human resources, finance, IT, and safety. Within these spaces, they can create and share:

- **Policy Documents:** Clearly outline company policies on various topics, such as employee conduct, discrimination, harassment, and leave of absence.
- **Procedure Documents:** Provide step-by-step instructions on how to perform specific tasks, such as requesting time off, submitting expense reports, or resolving IT issues.
- **Guidelines:** Offer guidance on best practices for various aspects of the job, such as communication, collaboration, and problem-solving.

Real-World Example: An operations team uses Confluence to document the procedures for handling customer complaints. The procedure document outlines the steps for receiving, investigating, and resolving customer complaints.

Company Intranet

Confluence can be used to create a comprehensive internal company intranet, providing a central platform for communication, collaboration, and information sharing. Teams can create spaces for different departments, projects, and teams. Within these spaces, they can share:

- **Company News and Announcements:** Keep employees informed about important company news, events, and changes.
- **Team Updates and Projects:** Share updates on team projects, milestones, and achievements.
- **Employee Resources:** Provide access to employee resources, such as benefits information, payroll information, and training materials.
- **Discussion Forums:** Facilitate communication and collaboration among employees by creating discussion forums on various topics.

Real-World Example: A company uses Confluence to create an internal intranet for its employees. The intranet includes information about the company, its products and services, its employees, and its benefits. It also includes a directory of employees, a calendar of events, and a discussion forum.

By leveraging Confluence's collaborative features and versatile content creation tools, HR and operations teams can improve communication, streamline their processes, and create a more organized and efficient workplace.

Confluence for IT and Support Teams

Confluence provides a robust platform for IT and support teams to streamline their processes, document knowledge, and collaborate effectively. Its versatile features and integrations with other tools like JIRA make it an indispensable asset for managing IT operations and providing efficient support.

Incident and Problem Management

Confluence serves as a central repository for documenting and tracking IT incidents and problems. Teams can create dedicated spaces for incident management and use pages to:

- **Log Incidents:** Record detailed information about each incident, including its description, impact, affected users, and timeline.
- **Investigate Causes:** Document the investigation process, including troubleshooting steps, analysis of logs and metrics, and communication with stakeholders.
- **Document Resolutions:** Record the steps taken to resolve the incident, the solution implemented, and any lessons learned.
- **Track Problems:** Identify and document recurring incidents that might indicate underlying problems. This helps prioritize investigations and implement long-term solutions.

Real-World Example: An IT team uses Confluence to create an incident report template. Whenever an incident occurs, they create a new page based on the template and fill in the relevant details. This ensures consistent documentation and allows them to track the progress of each incident.

Change Management

Confluence facilitates effective change management by providing a structured platform for documenting and tracking changes to IT systems and infrastructure. Teams can use Confluence to:

- **Document Change Requests:** Create change request templates that capture essential information like the purpose of the change, the affected systems, potential risks, and the implementation plan.
- **Track Approvals:** Use Confluence's commenting and approval features to streamline the approval process for change requests.
- **Document Implementation:** Record the details of change implementation, including steps taken, results, and any issues encountered.
- **Maintain Change History:** Keep a detailed log of all changes made to systems and infrastructure, providing valuable context for future troubleshooting and analysis.

Real-World Example: An IT team uses Confluence to document a change request for upgrading a critical software component. The change request includes detailed information about the upgrade process, potential risks, and rollback procedures. The team also uses Confluence to track approvals and document the actual implementation of the change.

Knowledge Base

Confluence is an ideal platform for building an internal knowledge base for IT teams. By creating and organizing pages with solutions to common IT problems, teams can:

- **Reduce Repetitive Support Requests:** Empower users to self-resolve issues by providing easy-to-access troubleshooting guides and FAQs.
- **Improve Onboarding:** Create onboarding materials for new IT team members, providing them with essential information about systems, processes, and procedures.
- **Share Best Practices:** Document best practices for system administration, software configuration, and incident response.

Real-World Examples:

- An IT team creates a Confluence space for their knowledge base, organizing pages by topic (e.g., networking, server administration, software troubleshooting).
- A support team uses Confluence to create detailed runbooks for common troubleshooting scenarios, providing step-by-step instructions for resolving issues.
- A system administrator documents system configurations and network diagrams in Confluence to ensure that the information is easily accessible for reference and troubleshooting.

By leveraging Confluence for IT and support, teams can improve their efficiency, enhance collaboration, and ultimately deliver a more reliable and responsive service to their users.

Confluence for Education and Research

Confluence is a versatile tool that can be applied beyond business and IT environments to educational and research settings. Its collaborative features and ability to organize information make it an excellent platform for knowledge sharing, collaboration, and documentation in academic and research contexts.

Course Materials

Confluence can revolutionize the way course materials are created, organized, and shared. Instructors can use Confluence spaces to create a dedicated hub for each course, where they can:

- **Create and Share Lecture Notes:** Create detailed lecture notes with rich formatting, images, and multimedia elements. These notes can be easily shared with students, providing them with comprehensive study material.
- **Organize Assignments:** Create assignments, specify due dates, grading criteria, and submission instructions. Students can access and submit assignments directly within Confluence, streamlining the process.
- **Facilitate Discussion:** Enable student collaboration by encouraging them to comment on pages, ask questions, and share their insights.
- **Create Study Guides and FAQs:** Develop study guides and FAQs to help students prepare for exams and understand complex concepts.

Research Collaboration

In the research world, collaboration is essential for driving innovation and discovery. Confluence provides a powerful platform for researchers to collaborate on joint projects, regardless of their location.

- **Share Data and Findings:** Create shared spaces for research projects where team members can upload and share data, analysis results, and research findings.
- **Document Research Processes:** Use Confluence pages to document research methodologies, protocols, and experiments. This ensures reproducibility and allows for knowledge transfer within the team.
- **Collaborate on Publications:** Co-author research papers, grant proposals, and other publications in Confluence. Utilize collaborative editing features to streamline the writing and review process.
- **Create Project Wikis:** Build wikis to document project goals, timelines, deliverables, and milestones. This helps keep everyone on the same page and ensures that the project stays on track.
- **Organize Literature Reviews:** Create pages to summarize and synthesize research findings from relevant literature, making it easier for the team to stay informed about the latest developments in their field.

By leveraging Confluence's collaborative features and information management capabilities, educational institutions and research teams can enhance knowledge sharing, streamline processes, and foster a more efficient and productive research environment.

Confluence for Personal Use

While Confluence is renowned for its collaborative capabilities, its utility extends beyond the team environment. Individuals can harness Confluence's versatile features for personal knowledge management, organization, and self-expression.

Note-taking

Confluence serves as a powerful note-taking tool, allowing you to capture and organize information from various sources. You can create pages for different topics or projects, add notes from meetings, lectures, or readings, and embed multimedia elements like images, videos, or audio recordings.

With Confluence's rich text editor and flexible formatting options, you can structure your notes in a way that makes sense to you. Use headings, lists, and tables to organize your thoughts, and highlight important points with bold or italics. You can also add labels to your notes to categorize them and make them easier to find later.

Personal Wikis

A personal wiki is a private knowledge base where you can document your hobbies, interests, or personal projects. Confluence's intuitive interface and collaborative features make it easy to create and maintain a personal wiki. You can create pages for different topics, link them together, and embed various types of content to create a rich and informative resource.

For example, if you're passionate about cooking, you can create a personal wiki to store your favorite recipes, cooking tips, and meal plans. If you're learning a new language, you can create a wiki to track your progress, store vocabulary lists, and practice grammar exercises.

Journaling

Confluence can also serve as a digital journal, where you can reflect on your experiences, thoughts, and feelings. You can create private pages to write daily entries, track your goals, or document your personal growth. The flexibility of Confluence allows you to personalize your journal with images, quotes, or other meaningful content.

By using Confluence for note-taking, personal wikis, and journaling, you can create a centralized and organized repository of your knowledge and ideas. This not only helps you keep track of information but also fosters self-reflection, creativity, and personal growth.

Chapter Summary

In this chapter, we explored the versatility of Confluence by delving into real-world use cases across various industries and teams. We showcased how Confluence empowers teams to collaborate, document, and share knowledge effectively.

We began by examining Confluence's pivotal role in software development, where it supports requirements gathering, technical documentation, and knowledge sharing throughout the SDLC. We discussed how Confluence pages can house product requirements, design documents, API specifications, deployment guides, best practices, and troubleshooting tips.

Next, we shifted our focus to marketing and sales teams, highlighting how Confluence can streamline campaign planning, enable sales teams with playbooks and battlecards, and facilitate the creation of customer-facing documentation like user guides and knowledge base articles.

We then explored Confluence's applications in HR and operations, showcasing how it can streamline onboarding and training processes, centralize policy and procedure documentation, and serve as a comprehensive company intranet.

We also discussed how IT and support teams can leverage Confluence for incident and problem management, change management, and knowledge base creation, leading to improved efficiency and faster issue resolution.

Moreover, we touched upon Confluence's usefulness in education and research, where it can be used to organize course materials, foster research collaboration, and document findings.

Finally, we illustrated how individuals can utilize Confluence for personal knowledge management, note-taking, creating personal wikis, and journaling.

By showcasing these diverse use cases, we aimed to demonstrate the wide-ranging applicability of Confluence across different industries and teams. Whether you're a software developer, marketer, HR professional, IT specialist, educator, researcher, or individual, Confluence can be tailored to meet your unique needs and enhance your productivity.

Lessons Learned and Tips for Success

Outline

- Lessons Learned from Real-World JIRA and Confluence Implementations
- Tips for Successful JIRA and Confluence Adoption
- Additional Tips for Maximizing Productivity
- Common Pitfalls to Avoid
- Embracing a Continuous Improvement Mindset
- Chapter Summary

Lessons Learned from Real-World JIRA and Confluence Implementations

JIRA and Confluence are powerful tools, but their successful implementation is not always a smooth journey. Real-world experiences have taught us valuable lessons about the challenges and pitfalls that can arise during the adoption process. By understanding these lessons, you can navigate your own implementation more effectively and avoid common mistakes.

Common Challenges

- **Resistance to Change:** Introducing new tools like JIRA and Confluence often faces resistance from team members who are accustomed to their existing workflows. This resistance can stem from fear of the unknown, concerns about the learning curve, or simply a preference for familiar tools.
- **Lack of Training and Support:** Inadequate training and support can hinder user adoption and lead to frustration and resistance. Users need to understand the benefits of the tools, how they work, and how they can be applied to their specific tasks.
- **Overcomplication:** JIRA and Confluence are highly customizable, but overcomplicating workflows, fields, and screens can overwhelm users and make the tools difficult to use. Start with a simple setup and gradually add complexity as needed.
- **Data Migration Issues:** Migrating data from existing systems to JIRA or Confluence can be a complex process. Inaccurate or incomplete data migration can lead to errors, confusion, and delays.
- **Integration Challenges:** Integrating JIRA and Confluence with other tools can be tricky, especially if the tools are not designed to work together seamlessly. This can result in data inconsistencies, workflow disruptions, and frustration for users.

Lessons Learned

- **Communication is Key:** Effective communication is crucial throughout the implementation process. Clearly articulate the benefits of JIRA and Confluence to your team, provide ample training and support, and address any concerns or questions promptly.
- **Start Simple, Scale Gradually:** Don't try to implement all features at once. Start with a simple setup that addresses the most critical needs, and gradually add more complexity as your team becomes familiar with the tools.
- **Focus on User Adoption:** Make the tools easy to use and relevant to your team's work. Gather feedback regularly and make adjustments to the setup based on user input.
- **Data Migration Requires Diligence:** Plan your data migration carefully and thoroughly test the process before going live. Consider using data migration tools or seeking professional help if needed.

- **Test Integrations Thoroughly:** Before deploying any integration to production, test it thoroughly in a staging environment to ensure it works as expected and doesn't cause any conflicts or errors.

Practical Advice

- **Get Buy-In:** Involve stakeholders and end-users in the planning process to get their buy-in and ensure that the tools meet their needs.
- **Provide Ample Training:** Offer comprehensive training sessions, create user guides, and provide ongoing support to help users master the tools.
- **Start with a Pilot Project:** Implement JIRA and Confluence on a small scale first to test the waters and identify any issues before rolling out to the entire organization.
- **Monitor and Measure:** Track usage and adoption metrics to identify areas where users are struggling and make necessary adjustments.
- **Celebrate Success:** Highlight the successes and benefits of using JIRA and Confluence to encourage further adoption and engagement.

By learning from real-world experiences and implementing these best practices, you can increase your chances of a successful JIRA and Confluence implementation, transforming the way your team works and achieving your project goals more efficiently.

Tips for Successful JIRA and Confluence Adoption

Successfully adopting JIRA and Confluence into your organization's workflow requires more than just installing the software. It's a process that involves careful planning, effective communication, ongoing training, and continuous improvement. Here are some practical tips to help you achieve a smooth and successful adoption:

Clear Communication and Training

- **Educate Users on Benefits:** Clearly articulate the benefits of JIRA and Confluence to your team. Explain how these tools can streamline workflows, enhance collaboration, and improve productivity. Highlight specific features and functionalities that will be most relevant to their work.
- **Provide Comprehensive Training:** Offer comprehensive training sessions to all users, covering the basics of JIRA and Confluence as well as more advanced features. Use a variety of training methods, such as live demonstrations, interactive workshops, video tutorials, and written documentation, to cater to different learning styles.
- **Foster Open Communication:** Encourage open communication and feedback channels where users can ask questions, raise concerns, or suggest improvements. This helps address any issues early on and fosters a sense of ownership and engagement among users.

Gradual Rollout

- **Start with a Pilot Project:** Begin by implementing JIRA and Confluence in a pilot project or with a small team. This allows you to test the tools in a controlled environment, gather feedback, and identify any potential issues before rolling them out to the entire organization.
- **Expand Gradually:** Once the pilot project is successful, gradually expand the use of JIRA and Confluence to other teams or departments. This allows you to iterate on your implementation based on the feedback received and ensures a smoother transition for the wider organization.

Customization and Configuration

- **Tailor to Your Needs:** JIRA and Confluence are highly customizable. Take advantage of this flexibility to tailor the tools to your organization's specific needs and processes. This might involve creating custom fields, workflows, screens, or integrations with other tools.

- **Keep It Simple:** Avoid over-customizing the tools initially. Start with a simple configuration that meets your core requirements and gradually add complexity as needed.
- **Engage Experts:** If you have complex customization needs, consider engaging JIRA and Confluence experts or consultants who can help you tailor the tools to your specific environment.

Continuous Feedback and Iteration

- **Regularly Collect Feedback:** Continuously gather feedback from users to identify any issues, challenges, or areas for improvement. You can use surveys, feedback forms, or direct conversations to collect input.
- **Act on Feedback:** Analyze the feedback received and make necessary adjustments to your JIRA and Confluence setup. This could involve refining workflows, adding new features, or providing additional training.
- **Iterate and Improve:** View adoption as an ongoing process of continuous improvement. Regularly evaluate the effectiveness of your JIRA and Confluence implementation and make incremental changes to optimize their use and ensure long-term success.

By following these tips, you can significantly increase the chances of a successful JIRA and Confluence adoption within your organization. Remember, the key is to focus on user needs, provide adequate support, and continuously adapt your implementation based on feedback and evolving requirements.

Additional Tips for Maximizing Productivity

Beyond the fundamentals of JIRA and Confluence adoption, there are several additional tips and tricks that can significantly enhance your team's productivity and make the most of these powerful tools.

Keyboard Shortcuts

JIRA and Confluence offer a wealth of keyboard shortcuts that can save you valuable time and streamline your workflow. By learning these shortcuts, you can navigate the interfaces, create and edit content, and perform common actions with lightning speed. Some essential shortcuts include:

- **JIRA:**
    - c: Create issue
    - e: Edit issue
    - /: Quick search
    - g + g: Go to dashboard
- **Confluence:**
    - c: Create page
    - e: Edit page
    - /: Quick search
    - b: Insert/edit link
    - {: Insert macro

Refer to the JIRA and Confluence documentation for a comprehensive list of available keyboard shortcuts.

Templates and Blueprints

Templates and blueprints are pre-designed page layouts or step-by-step guides that save you the hassle of creating content from scratch. They ensure consistency in formatting and structure, and they often include placeholder content and prompts to guide you through the creation process. Utilize templates for common document types like meeting notes, project plans, and status reports. Employ blueprints for more complex documents, such as product requirements or technical specifications.

Automation

Automation is a productivity powerhouse. JIRA's automation features allow you to create rules that automatically perform actions based on specific triggers or conditions. This can significantly reduce manual effort and streamline your workflows. For example, you can set up rules to automatically assign issues to the right team member, send notifications when deadlines approach, or update fields based on certain events.

Integrations

Integrating JIRA and Confluence with other tools you use regularly can create a more cohesive and efficient work environment. For instance, integrating with Slack or Microsoft Teams allows you to receive JIRA notifications and discuss issues directly within your chat channels. Integrating with development tools like Bitbucket or GitHub allows you to link JIRA issues to code commits and pull requests, providing traceability and context. Explore the various integrations available to connect your tools and streamline your workflows.

By incorporating these tips into your daily routine, you can maximize your team's productivity with JIRA and Confluence. These tools are designed to make your work easier and more efficient, and with a little practice and experimentation, you can unlock their full potential.

Common Pitfalls to Avoid

While JIRA and Confluence are powerful tools, their implementation and usage can be riddled with pitfalls that can hinder productivity and diminish their value. Here are some common mistakes to watch out for:

- **Overcomplicating Workflows:** In the pursuit of perfectly mirroring every nuance of your process, it's easy to create overly complex workflows with numerous statuses, transitions, and conditions. This can lead to confusion among users, slow down progress, and make it difficult to track and manage issues effectively. Start with a simple workflow and gradually add complexity only when absolutely necessary.
- **Ignoring User Feedback:** Your team members are the ones who use JIRA and Confluence daily, so their feedback is invaluable. Ignoring their concerns or suggestions can lead to frustration, low adoption rates, and ultimately, an inefficient system. Regularly solicit feedback from users, take their input seriously, and make adjustments as needed to ensure the tools are meeting their needs.
- **Neglecting Maintenance:** JIRA and Confluence are complex software platforms that require regular maintenance, updates, and backups. Neglecting these tasks can lead to performance issues, security vulnerabilities, and data loss. Schedule regular maintenance windows to apply updates, optimize performance, and create backups of your data.
- **Over-reliance on Customization:** JIRA and Confluence offer extensive customization options, but excessive customization can be a double-edged sword. While it allows you to tailor the tools to your specific needs, it can also make them complex, difficult to manage, and prone to performance issues. Strive for a balance between customization and simplicity. Only customize when it truly adds value and avoid unnecessary complexity.

Additional Pitfalls

- **Lack of Planning:** Failing to properly plan your JIRA and Confluence implementation can lead to confusion, delays, and missed opportunities for optimization. Take the time to define your goals, gather requirements, and develop a clear implementation plan.
- **Insufficient Training:** Inadequate training can leave users feeling lost and frustrated. Provide comprehensive training on how to use the tools effectively, including both basic and advanced features. Offer ongoing support to answer questions and address any challenges that arise.

- **Lack of Governance:** Without clear guidelines and governance, your JIRA and Confluence instances can become disorganized and chaotic. Establish clear policies for naming conventions, content organization, and permission management.

By being aware of these common pitfalls and taking proactive measures to avoid them, you can ensure a smoother and more successful JIRA and Confluence implementation. Remember, these tools are meant to enhance collaboration and productivity, not hinder them. With careful planning, ongoing maintenance, and a focus on user needs, you can unlock the full potential of JIRA and Confluence for your team.

Embracing a Continuous Improvement Mindset

JIRA and Confluence are not static tools; they are constantly evolving platforms with new features, updates, and enhancements being released regularly. To truly master these tools and maximize their value, it's essential to adopt a continuous improvement mindset. This means constantly evaluating the effectiveness of your JIRA and Confluence setup, seeking feedback from users, and making incremental adjustments to optimize their use and ensure long-term success.

Regular Evaluation

Set aside time to periodically evaluate how JIRA and Confluence are being utilized in your organization. Analyze usage metrics, track key performance indicators (KPIs), and assess whether the tools are meeting your team's needs. Look for areas where workflows can be streamlined, processes can be automated, or user experience can be enhanced.

Gathering Feedback

Regularly solicit feedback from users to understand their pain points, challenges, and suggestions for improvement. This can be done through surveys, feedback forms, interviews, or informal conversations. Encourage open and honest communication, and create a safe space for users to share their thoughts and experiences.

Incremental Improvements

Based on your evaluation and user feedback, identify areas where you can make incremental improvements. These could be small changes, such as adding a new custom field, tweaking a workflow transition, or creating a new dashboard gadget. Or they could be larger changes, such as reorganizing your space hierarchy in Confluence or implementing a new JIRA automation rule.

The Iterative Process

Continuous improvement is an iterative process. It involves constantly evaluating, gathering feedback, and making small adjustments to optimize your JIRA and Confluence setup over time. There is no one-size-fits-all solution, so what works for one team or organization may not work for another. Be willing to experiment and try new things, and don't be afraid to make changes if something isn't working as expected.

The Benefits of Continuous Improvement

By embracing a continuous improvement mindset, you can:

- **Maximize Efficiency:** Streamline workflows, automate repetitive tasks, and reduce manual effort.
- **Improve User Experience:** Create a user-friendly environment that makes it easy for your team to collaborate and access the information they need.
- **Increase Adoption:** Encourage users to embrace JIRA and Confluence by continuously improving their experience and addressing their concerns.

- **Ensure Long-Term Success:** As your organization grows and evolves, your JIRA and Confluence setup should adapt to meet changing needs. A continuous improvement mindset ensures that your tools remain relevant and valuable for years to come.

Remember, mastering JIRA and Confluence is not a destination but a journey. By embracing a culture of continuous improvement, you can empower your team to achieve their goals and maximize the potential of these powerful tools.

Chapter Summary

In this chapter, we explored the key lessons learned from real-world implementations of JIRA and Confluence. We discussed common challenges faced during adoption, such as resistance to change, lack of training and support, overcomplication, data migration issues, and integration challenges. We also highlighted valuable lessons learned, emphasizing the importance of communication, starting simple, focusing on user adoption, and diligently managing data migration and integrations.

To ensure successful adoption, we offered practical tips, including clear communication and training, a gradual rollout approach, customization and configuration to meet specific needs, and a focus on continuous feedback and iteration. We also provided additional tips for maximizing productivity, such as using keyboard shortcuts, templates and blueprints, automation rules, and integrations with other tools.

Moreover, we highlighted common pitfalls to avoid, such as overcomplicating workflows, ignoring user feedback, neglecting maintenance, and over-relying on customization. By being aware of these pitfalls and taking proactive measures, you can navigate your JIRA and Confluence implementation more smoothly.

Finally, we encouraged readers to embrace a continuous improvement mindset, emphasizing the need to regularly evaluate the effectiveness of the tools, gather feedback from users, and make incremental adjustments to optimize their use and ensure long-term success. By incorporating these lessons and tips into your JIRA and Confluence journey, you can create a collaborative and productive environment that empowers your team to achieve their goals.

Appendices

Appendix A: JIRA Cheat Sheet

This cheat sheet provides a quick reference for essential JIRA commands, shortcuts, and features. It is designed to help you navigate the JIRA interface, create and manage issues, use Agile boards, and leverage JQL for advanced searches.

Basic Navigation

Command	Action
g + g	Go to dashboard
c	Create issue
e	Edit issue
/	Quick search
.	View next issue
,	View previous issue
Ctrl + Shift + S	Save issue
Shift + Enter	Add comment and submit

Issue Management

Command	Action
a	Assign issue
l	Link issue
m	Move issue to another project
v	View issue in new tab/window
w	Watch/unwatch issue

Agile Boards

Command	Action
w	Move issue to next column
q	Move issue to previous column

Shift + Click	Select multiple issues

JQL (JIRA Query Language)

Operator	Description
=	Equals
!=	Not equals
>	Greater than
<	Less than
>=	Greater than or equal to
<=	Less than or equal to
AND	Both conditions must be true
OR	At least one condition must be true
NOT	Excludes issues that match the condition
IN	Matches any value in a list of values
NOT IN	Excludes any value in a list of values
IS	Checks if a field has a value
IS NOT	Checks if a field does not have a value
ORDER BY	Sorts results by a specific field

Common JQL Functions

Function	Description
currentUser()	Returns the current user's username
membersOf("group")	Returns members of a specified group
startOfDay()	Returns the start of the current day
endOfDay()	Returns the end of the current day

Note: This cheat sheet is not exhaustive and only includes some of the most common JIRA commands and JQL operators. Refer to the official JIRA documentation for a complete reference.

Appendix B: Confluence Cheat Sheet

This cheat sheet provides a quick reference for essential Confluence commands, shortcuts, and features. It is designed to help you navigate the Confluence interface, create and edit pages, format content, and collaborate effectively with your team.

Basic Navigation

Command	Action
c	Create a new page
e	Edit the current page
s	Save the current page
/	Quick search
[	Go to the previous page in the hierarchy
]	Go to the next page in the hierarchy
Ctrl + S	Save page (Windows/Linux)
Cmd + S	Save page (Mac)

Text Formatting

Command	Action
Ctrl + B	Bold text (Windows/Linux)
Cmd + B	Bold text (Mac)
Ctrl + I	Italicize text (Windows/Linux)
Cmd + I	Italicize text (Mac)
Ctrl + U	Underline text (Windows/Linux)
Cmd + U	Underline text (Mac)
#	Heading 1
##	Heading 2
###	Heading 3
* list item	Bulleted list
1. list item	Numbered list
[link text](url)	Insert link

code block	Code block

Table Formatting

Command	Action
`/table`	Insert table
`Ctrl + Shift + T`	Insert table (Windows/Linux)
`Cmd + Shift + T`	Insert table (Mac)

Collaboration

Command	Action
`@username`	Mention a user
`[ ]`	Create a task

Macros

Macro	Description
`toc`	Table of Contents
`code`	Code Block
`drawio`	Draw.io Diagram
`jira`	Jira Issues
`status`	Status Indicator

Note: This cheat sheet is not exhaustive and only includes some of the most common Confluence commands and macros. Refer to the official Confluence documentation for a complete reference.

Appendix C: Additional Resources for Further Learning

This appendix provides a curated list of resources to help you deepen your knowledge and expertise in JIRA and Confluence. Whether you're a beginner looking for introductory tutorials or an experienced user seeking advanced tips and tricks, these resources will provide valuable insights and guidance.

Official Atlassian Resources

- **Atlassian Documentation:** The official documentation for JIRA and Confluence is a comprehensive resource for learning about the platforms' features, functionalities, and best practices.
    - JIRA Documentation: https://support.atlassian.com/jira-software-cloud/
    - Confluence Documentation: https://support.atlassian.com/confluence-cloud/
- **Atlassian University:** Atlassian offers online training courses and certifications on JIRA and Confluence, covering various topics from beginner to advanced levels.
    - Atlassian University: https://university.atlassian.com/
- **Atlassian Community:** The Atlassian Community is a vibrant online forum where you can ask questions, share ideas, and learn from other JIRA and Confluence users.
    - Atlassian Community: https://community.atlassian.com/

Blogs and Websites

- **The Atlassian Blog:** Stay up-to-date with the latest news, product updates, and best practices from Atlassian.
    - The Atlassian Blog: https://www.atlassian.com/blog
- **JIRA Training Hub:** A collection of JIRA training resources, including tutorials, webinars, and articles.
- **Confluence Training Hub:** A collection of Confluence training resources, including tutorials, webinars, and articles.
- **The Jira Guy:** A popular blog by Rachel Wright, a JIRA expert, offering tips, tricks, and tutorials.
    - The Jira Guy: https://thejiraguy.com/

Books

- **Practical JIRA Administration (3rd Edition):** A comprehensive guide to JIRA administration, covering installation, configuration, customization, and maintenance.
    - By Matthew Doar
- **JIRA Strategy Admin Workbook:** A practical workbook with exercises and examples to help you develop a JIRA strategy.
    - By Rachel Wright

Other Resources

- **Atlassian Marketplace:** Explore the Atlassian Marketplace for thousands of apps and add-ons that can extend the functionality of JIRA and Confluence.
    - Atlassian Marketplace: https://marketplace.atlassian.com/
- **LinkedIn Groups:** Join JIRA and Confluence groups on LinkedIn to connect with other users and share knowledge.
- **YouTube Channels:** Many YouTube channels offer tutorials and demos on JIRA and Confluence.

By actively utilizing these additional resources, you can stay up-to-date with the latest JIRA and Confluence developments, expand your knowledge, and continue to master these powerful tools for your agile project management needs.

Conclusion

In this comprehensive guide, "Mastering JIRA for Agile Projects: A Practical Guide with Real-World Examples (Confluence Included)," we have embarked on a journey to unlock the immense potential of JIRA and Confluence for seamless collaboration and efficient project management. We began by establishing a solid foundation, understanding the core concepts of these tools and how they can revolutionize your team's workflow.

We then delved into the practical aspects of setting up your JIRA account and project, navigating the interface, creating and managing issues, using agile boards, and configuring workflows. You learned how to harness JIRA's robust search capabilities and utilize JQL to pinpoint specific information. We also explored the intricacies of JIRA administration, covering user and group management, project roles and permissions, customization, and automation.

In the realm of Confluence, we discovered how to create and manage spaces, build and organize pages, leverage templates and blueprints, and foster collaboration among team members. We also discussed advanced Confluence features like user and permission management, integration with JIRA, and advanced formatting and macros.

Throughout this journey, we shared real-world examples and case studies that illustrated the practical applications of JIRA and Confluence across various industries and use cases. These examples showcased how these tools can be adapted to the unique needs of software development teams, marketing teams, HR departments, IT service management, educational institutions, nonprofits, and even individuals.

As you continue to explore and experiment with JIRA and Confluence, remember that mastering these tools is an ongoing process. Embrace a continuous improvement mindset, seek feedback from your team, and adapt your workflows as needed. With dedication and practice, you can harness the full power of JIRA and Confluence to achieve unprecedented levels of collaboration, efficiency, and success in your projects.

We hope that this guide has been a valuable resource on your journey to mastering JIRA and Confluence. As you embark on your own projects, we encourage you to refer back to this book as a reference and a source of inspiration. May your projects be well-organized, your teams be highly collaborative, and your results be exceptional. Happy JIRA-ing!

Made in the USA
Coppell, TX
10 April 2025